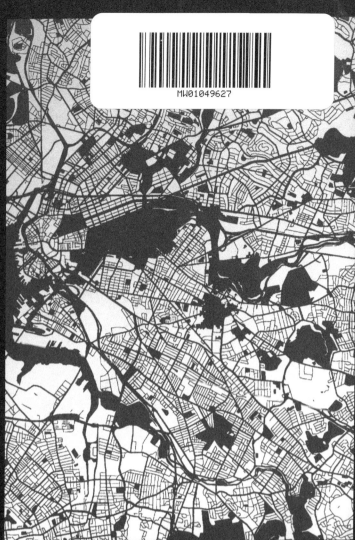

Geographic Information Science
INTRODUCTORY CONCEPTS & APPLICATIONS

Kendall Hunt
publishing company

Rick Bunch | Elisabeth Nelson | James Nelson

www.kendallhunt.com
Send all inquiries to:
4050 Westmark Drive
Dubuque, IA 52004-1840

Copyright © 2020 by Kendall Hunt Publishing Company

ISBN: 978-1-5249-8962-0

Published in the United States of America

CONTENTS

PREFACE

We began teaching an introductory course in Geographic Information Science in 2004. During those early years, one of the most difficult issues we faced was finding a textbook that we considered appropriate for our course. We wanted one book that covered the basic theoretical concepts behind cartography, GIS, and remote sensing. We wanted those concepts presented in a language that was student-friendly to those outside the discipline of geography, and we wanted appropriate exercises to emphasize theoretical concepts in a hands-on learning environment. After several years of searching and coming up short, we decided to write our own. With our combined backgrounds in GIScience and computer technology, we were able to produce a book that presents the basic tenets that undergird the geospatial technologies of cartography, GIS, and remote sensing using an historical perspective as the link that ties the technologies both to each other and to GIScience. Our training also allowed us to include hands-on exercises at the end of each chapter. These exercises are designed to explore the concepts presented and take advantage of a variety of software packages, including ESRI's *ArcGIS Pro* and Purdue University's *MultiSpec*.

ACKNOWLEDGMENTS

We would like to thank the many students and colleagues at UNC Greensboro who have offered their thoughts and suggestions on the topics and exercises covered in our text. We are especially indebted to those instructors and professors who have used our text and taken the time to discuss their experiences. A huge thank you goes out to Kaitlyn Jessee and Elaina Kauzlarich for providing suggestions and edits that greatly improved the book. Lastly, thank you to the hard-working people at Kendall-Hunt for guiding us through all the stages of writing and revising our text.

ABOUT THE AUTHORS

Rick Bunch is a Professor of Geography at UNC Greensboro. His interests are in Geographic Information Systems (GIS) and the conceptualization, modeling and analysis of geographically referenced data. He serves on the editorial board for the journals of *Cartography and Geographic Information Science* and the *International Journal of Applied Geospatial Research*.

Elisabeth Nelson was conferred emeritus faculty status as an Associate Professor of Geography at UNC Greensboro in 2018. A former editor of *Cartography and Geographic Information Science*, her research specialty lies within the realm of cartography. She has been published in *Cartography and Geographic Information Science, Cartographica,* and *Cartographic Perspectives.*

Jim Nelson is the Lab Director for the Department of Geography at UNC Greensboro. With interests in cartography, urban planning, and GIScience, he excels at helping students navigate the complexities of geospatial technologies. He also enjoys challenging students of all levels with unique lab exercises.

CHAPTER 1
Geography and Geographic Information Science

Geographic information science (GIScience) is the fusion of multiple areas of study, but **geography** is its heart. As a core concept of our civilization, geography has often been characterized as the "mother of all sciences." Such a broad view has made it a difficult field to define succinctly, particularly as it has sought to keep pace with our rapidly changing worldview. First coined by *Eratosthenes*, head of the Great Library in Alexandria, Egypt, the term "geography'" is literally translated as "earth writing" in Greek. As a definition, this might suggest that geography is more an amalgamation of subjects related to the Earth, from the physical to the cultural, rather than a discipline or subject in and of itself. What is it, then, that binds geographers and their various studies together?

One of the more influential arguments in favor of geography as a subject can be found in the classic work **The Four Traditions of Geography** (Pattison, 1990). Interestingly, this article doesn't attempt to define geography as much as it does to categorize it into related, but distinct, traditions. In doing so, Pattison highlights that geographic studies are bound together into a single discipline via a common theme. The four traditions he outlines as central to geography are *Area Studies*, *Earth Science*, *Man-Land*, and *Spatial*. The Area Studies Tradition provides the home for world regional geography. Its focus is on describing regions and their characteristics, highlighting both similarities and differences between areas and examining relationships between them. The Earth Science Tradition, on the other hand, is the home of physical geography. As such, it specializes in the physical features and natural processes of the Earth, stressing the earth–sun interactions and the core concepts of the Earth's four physical systems or "spheres": atmosphere, biosphere, hydrosphere, and lithosphere. The tradition of Man-Land forms a bridge between Area Studies and Earth Science with its emphasis on the relationship between human societies and the environment. How humans influence and/or perceive the environment as well as how nature may affect them (i.e., natural hazards) are themes examined under this tradition.

The common thread among these traditions, and the emphasis of the fourth and final Spatial Tradition, is the *exploration of spatial relationships*. The Spatial Tradition is devoted to developing tools and theoretical frameworks for studying spatial relationships in general; its focus is on the use of **spatial analysis** to research and solve geographic problems. Thus, while it comprises a unique area of geographic study, the focus of this tradition and the use of the tools, frameworks, and analyses derived from it, is what all the traditions have in common. The key to all things geographical is that they all study and exploit spatial relationships.

Eratosthenes may have been the first to recognize geographical studies as unique, but the idea of a spatial perspective wasn't actually considered a formal category of knowledge until the 1700s. At that time, philosophers began to consider concepts such as distance, direction, and position as a specific perspective on the world. German philosopher *Immanuel Kant* was the first to identify geography as a unique form of knowledge. He considered geography, along with history and the "subject matter" of sciences (i.e., biology), to each be separate realms of intellectual inquiry (May, 1970). To grasp why Kant believed geography to be unique, visualize yourself studying the world through a *spatial lens*. When you do this, your focus shifts to one in which you are interested in *connections*—how the physical and cultural aspects of our planet relate to each other.

Kant, for example, would have argued that the biologist, the historian, and the geographer would all have different approaches to studying an historic site such as the Guilford Courthouse National Military Park in Greensboro, North Carolina. The biologist, for instance, might focus on specific life forms associated with the park by planning and emphasizing bird conservation. The historian, on the other hand, would be more interested in the importance of the battle to the outcome of the Revolutionary War. These are two very different approaches to the study of the park, and although both might incorporate spatial components in their research, neither would most likely make the spatial component the primary emphasis of their work. The geographer is unique in that he or she would be most interested in the park's spatial relationship to surrounding geographic features. For example, Stine, Nelson, and Swaim (2006) examined the locations of battle lines within the park in the context of Greensboro's current landscape, with the goal of enhancing a visitor's understanding of the spatial elements of the battle when they visit the park.

The Spatial Tradition and GIScience

Pattison's categorization of geographical studies into the four traditions clarifies how and why geography is a unique form of intellectual inquiry. It also highlights the role of GIScience in geography, which parallels the Spatial Tradition in its emphasis on developing tools and theoretical frameworks for studying spatial relationships. The tool that the Spatial Tradition and GIScience traditionally used in analog problem-solving and data presentation has been the **map**. Defined by Robinson et al. (1995, 9) as a "…graphic representation of the geographical setting…," the map is an effective method of transmitting information and providing a venue for the analysis of spatial relationships. It is a well-suited vehicle for these uses because it deliberately simplifies real-world situations and presents results using abstract, but easily identified, symbology.

Today's map is set in a dynamic, computerized setting that has provided cartographers and geographic information scientists (GIScientists) with the opportunity to design new types of maps and to allow users to explore and interact with the spatial data comprising them. The addition of interaction encourages spatial and visual thinking processes as users explore spatial data relationships and patterns (Menno-Kraak, 2006).

If anything, then, the map has become even more powerful and indispensable to geography as the discipline has moved into the digital environment.

Characterizing the map and its ability to capture spatial relationships in graphic form highlights its use of *spatial structure*, which emphasizes **location** and **attributes**, two key characteristics of any map (Robinson et al. 1995). **Location** is a place characteristic defined by using coordinate systems to designate a place's position on Earth. **Attributes** represent a name, label, measurement, or value associated with a location or pair of coordinates (Figure 1.1). The combination of location and attributes comprises **geospatial data**. It is from these two basic data elements that you can begin to explore relationships: relationships between locations, such as distances; relationships between attributes, like income and education in Memphis, TN; or relationships between an attribute at multiple locations, such as varying rainfall amounts between Memphis and New Orleans. The result is a study of patterns and interactions—**spatial analysis**—that occurs over a given geographic region.

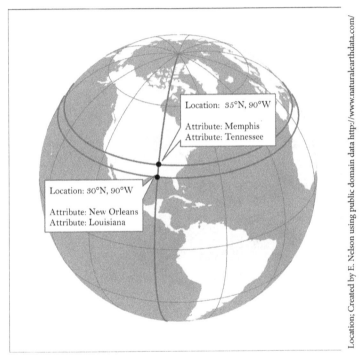

Location; Created by E. Nelson using public domain data http://www.naturalearthdata.com/

FIGURE 1.1
Location and attributes.

The processes of collecting, analyzing, and visualizing geospatial data are all shaped by constant changes in computer technology. The initial movement of the mapping process into this environment has its roots in the early 1960s. It was during this timeframe that **Geographic Information Systems (GIS)**, envisioned as a "digital toolbox for handling maps" (Goodchild, 2004, 709), were first implemented with the goal of alleviating the more monotonous and often expensive tasks cartographers and surveyors performed when working with spatial data. Considered one of the core systems under the current geospatial technology umbrella, GIS is a computerized information system designed specifically to capture, store, manage, analyze, and present spatial data.

The maps produced in a GIS are often described as layers of information created from different types of spatial information. These layers might include water features, parcels, elevation, roads, and so on (Figure 1.2). When the layers take the form of a static printed map, you can visually examine the spatial relationships between them. You might examine a county map, for example, to locate and count the number of elementary schools. You could also visually estimate the clustering, or distances between these schools, and perhaps infer from that the population densities of the areas around them. Imagine now that these layers of information can be accessed and displayed on your home computer. Within the digital environment of a GIS, you can use built-in functions to have the computer analyze these layers. The GIS can tell you not only how many elementary schools there are within the county but also how many are within, say, 7 miles of the largest city in the county, which ones are within specific census tract areas, and the demographics of the populations within those tracts.

Source: *National Weather Service* (https://www.weather.gov/bmx/gis).

FIGURE 1.2
GIS conceptualization of spatial features as layers of information.

These types of built-in functions took time to develop; the GIS of today has benefitted from a 50-year evolutionary process. From the beginning, those involved in the development of these systems faced both computational and conceptual challenges. As the field matured, some began to question whether there might be a science behind the technology comprising an academic subdiscipline. In 1992, Michael Goodchild of the University of California at Santa Barbara published one of the first lists of GIS-related research priorities. The title of the paper was *Geographical Information Science*, and while a definition of GIScience was not offered, Goodchild did present the academic community with proposed components of the underlying science. These included *data collection, data capture, spatial statistics, data modeling, data structures, data display, analytical tools,* and *managerial and ethical issues.* One, if not the first, definition of GIScience came from the University Consortium for Geographic Information Science (UCGIS). This entity was formed in

1994 by a group of academics who came together to form the first committee for basic GIS research (Mark, 2003). They defined their group, and thus, indirectly, GIScience, as "…dedicated to the development and use of theories, methods, technologies, and data for understanding geographic processes, relationships, and patterns" (UCGIS, 2018).

GIScience Today

In 2006, the UCGIS sought to formalize the difference between geographic information systems (GIS) and geographic information science (GIScience). Early GIS, along with cartography and remote sensing, were technologies that initially evolved separately, both in product design and research agendas. As they have all moved to the digital environment, however, they have begun to "…serve overlapping applications, and face similar issues of representation, database design, accuracy, and visualization" (Goodchild, 2004, 710). GIScience is the subdiscipline that addresses these issues and the principles of spatial information processing under which current GIS, cartographic, and remote sensing technologies operate.

The UCGIS now considers geospatial technology and GIScience to be two of three interrelated subdomains of *Geographic Information Science and Technology*, a broader framework proposed to address the continually evolving discipline of GIScience (DiBiase, 2006, 5). The third subdomain is *Applications of GIS&T*. Within the framework, which is also often referred to as *geospatial technologies* or *geotechnology*, GIScience represents the conceptual underpinnings of GIS, while geospatial technology refers to the set of specialized technologies that handle spatial data. Applications cover the myriad of uses of these technologies in different sectors of employment and across different disciplines. It is noteworthy that the U.S. Department of Labor named *geotechnology* as "…one of the three most important emerging and evolving fields, along with nanotechnology and biotechnology" in 2004 (Gewin, 2004).

GIS&T, then, is presented as an integrative realm, one that ties research together across many related disciplines and expands how we think about GIScience. Two events resulted from this change in perspective. First, UCGIS called for a greater need to teach students the concepts that form the foundation of GIS&T, as well as the expertise in how to apply these technologies, as acknowledged by the U.S. Department of Labor. Second, this group has formally expanded the view of what it means to "do" GIS. GIS is now one component of a much larger knowledge realm, and understanding each component in this realm is essential to fulfilling the need for this pool of labor the government has forecast.

This book, *Geographic Information Science: Introductory Concepts and Applications*, emphasizes the conceptual understanding required to work with GIS, cartography, and remote sensing properly at a basic level. Marble (1999, 31) has argued early on that GIScience education lacked depth and breadth. He notes, "*Existing GIS education fails to provide the background in GIScience that is necessary to meet the needs of either users of GIScience technology or of the scientific community engaged in basic GIScience research and development.*" Marble (1998) identified and outlined competency levels that he felt degree programs should provide (Figure 1.3). The base of the pyramid, *Basic Spatial and Computer Understanding*, is the focus of this book. The pervasiveness of GIS across disciplines, he argues, demands that geography step up and critically engage students at this level before allowing them to move upward. Primary concerns include learning how to *think spatially* and how to strike a balance between learning complex software and forming an understanding of the foundational concepts common to the geospatial technologies. Both are crucial to minimizing errors and efficiently using GIS at more advanced levels.

Source: E. Nelson

FIGURE 1.3
Marble's Competency Levels for Degree Programs, 1998.

Key Terms

Geographic information science

Geography

The Four Traditions of Geography

Map

Location

Attributes

Geospatial data

Spatial analysis

Geographic information systems

Questions

1. What is geographic information science?

2. Who was Eratosthenes, and why was he important?

3. What is the definition of geography?

4. What are the four traditions of geography, according to Pattison?

5. Who was Immanuel Kant, and why was he important?

6. What is the definition of a map?

7. What is spatial structure, and what are two key characteristics?

8. What is spatial analysis?

9. What is a geographic information system?

Bibliography

The American Heritage Dictionary of the English Language. 1993. 3rd ed. Boston MA: Houghton Mifflin.

Bonnet, A. 2008. *What is Geography?* Los Angeles, CA: Sage Publications.

Brown, L.A. 1977. *The Story of Maps*. New York, NY: Dover Publications, Inc.

Campbell, J. 1998. *Map Use & Analysis*. 3rd ed. Boston, MA: WCB McGraw-Hill.

Clarke, K.C. 2003. *Getting Started with Geographic Information Systems*. 4th ed. Upper Saddle River, NJ: Pearson Education, Inc.

Dent, B.D., Torguson, J.S., and T.W. Hodler. 2009 *Cartography: Thematic Map Design*. 6th ed. New York, NY: McGraw-Hill.

DiBiase, D., DeMers, M., Johnson, A., Kemp, K., Luck, A.T., Plewe, B., and E. Wentz., eds. 2006. *Geographic Information Science and Technology Body of Knowledge.* 1st ed. Washington, DC: Association of American Geographers.

Gewin, V. 2004. "Mapping Opportunities." *Nature* 427: 376–377.

Goodchild, M. 1992. "Geographical Information Science." *International Journal of Geographical Information Systems* 6(1): 31–45.

Goodchild, M. 2004. GIScience, geography, form, and process. *Annals of the Association of American Geographers* 94(4): 709–714. [410]

Kraak, M. J. 2006. Beyond geovisualization : visualization viewpoints. *IEEE Computer Graphics and Applications, 26*(4), 6-9.

Marble, D.F. 1998. "Rebuilding the top of the pyramid." *ArcNews*, 20(1): 28–29.

Marble, D.F. 1999. "Developing a model, multipath curriculum for GIScience." *ArcNews* 21(1): 31.

Mark, D. 2003. "Geographic information science: Defining the field." In *Foundations of Geographic Information Science*, edited by M. Duckham, M. Goodchild, M. Worboys. New York, NY: Taylor and Francis.

May, J.A. 1970. *Kant's Concepts of Geography and Its Relation to Recent Geographical Thought.* Toronto, Canada: University of Toronto Press.

National Academy of Sciences. 2006. *Beyond Mapping: Meeting National Needs Through Enhanced Geographic Information Science.* Washington DC: National Academies Press.

Pattison, W. 1990. "The Four Traditions of Geography." *Journal of Geography*, September-October, 202–206.

Robinson, A.H., Morrison, J.L., Muehrcke, P.C., Kimerling, A.J., and S.C. Guptill. 1995. *Elements of Cartography.* 6th ed. New York, NY: John Wiley & Sons, Inc.

Slocum, T.A., McMaster, R.B., Kessler, F.C., and H.H. Howard. 2005. *Thematic Cartography and Geographic Visualization.* 2nd ed. Upper Saddle River, NJ: Pearson Education, Inc.

Stine, R., Nelson, E., and M. Swaim. 2006. "The Battle of Guilford Courthouse: Using Cartographic Animation to Enhance Understanding of Historic Landscapes." *Research in Geographic Education* 8: 73–89.

UCGIS. (2018). Bylaws of the University Consortium for Geographic Information Science. Pg 16, Retrieved October 20, 2019 from https://www.ucgis.org/assets/docs/UCGIS_ByLaws_April2018.pdf

Introducing ArcGIS Pro

In this exercise, you will explore the ArcGIS Pro environment. You will also add, symbolize, and explore data associated with your map using basic tools.

OBJECTIVES

- Identify the major components of the ArcGIS Pro Interface
- Learn how to use navigation and layer tools
- Learn how to explore spatial data
- Become familiar with the *Catalog Pane* and *Content Pane*

SOFTWARE

This exercise uses ESRI's ArcGIS Pro 2.3.2. Your instructor will provide instructions on the steps needed to access the software.

DATA

The data for this exercise are available from the Kendall Hunt Student Ancillary site. See the inside front cover for access information. You may also be directed to download the data from a different location by your instructor.

1. Download the data as directed by your instructor
2. Save the file to a location where you have read/write privileges

The files are compressed and must be decompressed prior to use.

The ArcGIS Pro Interface

CONCEPT

To use **ArcGIS Pro** efficiently, you must learn how to navigate its graphical user interface (GUI). The GUI is organized into four general components. These components are called the *Ribbon*, *Contents Pane*, *View*, and *Catalog Pane* (Figure 1.1).

The *Ribbon* is an application-based concept used to organize functionality by themes using tabs. *Map, Insert, Analysis, View, Edit, Imagery,* and *Share* are all tabs that contain commands and tools that are further grouped together by related commands.

The *Contents Pane* shows the data and layers contained in the active view.

The *View* is the window where you can explore and work with your maps. Do not confuse the *View* tab with the *View* window. The *View* is a window where you see your map, whereas the *View* tab provides a group of commands that allow you access to additional ArcGIS Pro functionality.

The *Catalog Pane* provides access to data and items associated with your project.

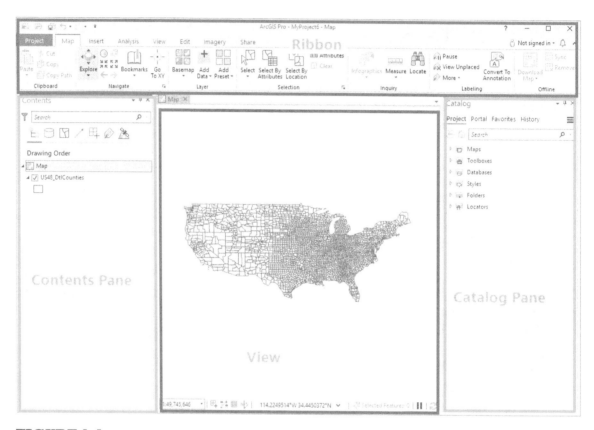

FIGURE 1.1

1. Start ArcGIS Pro.
2. In the dialog box, select *Open another project*. The option is in the lower left corner of the dialog screen (Figure 1.2).

Open another project

Settings

FIGURE 1.2

3. Navigate to the *Chapter01* folder in the provided class folder and select *Exercise_01.aprx*.
4. You should see a map of the counties for the 48 U.S. states (Figure 1.3).
5. Click on each tab of the *Ribbon* to explore the different groups of tools, commands, and functions available in this component.

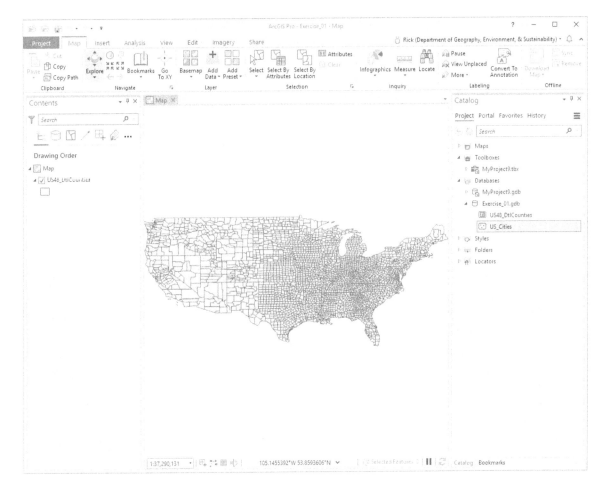

FIGURE 1.3

The application-based concept that uses tabs to organize components by themes and that groups tools by related commands and functions in ArcGIS Pro is called:

a. Catalog pane
b. View
c. Ribbon
d. Contents pane

Exploring Spatial Data Using Map Tab Tools

The *Map* tab is the place where you can query, explore, and add spatial data. When you interact with spatial data in this environment, you are working with real-world coordinates. In this section, you will explore and add spatial data using the group of *Navigate* and *Layer* tools found in the *Map* tab.

1. Click on the *Map* tab and locate the group of *Navigate* tools (Figure 1.4).

FIGURE 1.4

2. Hover and hold your mouse cursor over each item to read their descriptions.
3. Move your mouse pointer over the map in the *View* window.
4. Click and hold your left mouse button and move your cursor around. The map should move with your cursor.
5. Roll your middle mouse roller. Your map should zoom in and out as you scroll back and forth.
6. Now press the *World* icon in the group of *Navigate* tools. This tool places the map back to its full extent.

What are the functions of the two *Navigate* tools highlighted in yellow in the following illustration?

a. Full extent
b. Previous extent
c. Next extent
d. Fixed zoom in and Fixed zoom out

7. Navigate to and zoom in on the state of Maine in the top right-hand portion of the map.
8. Click on the *Bookmarks* icon and select *New Bookmark* and name it *Maine*.
9. Now press the *World* button to view the full extent of your map.
10. Again, click on the *Bookmarks* icon and select the saved bookmark called *Maine*. The bookmark takes you right back to Maine.
11. Hover your mouse cursor over the northernmost or top-most county in Maine and click to identify it. A new window will open, showing you the data that have been collected and stored for this county, including its name.

QUESTION 1.3

What is the name of the county in Maine that is being displayed in the pop-up box from step 11?

a. Washington
b. Somerset
c. Aroostook
d. Penobscot

QUESTION 1.4

How many households are there in the county that you identified in QUESTION 1.3?

a. 30,356
b. 20,436
c. 14,678
d. 56,342

QUESTION 1.5

What is the name of the southernmost county in Texas?

a. Cameron
b. Zapata
c. Hidalgo
d. Willacy

12. Now press the *World* icon in the group of *Navigate* tools. This tool places the map back to its full extent.
13. Select *Go To XY* under the *Navigate* group of tools (Figure 1.5).
14. Type -112 for longitude (long.): and 36 for latitude (lat.) in the dialog box that appears (lower middle portion of your *View* window).
15. Leave the unit format as *dd*.
16. Press the *Flash* location button (just left of the hand or *Pan* icon) and zoom in to the flash point.

Explore   Bookmarks   Go
                        To XY

Navigate

FIGURE 1.5

What is the name of the county identified by the geographic locations you specified in Step 13 using the *Go To XY* tool?

    a.   Unitah
    b.   Nevada
    c.   Coconino
    d.   Grand

17. The group of *Layer* tools allows us to add additional data to our map. Click on the *Add Data* icon.
18. Navigate to your *Exercise_01.gdb* and select *US_Cities* and click *OK* to add the data.

How many cities are in Miami-Dade County (the southeastern most county in Florida)?

    a.   1
    b.   2
    c.   3
    d.   4

19. Now press the *World* icon in the group of *Navigate* tools. This tool places the map back to its full extent.

Exploring the Catalog Pane

The *Catalog pane* is used to access and manage your data. The *Catalog pane* allows you to browse and search for layers to add to a map, connect to databases and folders, and create and import maps. The *Catalog pane* is essential to maintaining, organizing, and creating spatial data for projects. In this section, we will begin exploring the *Catalog pane* by connecting to your class exercise folder, opening a geodatabase, and importing a feature class.

1. Find your *Catalog pane.*
2. Right-click on the *Folders* icon and select *Add Folder Connection.*
3. Navigate to your *Chapter01* folder, select it, and click *OK.*
4. Expand the *Folders* by clicking on the arrow to the left of the *Folders* icon. You should see your *Chapter01* folder.
5. Click the arrow to the left of your *Chapter01.* You should see a folder called *Index* which contains a thumbnail map for your project. You should also see a *More Data* folder and your geodatabase called *Exercise_01.gdb.*
6. Expand the *Databases* folder and the *Exercise_01.gdb* by clicking on the arrows next to each icon
7. You should see all the items highlighted in Figure 1.6.

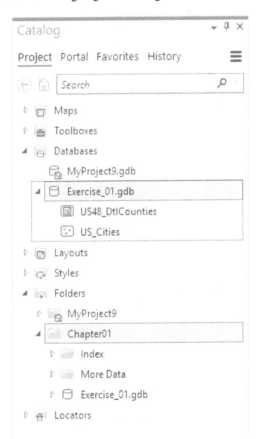

FIGURE 1.6

What is the name of the file listed in the *More Data* folder?

    a.   US48_DtlCounties
    b.   Exercise_01.gdb
    c.   World_Boundaries.shp
    d.   US_Cities

8. Right-click on the *Exercise_01.gdb* under the *Databases* Folder.
9. Select *Import > Feature Class* (Figure 1.7).

FIGURE 1.7

10. Under *Input Features,* navigate to your *More Data* Folder by clicking on the *Folder* icon, then select *World_Boundaries.shp*.
11. Click *OK*.
12. *Output Location* should be *Exercise_01.gdb* by default.

13. Under *Output Feature Class*, name your feature class *MyWorld_Boundaries*.
14. Click the Run button in the bottom right-hand corner of the *Geoprocessing* dialog box.
15. Close the *Geoprocessing* dialog box by clicking on the X and examine your *Exercise_01.gdb*. Your imported feature class should be listed in the *Contents pane* and appear in your map and in the *Exercise_01.gdb* geodatabase.

Exploring the Contents Pane

CONCEPT

The *Contents pane* lists the layers contained in the map. It allows you to manage how your layers are displayed, ordered, and listed. You can also manage the symbology and properties of layers in the *Contents pane*. In this section, you will explore the basic functions of *Listing, Drawing Order*, and *Labeling* in the *Contents pane*.

1. Locate the *Listing* icons in your *Contents pane* (highlighted in Figure 1.8).

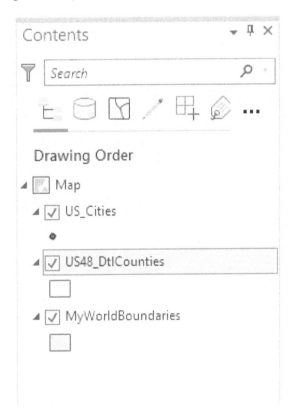

FIGURE 1.8

2. Roll your mouse over each icon and pause to read their descriptions.
3. Press each icon button and view the different characteristics of each listing option.

Which listing option allows you to see the path where the data are stored?

    e.   List by drawing order
    f.   List by data source
    g.   List by selection
    h.   List by snapping

4.   Select the *List By Drawing Order* icon.
5.   To change your drawing order, scroll over the layers in the *Contents pane.* Left-click and hold your mouse button on a layer to drag the layer up or down to match the drawing order illustrated in Figure 1.9.

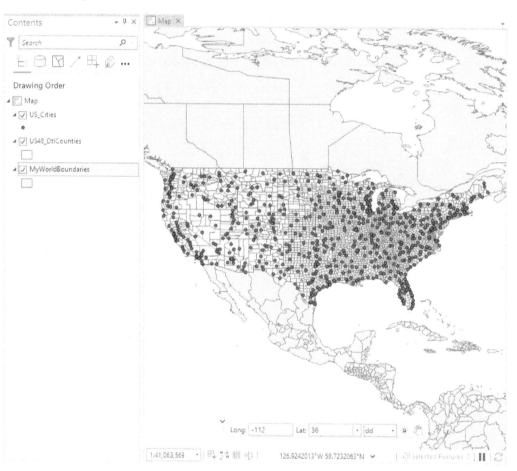

FIGURE 1.9

Which layer in Figure 1.9 is drawn last?

  a. US_Cities
  b. US48_DtlCounties
  c. MyWorld_Boundaries
  d. Map

6. Click on the check box next to the *US_Cities* and *MyWorld_Boundaries* layers to turn them off.
7. Double-click on the rectangular box just under the check box for the *US48_DtlCounties* layer to view color choices.
8. Type yellow in the *Type here to search* prompt, then press Enter. Select *Yellow (Pastel)*.
9. Right-click on the *US48_DtlCounties* layer and select *Label*.
10. Right-click on the *US48_DtlCounties* and select *Properties*.
11. Change the visibility range to 1:5,000,000 in the *Out beyond (minimum scale)* box prompt.
12. Click OK.
13. Turn on all layers by checking the box next to each of their names.
14. Right-click on the *US48_DtlCounties* layer and select *Zoom to Layer*.
15. Since you set the visibility scale of the *US48_DtlCounties* layer, it will not appear until you zoom in close enough to each the *Out beyond (minimum scale)* limit.
16. Zoom in closer to a state of your choice (e.g., North Carolina). You should see the counties and their names appear.
17. Save your project to your *Chapter01* folder as *Ex01_yourlastname*.

CHAPTER 2
Spatial Representation

I n Chapter 1, we defined a map as a "… graphic representation of the geographical setting…" (Robinson et al., 1995, 9). In this setting, the word *representation* may refer to a likeness of the environment, such as the image of the United States in Figure 2.1, or to an abstract concept, such as the spatial variation of those aged 35 and older who are enrolled in school (Figure 2.2). In both instances, the result is a method of communication that relies on one of four fundamental forms of intelligence. The method is called **graphicacy**, and the type

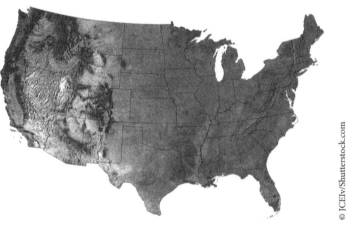

© JCEtv/Shutterstock.com

of intelligence upon which it relies is known as **visuospatial intelligence**. Communicating via graphicacy requires that we be able to generate and understand graphics and images, including photographs, diagrams, maps, charts, and plans, among others.

As a vehicle for communication, graphicacy is surely one of the earliest methods humans used; unfortunately, its power often goes undetected in American education, where developments in *verbal*, *social*, and *numerical* intelligences (and corresponding communication methods of *literacy*, *articulacy*, and *numeracy*) dominate (Aldrich and Sheppard, 2000). This is unfortunate, because developing graphicacy skills and visuospatial intelligence are particularly important in today's graphics-intensive, technologically driven world. A *picture is worth a thousand words* is often repeated for a reason, and Balchin and Coleman (1965, 25)

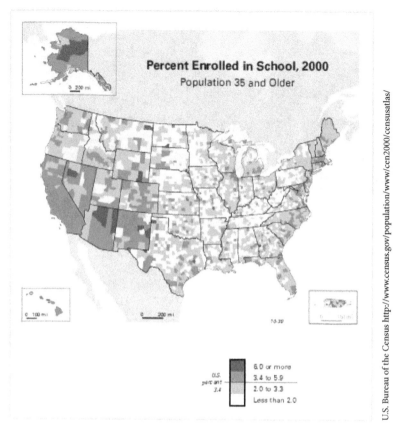

Percent Enrolled in School, 2000
Population 35 and Older

6.0 or more
3.4 to 5.9
2.0 to 3.3
Less than 2.0

U.S. percent 3.4

U.S. Bureau of the Census http://www.census.gov/population/www/cen2000/censusatlas/

FIGURE 2.2
Percent of population 35 and older enrolled in school in 2000.

make the argument beautifully when they say that "…neither words nor numbers nor diagrams are simpler or more complex, superior or inferior. They are only more suitable or less suitable for particular purposes."

Maps and Graphicacy

In the world of GIScience, Jack Dangermond, founder of ESRI (Environmental Systems Research Institute), has declared the map to be "…one of humanity's most sophisticated conceptual creations" (Kimerling et al. 2009, foreword). Although not always recognized as such, a map is a very complex graphic format. More than a photograph, the map is a purposefully simplified picture of the world; it is created to highlight certain aspects of reality, to provide an alternative that is less complicated, so the users may easily focus on the highlighted spatial relationships the cartographer wishes them to consider. Compare, for example, two maps of Pakistan prepared by the Central Intelligence Agency. The physiographic map (Figure 2.3) is designed to highlight the physical features of the country: the river systems, the mountain ranges, and their relationships

FIGURE 2.3
Pakistan's Physiography.

to the major population centers and historical and archaeological sites. In the design of the transportation map (Figure 2.4), on the other hand, the cartographer has opted to remove the relief and the mountain range designations, as well as the historical and archaeological sites. Instead, railroads, airports, canals, and roads have been emphasized, as well as their relationships to both major and minor population centers to highlight interconnectivity. Maps such as these are also distinctive because they offer us a view of the world that is outside our normal range of view, allowing us to visualize and understand spatial relationships over distances that are larger than we can see.

Maps can simplify the communicating of key spatial relationships, but that built-in simplicity can be deceptive if the map's design is poorly executed, or if the user lacks knowledge that would increase their like-

FIGURE 2.4
Transportation geography of Pakistan.

lihood of misinterpreting the presented reality. Think about it: How many ways are there to present a less complicated view of your environment? The answer can be unnerving, not only in *what* to show but in *how* to show it. As Harvey (2008) points out, this fuzziness in what to represent—as well as how to best represent it—leaves many feeling that these simplified representations are too complex, with the result that maps are easily misunderstood or perhaps even perceived as just too difficult to learn how to interpret properly. Like Harvey, however, I agree that taking the time to familiarize yourself with the principles and conventions of cartography and GIScience will significantly sharpen your visuospatial intelligence. It will also provide you with the information you need to understand geospatial information, GIScience, and cartographic products, all of which are an increasingly important part of our everyday experiences.

Key Map Characteristics

Our fascination with maps has been part of our makeup since the ancient Greeks began investing time and energy in studying the size and shape of our planet, developing better methods of locating features, and plotting those locations on two-dimensional surfaces. As those methods have evolved, so has the variety of maps that can be produced, and the end products are often so different that there are times when one might question whether they all stem from the same set of principles. Luckily, they do, and one place we can start our journey in exploring the underpinnings of GIScience is with those principles. In one sense, what we are broadly doing is defining the *prototype* for a map. The prototype will have all of the following six characteristics, as noted in Robinson et al. (1995):

1. SPATIAL STRUCTURE

Our definition for the *map* is quite broad and one of the reasons it works so well is because it highlights the idea of **spatial structure**, which emphasizes *location* and *attributes*, two key map characteristics we first introduced in Chapter 1 (Figure 2.5). *Location* is a place characteristic defined by using coordinate systems to designate a place's position on Earth. *Attributes* represent a name, label, measurement, or value associated with a location or pair of coordinates.

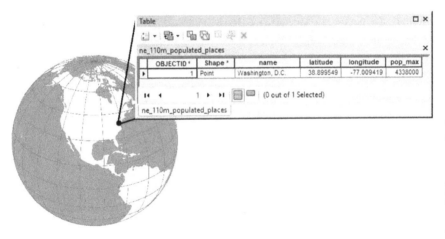

Source: E. Nelson, using data from http://www.naturalearthdata.com/

FIGURE 2.5
Spatial Structure: Locations and Attributes.

These two characteristics are required of all maps because they are the basis upon which we form spatial relationships. With location and attributes, we can work with distances and directions and evaluate patterns and interactivity. We will delve more deeply into location and the coordinate system of latitude and longitude in Chapter 3.

2. PROJECTION

Representing geographic information in two dimensions means that we must mathematically transform it from its three-dimensional source, the Earth. The systematic translation of locations on Earth's three-dimensional surface to their corresponding locations on a flat surface is called a *map* **projection**. Moving from a spherical coordinate system to one in which space is visualized using Euclidean geometry creates distortions in the spatial relationships between features being mapped (Figure 2.6). Map projections, then, play a vital role in map development. The projection that you choose to use will have consequences on your map's accuracy and the tasks for which it is designed. We will be learning more about map projections and their role in GIScience in Chapter 4.

3. SCALE

Maps are not reality, but spatial surrogates; thus, they have a proportional relationship to the real world they represent. The relationship between the size of the area on the map and the size of the area in reality is described by the **map scale**. Mathematically, a map's scale is a *ratio* and is defined as *Map Distance/Ground Distance*. When Map Distance is represented by a measurement of 1, this ratio is called a **representative fraction** (RF), and it is one of three ways of describing **scale** on a map (Figure 2.7). Take, as an example, a map that has a scale of 1/24,000 (or

Source: E. Nelson, using data from http://www.naturalearthdata.com/

FIGURE 2.6
The concept of a map projection.

SCALE 1:24 000

Source: E. Nelson, using data from U.S. Geological Survey, Department of the Interior.

FIGURE 2.7
Map scale and the representative fraction.

1:24,000). On this map, 1 in. on the map represents 24,000 in. on the ground. In the case of Figure 2.7, the length of the road segment between Dogwood Drive and Starmount Drive, on the map, is approximately 1 in. Since the scale is listed as 1:24,000, we know that the real-world distance is 24,000 in.

Using the English system of measurement, we could easily divide this ground distance (24,000 in.) by 12 in. to find that "1 in. represents 2,000 ft." With this conversion, we have moved away from the RF, which as a fraction requires that both the denominator and numerator be in the same units of measurement, to a *verbal statement*. Verbal statements are usually easily grasped by most map users. Representative fractions, while standard for some map types, are not particularly user-friendly to those new to mapping, as scale is often more difficult to visualize in that form.

RFs are useful, however, because they are not tied to any particular unit of measurement. By keeping both sides of the fraction in the same units, any system of measurement may be used. Thus, the 1/24,000 could mean "1 in. represents 24,000 in.," "1 ft represents 24,000 ft," or even "1 m represents 24,000 m." Imagine the following: You have an image on which the length of an American football field is approximately 1 in. (Figure 2.8). The actual ground distance of that field is approximately 360 ft., or 4,320 in. (360 ft. × 12 in.). The representative fraction of the image, then, according to our definition, is 1/4,320, which may also be written as 1:4,320.

Source: E. Nelson, using data from U.S. Geological Survey, Department of Interior.

FIGURE 2.8
Setting up the representative fraction.

If you were to measure that same football field in centimeters, it would be 2.54 cm in length. The actual ground distance, using the metric system, is 109.73 m or 10,973 cm (109.73 m × 100 cm). That leaves us with a fraction of 2.54/10,973. To find the RF, the numerator must be 1, which requires us to divide both the numerator and denominator of the fraction by the numerator value (2.54 in this case). When you do that the resulting RF is 1/4,320, which may also be written as 1:4,320.

Another more user-friendly format for scale is the **graphic scale**. A graphic scale is simply a line on the map that is subdivided into major units representing ground distance. In Figure 2.9a, a line 1-in. long has been drawn to represent map distance. It is labeled with the corresponding ground distances for our football field example, as specified by the RF and/or verbal statement. By measuring the length of the line, and associating that length with the ground distance, one may easily convert it back to a word statement of RF (in this case, 1 in. represents 360 ft.).

In Figure 2.9b, you can see that both the length of the graphic scale and its overall design may vary; these are decisions made by the producer of the map. In this instance, the cartographer slightly lengthened the graphic scale (to about 1.4 in.) to round the ground distance it represents to an even 500 ft. Graphic scales have an advantage in that they retain accuracy even if a map user prints the map then enlarges or reduces it for later use. The same cannot be said of the representative fraction or verbal statements; because they are numerical and not graphical, reducing or enlarging the map does not reflect the change in numbers that should occur with these manipulations.

Map scale may also be expressed more generically as a *relative scale* (Campbell, 1998), which is useful when one wants to compare maps at different scales. A relative scale,

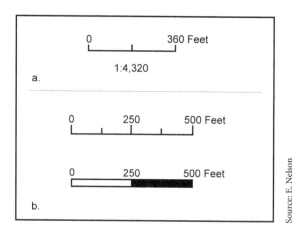

Source: E. Nelson

FIGURE 2.9
Examples of scale designs for a map with a scale of 1:4,320. (a) 1-inch scale length, and b) modified scale lengths to show rounded ground distances)

expressed as *large-scale, small-scale,* or *intermediate-scale,* gives one an idea of the level of detail expressed on the map, as well as the size of the area covered. Using the representative fraction (RF) as the foundation, a large-scale map is one with a large RF. This, however, is not as simple as it sounds. Think of fractions that you work with on a daily basis: 1/2 is a larger fraction than 1/4, but the scale itself has a *smaller* number in the denominator; this fact can cause confusion when working with scale cartographically.

There are also no concrete rules on what constitutes a large- versus a small-scale map; scale, in fact, is best thought of as a continuum (Figure 2.10). That said, generally, a large-scale map is 1:50,000 or larger; it covers a limited area, but is able to provide a lot of detail about the place being mapped (Robinson et al., 1995). A small-scale map, on the other hand, is typically 1:500,000 or smaller; it covers extended areas and provides minimal detail about the mapped features. Those in-between are labeled medium-scale. Because map scale directly affects the level of detail that can

Source: E. Nelson, using data from U.S. Geological Survey, Department of the Interior.

FIGURE 2.10
Scale as a relative concept.

be represented on a map, this concept, along with map projection, is another important key to understanding map accuracy.

4. GENERALIZATION

Since every map is, by necessity, smaller than the real world it represents, there is no way to show every detail of reality, even on a large-scale map. This basic fact about maps means that the level of detail provided on any given map must be manipulated to suit its purpose. Think of it like this—on a map of 1:65,000, you want to show a park that is approximately 1 mile along its widest length in the real world. How big should that park be on your map? According to the RF, 1 in. on the map represents 65,000 in. on Earth. If we divide 65,000/12, we know that 1 in. on this map represents 5,417 ft (or slightly longer than a mile) on the longest side (Figure 2.11, bottom), which would make the park a little less than 1 in. along its longest side.

That's quite a reduction from the real-world size, but let's not stop there. Let's see what we would have to do to symbolize the park on the map at a scale of 1:650,000. Our RF here stipulates that 1 in. represents 54,167 ft. On this map, then, 1 in. represents much more than 1 mile, so we can no longer draw the park as 1 inch in length. If we divide 54,167 ft/5,280 ft, we see that 1 in. on this map actually represents about 10.3 miles. To fit the park on this map, then, at a size commensurate with the scale, the long side of the park would have to be about 1/10 the length on the previous map, or about 0.1 in. in length. The 1:650,000 map is much smaller-scaled and can't support the same level of detail as the 1:65,000. How, then, should we represent the park on this new map? One possibility would be to change the symbology from an area symbol to a point symbol (Figure 2.11, top). This is the essence of **cartographic generalization**, which is a suite of processes cartographers use to select

Source: E. Nelson, using data from U.S. Census Bureau; National Park Service.

FIGURE 2.11
Examples of the influence of scale on map design: map of Guilford County National Military Park at 1:65,000 (bottom); map reduced to 1:650,000 with change of symbology to accommodate smaller scale (top).

which information to retain for a given map and to determine how to represent that information within the context of the final maps scale.

Many GIScientists have studied cartographic generalization, and several have proposed formal models of the process to help cartographers understand its implications for map creation and map use. Of all the operations that are part of this process, there seem to be a core few that everyone includes and that you should be aware of as you explore the world of GIScience. These are **selection, simplification, symbolization**, and **classification** (Dent et al., 2009). This section of the chapter will discuss the generalization processes of *selection* and *simplification*. Symbolization and classification are also part of the generalization process, but, as noted by Robinson, they are also key map characteristics, so they will be discussed later on in the chapter (see sections Symbolization and Classification). Implementing each of these processes results in a reduction of the amount of detail included on a map. How much reduction is largely a function of the map's scale, with small-scale maps requiring more generalization due to space limitations than their larger-scale counterparts. While generalization provides a simpler picture of reality, if done correctly it will retain the distinguishing characteristics of the mapped features and leave the user with enough information to grasp the conceptual meaning of the map.

Selection. Cartographic generalization begins with the process of *selection*; in fact, Robinson and colleagues (1995) see selection as a precursor to other geometric and statistical generalization operations. Selection is simply choosing which features to show and which to eliminate. The choices that are made depend on the purpose of the map and the final scale, that is, how much room there is to show detail. Consider, for example, the difference between a road map for the state of Colorado versus one focusing on the Denver, Colorado region (Figure 2.12). The scale of a map of Colorado (top), designed for a 2.75 × 2.125 in.

FIGURE 2.12

The process of selection in cartographic generalization: (top) map of the state of Colorado at 1:9,000,000; (bottom) map of the city of Denver, Colorado region at 1:2,000,000.

space, would be around 1:9,000,000 (1 in. represents 142 miles). At this scale, you could show the major cities of the state, the interstate system, and some of the other regionally important roads. A map of the Denver region of Colorado (bottom), however, using approximately the same page constraints, would result in a final map scale of approximately 1:2,000,000. Not only could you show the major cities, interstates, and regionally important roads, but you could also display smaller cities and towns, minor roads with labels, and other labeled physical and cultural features, such as rivers, streams, parks, forests, historic sites, and outlines of urbanized areas.

Simplification. You may also find that some features need to be *simplified* at smaller scales. In the case of a United States reference map, for example, that might mean using less complex lines to represent coastal boundaries; these lines would retain the major characteristics of the coastline, but eliminate or smooth out fine details so that the final appearance is simplified and less cluttered. In Figure 2.13, the 1:50,000,000 database would represent such a simplified coastline. This database, however, would not be appropriate for mapping a much larger-scaled map, such as a portion of the North Carolina coastline. You would not choose to simplify shorelines to the same extent at this larger scale because the final appearance would look coarse and result in significant map errors and inaccuracies.

Source: E. Nelson, using data from http://www.naturalearthdata.com/ http://www.nws.noaa.gov/geodata

FIGURE 2.13
Simplification and the relationship of scale to GIS database choices.

To better visualize these potential problems, compare the coastal linework of the two database scales. The coarseness of the 1:50,000,000 database means that some of the smaller towns and cities on the coast, such as Beaufort, Swansboro, and Sneads Ferry, are located in the water. The cities and towns database was compiled at a larger scale than the 1:50,000,000 shoreline database, introducing error into a map comprised of these two layers. A much better choice would be to use the 1:10,000,000 database with the cities and towns data, as this pairing of data layers provides much more detail in the shape of the coastline and better matches the scale of the cities and towns database. It should be clear from these examples that, despite the tendency one has to treat GIS data as *scaleless*, that is most definitely not the case. You can zoom in and out on a GIS database, but that does not mean that the level of detail of the database changes. This example also serves to point out that today's GIS databases are very similar to traditional map output; that is, they are compiled (often from paper maps) at a specific scale, which limits them in their mapping applications to a range of scales around that original compilation scale. Similar to "buyers beware," there should also be a "mappers beware" notice to that effect; if the database scale is unsuitable for your needs, you will need to find a different, more appropriately scaled database before continuing with your mapping project.

5. SYMBOLIZATION

As the ability to include more detail increases, then, we can often choose symbology that looks more like the real-world feature. This can be seen with the coastlines in Figure 2.13 and with the change in symbolization for the park at different scales in Figure 2.11. Parks, after all, aren't really points; they all have boundaries and, thus, areal extents. It just isn't always convenient—or possible—to show that symbolically on a map, which leaves us with a more abstract and generalized symbol choice. Because of this added complexity, *symbolization* has a whole host of principles and conventions associated with it, so much so that it often is addressed not only as part of generalization but also as a basic characteristic of maps as well. What are some of these principles and conventions? Far from a random process, the selection of map symbols is influenced by the interaction of at least three factors: the **symbol dimension**, which is related to the map's final scale; the *level of measurement* of the attribute data that the symbol is representing; and the **visual variable** used to match that level of measurement in a logical fashion.

Symbol dimension. With the basic road map of Colorado in Figure 2.12, for instance, the locations of the major cities in the state are displayed using point symbols (Figure 2.12, top). Cities in the real world, however, have boundaries and cover varying areal extents so that someone may live inside the city limits of Denver, while another person lives outside those boundaries. Why do we display these features as points, then? There are a couple of reasons: (1) The scale of the map is so small it doesn't do a particularly good job of showcasing those boundaries, and (2) as a reference map for the state, all we really need to know is the coordinate location of the city, which can be symbolized using a point symbol. So, although the city itself has areal extent and may be shown as a polygon in its true form (see Denver in Figure 2.12, bottom), at smaller scales and for particular purposes, cartographers may choose to show it using a point symbol, which has location, but no extent. This is the concept of *symbol dimensionality.* All mapped features have a real-life dimensionality and a symbolized dimensionality, but the mapping from reality to symbol is not necessarily one-to-one, as we just saw. In most situations, you will work with either *points* (0-dimensions), *lines* (1-dimension with a length attribute), or *polygons* (2-dimensions with length and width attributes).

Visual variable. The choice of symbol dimensionality is made in concert with the choice of which *visual variable* to use in drawing the symbol. The term "visual variable" is associated with Jacques Bertin (1983), a French cartographer who used it to describe the characteristics of a symbol that might be harnessed to help map users perceive spatial variation in attributes across the mapped features. There are seven traditional visual variables that Bertin associated with map symbols: *position, shape, size, hue, value, orientation,* and *texture.* Other researchers have since supplemented those, but these will suffice for our explorations here. As Figure 2.14 shows, *position* simply denotes coordinate locations, in this case for cities, which have been symbolized here by using black dots, all of which are the same size.

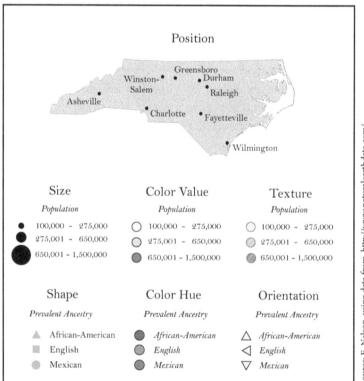

FIGURE 2.14
Bertin's original visual variables.

Source: E. Nelson, using data from http://www.naturalearthdata.com/ http://www.nws.noaa.gov/geodata

What if we wanted to indicate the prevalent ancestry of residents for each city? From Bertin's perspective, you could implement this in a variety of ways. For example, you might symbolize those cities reporting a prevalent African American ancestry with triangles, whereas you could use squares for those reporting a prevalent English ancestry. This type of choice takes advantage of the visual variable *shape*. Alternatively, you might symbolize each city with a circle, and then vary *color hue* of the circles (i.e., red, green, blue) to show that distinction. Would symbolizing prevalent ancestry by varying the *sizes* of the circles for each group be a more effective or less effective solution? The answer to this type of question lies in the attribute data's *level of measurement*.

Levels of measurement. Attributes may be described using many scales of measurement; they are often classified by both formal mathematical properties and by the operations we use during actual measuring (Stevens, 1946). The way in which an attribute has been measured and recorded directly affects how we may manipulate it statistically and visually. For instance, in the context of **levels of measurement**, four measures can be used to manipulate attribute symbolization: *nominal, ordinal, interval,* or *ratio*.

An attribute with a *nominal* level of measurement is one that only allows us to determine whether two or more categories are alike or different. In a case like Figure 2.14, we would have nothing more than a label, such as those describing prevalent ancestry for each city. Prevalent ancestry is not a descriptor that can be ordered; one type of ancestry is not better than another, and they do not differ numerically; they are different in kind or category. In mapping, one of the key goals is to create an intuitive and logical connection between an attribute's level of measurement and the visual variable of the map symbol that will be used to highlight the attribute's spatial variation across a region. We want map users to understand what we are trying to say quickly and with minimal effort. Here, we want the *categorical difference* of prevalent ancestry to stand out; one of the better solutions is to assign different *shapes* of the point symbol to each category.

Different symbol shapes are effective in this case because we do not perceive them as being ordered—squares, circles, and triangles are different, one is not associated as being better or numerically "more" than another. It would also be acceptable to use point symbols of different *color hues* or *orientations*, as they are not perceived as having an order either. Which do you think works best for this particular data set in Figure 2.14? Most cartographers would probably choose shape or hue; both produce a strong visual signal that is easily differentiated. Hue, or the aspect of color that we identify as red, green, blue, and so on, produces possibly an even stronger visual signal than shape, but may be more difficult to differentiate in small swatches, and a point symbol is typically a pretty small swatch. The orientation of a shape, such as a rectangle or triangle, might also work, but is a less exercised option, possibly due to the jarring effects that the varying orientations have on our eyes.

If our data set recorded not a label, but a number for each city's total population, also shown in Figure 2.14, then you would have a *ratio*-level attribute measurement. Ratio levels of measurement are associated with numbers; there is an explicit ordering of the cities on the map according to population size in this case, so there should be a corresponding order to the visualization of the attribute spatially. A classic option here would be to vary the *size* of the original circle symbol. Smaller to larger circles have a definite implied order with which all map users can identify. *Color value*, the relative lightness or darkness of a single hue, would also work. However, the size of the point symbol produces the same problem for value as it does for hue—it may not have enough of a canvas for map users to differentiate differences easily. *Texture*, the spacing of elements within a pattern, is also an ordered visual variable, but it typically does not work well with point symbols.

It should be pointed out here that there is a hierarchy implied in the concept of "levels of measurement" (Figure 2.15). Nominal data are characterized by the least amount of detail and ratio data the most. The next level above nominal is *ordinal*. Ordinal measurements are *rankings*; an example might be a ranking of each city's unemployed, such as below the national average, average, and above the national average. There is an order to the attribute that can be visualized symbolically, but the distance between the categories cannot be described numerically, just as more or less. Levels of measurement not attached to numbers, such as nominal and ordinal, are more broadly categorized as *qualitative data*. With ordinal-level data, you not only have a label, but a descriptive indication of ordering. In this case, you would most likely want to emphasize the difference in that rank-order on

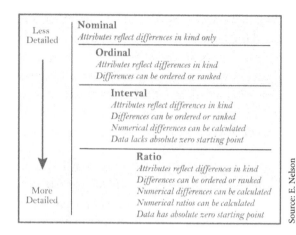

FIGURE 2.15
Levels of measurement hierarchy for attribute data.

your map, which means using a visual variable that map users intuitively "see" as having order. Despite the fact that no numbers are associated with ordinal data, the data variation itself is displayed quite similarly to ratio- and interval-level data and makes use of the same visual variables.

As you move from less detailed data to more detailed data, each specific level always includes all of the qualities of the less detailed levels that come before it. The next step up from ordinal-level data adds meaning to the numerical differences between categories. Both *interval*- and *ratio*-level attributes are examples of *quantitative data*—they are based upon numerical differences. In our example, if our data set included attributes that listed the number of unemployed for each city, then we would be able to calculate the precise difference in the number of unemployed between cities. This increased level of detail provides additional interpretative power to our visualizations.

In the previous paragraph, interval and ratio data were lumped together, but there is a key statistical difference between them, even if there is not necessarily a graphical difference to how we visualize the data. In our example, we moved from nominal to ordinal to ratio data, skipping interval. Why? When talking about the number of unemployed, there is an absolute zero involved; in other words, you can create meaningful fractions or ratios from the data. It would be, for instance, quite proper to state that one city has approximately 1.7 times as many unemployed as another. This is something that cannot be done with interval data, which do not have an absolute zero. Interval data are numerical; it just doesn't make sense to calculate fractions or ratios using it. The classical example of interval data is the Fahrenheit temperature scale. With temperatures, the intervals between the values are interpretable (there is a change of 20° between 20-40 and 40-60). However, because zero has no absolute meaning in this scale (i.e., no set number denotes a lack of temperature), you cannot say the 40° is twice as hot as 20°.

6. CLASSIFICATION

Classification refers to the process of grouping similar attribute values. Like symbolization, there are several principles and conventions associated with the process, making this not only an operation within the context of cartographic generalization but also a basic map characteristic. The goal of grouping similar attribute values is to reduce the complexity of the final map; thus, instead of trying to display each numeric value in the data set with a unique symbol, the cartographer uses a smaller set of symbols to display a limited number of groups that house similar values. The result, if conducted with care, improves the organization of information, making it easier for the map user to visualize the broader spatial patterns within the data. In Figure 2.14, for example, the major cities in North Carolina could be grouped or classified according to population size; in this case, cities with larger populations might be represented with larger symbol sizes than cities with smaller populations. We will explore classification in more detail in Chapter 6.

Functions of Maps

While all maps share the basic characteristics of spatial structure, scale, projection, generalization, classification, and symbolization, you will quickly find that they do not all look the same. The difference in appearance is linked to their function, a topic that Kimerling and colleagues (2009) cover quite nicely. They identify reference maps, thematic maps, and navigation maps as indicative of some of the basic functions maps serve. The following is largely derived from their treatment on the topic.

Reference maps are designed so that a map user can identify the locations of several different feature types quickly and easily, as well as determine the distances and directions between them. These maps tend to be larger in scale, accurate, and tend to include as much detail as possible. Another trademark design of these maps is their attempt to portray all mapped features as equally important from a visual perspective. The classic example of a general reference map is the topographic map, which is designed to highlight the physical and cultural characteristics of an area (Figure 2.16). In the United States, the United States Geological Survey (USGS) produces our topographical map series. These maps, which we will discuss in detail in Chapter 5, not only provide the map user with locations of such features as roads, shorelines, water features, and buildings, they also use specialized symbology to embed the shape of the land into the map.

Similar to reference maps, but designed for hands-on calculations, are navigation maps or charts. These are maps designed for navigators, who use them to plot courses and mark bearings (the topographic map also fits here, so you can see these functions are not exclusive of one another, but rather form a continuum of uses). Types of navigation maps include nautical charts and aeronautical charts among many others. Nautical charts are designed for water navigation and, thus, will have detailed shorelines and water-depth data available to the navigator. Air navigators use the aeronautical chart, which shows attributes such as heights of towers, possible obstructions, and specialized symbology for ground elevations. You could also include the standard road map in this group, although its "look" is a bit different from the chart. Nevertheless, a good road map supplies information necessary to route planning; road quality, distances, and places of interest.

Thematic maps, on the other hand, function quite differently (Figure 2.17). These maps have been likened to geographic essays in that they focus on one particular topic. The topic can be physical in nature, such as the distribution of soil types in North Carolina, or they can choose to emphasize a more abstract, cultural topic, such as the varying chances of contracting malaria worldwide. Because they visually emphasize one particular attribute over the rest of the geographical background, these maps communicate quite different information. Typically smaller in scale, they are not suited for estimating distances and directions or locating specific geographic features. Instead, thematic maps are built specifically to communicate information regarding the spatial structure of the topic emphasized.

FIGURE 2.16
Example of part of a 7.5 minute USGS topographic sheet.

FIGURE 2.17
Example of a thematic map.

GEOGRAPHIC INFORMATION SCIENCE

Maps in the Digital Environment

Moving from a real-world, printed map to a computer representation is known as *data modeling*. On the surface, this might not seem difficult—until you realize that computers can't "see" graphics and images like we can; computers deal only with numbers. One of the first challenges you confront then, is how to model our world so the computer can "see" what we as humans see and interpret when a map is put in front of us. How do you convert lines, shapes, and images into numbers? One solution is to use geometric shapes, such as points, lines, and areas, to represent different map features (Figure 2.18). This is called a *vector* model of reality, and the point—represented by an (x, y) coordinate tied to a spatial reference system (such as latitude and longitude)—is the simplest geographic feature. It could be a city, or an archaeological site, perhaps. Storing these features as (x, y) coordinates allows us to do at least three things: (1) transfer the data to the computer, (2) use the data to redraw the map digitally, and (3) perform some very basic calculations, such as finding the distance between two features. Lines in this model are represented by storing a string of coordinates that need to be connected by the computer. The computer reads the coordinates and then connects them by drawing line segments between them. Finally, areas or polygons are also represented by storing a string of coordinates, except in this case the first and last coordinate pairs are the same, resulting in a closed figure when drawn.

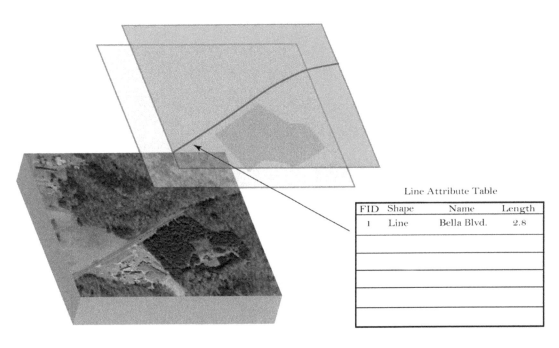

Line Attribute Table

FID	Shape	Name	Length
1	Line	Bella Blvd.	2.8

Source: E. Nelson, using photos and data from U.S. Geological Survey, Department of the Interior.

FIGURE 2.18
The world as seen in a vector model – points, lines, polygons.

Each set of features on a map (point, lines, and polygons) are stored in their own data file using these coordinates. GIScientists refer to these types of data files as files that contain "feature geometry." Stored in this manner, the computer can now draw the features, but it still has no way to differentiate them symbolically within any data file. For this to occur, we need to supply the computer with *attribute data* for each feature. Attribute data are recorded in a flat file, or spreadsheet form, for each geographic feature. This attribute file is linked to the file of feature geometry using a Feature ID Number (FID). The FID is included in both the geometry and attribute files and is a unique code supplied to each feature geometry (Figure 2.18). Because it exists in both files, the computer can use it to associate the correct attribute data with the correct geometry. For example, by linking city coordinates (points) to a table that lists the population for each city, we can use different circle sizes for each city, depending on how many people reside there. This setup, where we use multiple tables that are linked by FIDs, is called a *georelational database.*

Key Terms

Graphicacy
Visuospatial intelligence
Spatial structure
Projection
Map scale
Representative fraction
Scale
Graphic scale

Cartographic generalization
Selection
Simplification
Symbolization
Classification
Symbol dimension
Visual variable
Levels of measurement

Questions

1. What are the four fundamental forms of intelligence, and the corresponding forms of communication?

2. What are the six characteristics of the map prototype, as noted by Robinson?

3. What is a map projection?

4. What is map scale?

5. What is a representative fraction?

6. What is the advantage to using a graphic scale, instead of a representative fraction?

7. What are the differences between a large-scale and a small-scale map?

8. What is cartographic generalization?

9. What are the core cartographic generalization operations?

10. What factors influence the selection of map symbols?

11. What are the seven visual variables that Bertin associates with map symbols?

12. What are the four levels of measurement used to manipulate attribute symbols, and how are they different?

13. What are some examples of the different types of functions maps may have?

14. What is the major problem in moving to a digital map environment?

15. How are lines, shapes, and areas encoded in a computer?

16. What is a georelational database?

Bibliography

Aldrich, F., and L. Sheppard. 2000. "Graphicacy: The Fourth 'R'?" *Primary Science Review* 64: 8-11.

Balchin, W.G.V., and A. M. Coleman. 1965. "Graphicacy Should Be the Fourth Ace in the Pack." *The Times Educational Supplement* (Rpt. In *The Cartographer*, 1966) 3 (1): 23-28.

Bertin, J. 1983. *Semiology of Graphics: Diagrams, Networks, Maps.* Madison, WI: University of Wisconsin Press.

Campbell, J. 1998. *Map use and analysis.* 3rd ed, Boston, Mass., WCB McGraw-Hill.

Dent, B.D., Torguson, J.S., and T.W. Hodler. 2009. *Cartography: Thematic Map Design.* 6th ed. New York, NY: McGraw-Hill.

Harvey, F. 2008. *A Primer of GIS.* New York, NY: The Guilford Press.

Kimerling, A.J., Buckley, A.R., Muehrcke, P.C., and J.O. Muehrcke. 2009. *Map Use: Reading and Analysis.* 6th ed. Redlands, CA: ESRI Press Academic.

Poracsky, J., Young, E., and J.P. Patton. 1999. "The Emergence of Graphicacy." *The Journal of General Education* 48(2): 103-110.

Robinson, A.H., Morrison, J.L., Muehrcke, P.C., Kimerling, A.J., and S.C. Guptill. 1995. *Elements of Cartography.* 6th ed. New York, NY: John Wiley & Sons, Inc.

Stevens, S. S. 1946. On the Theory of Scales of Measurement. *Science.* Vol. 103, No. 2684, 677-680.

Visualizing Spatial Features

In this exercise, you will create a general reference map of South Carolina and use it to explore the map characteristics of location, attributes, map projection, map scale, and the processes of cartographic generalization.

OBJECTIVES

- Create a project
- Verify coordinate systems for layers
- Choose appropriate layers for your map
- Create appropriate map symbols

SOFTWARE

This exercise uses ESRI's ArcGIS Pro 2.3.2.

DATA

The data for this exercise are available from the Kendall Hunt Student Ancillary site. See the inside front cover for access information. You may also be directed to download the data from a different location by your instructor.

1. Download the data as directed by your instructor
2. Save the file to a location where you have read/write privileges

The files are compressed and must be decompressed prior to use.

Creating a Project in ArcGIS Pro

1. Start ArcGIS Pro.
2. Select *Map* under *New > Blank Templates* in the dialog box.
3. Leave the defaults for *Name* and *Location*. Click *OK*. ArcGIS Pro creates a default folder to store all components of a project, but, for this lab, we will use the folder provided in the class data.
4. Right-click on the *Topographic* layer in the *Contents pane* and select *Remove*. This base map automatically loads anytime you start a new project. We do not need the base map for this exercise.
5. In the *Catalog pane*, right-click the *Folders* icon and select *Add Folder Connection*.
6. Navigate to and select your *Chapter02* class folder.
7. Click OK.
8. Expand your *Folders* and *Chapter02* folders and your *Exercise_02.gdb* by clicking on the arrow to the left of each icon to view the contents (Figure 2.1).

FIGURE 2.1

9. Click on *Project* (upper left corner of your session) and select *Save As*.
10. Navigate to your *Chapter02* class folder and save the project as Ex02_*yourlastname*.

Verifying Coordinate Systems

Representing geographic information in 2-dimensions means that we must mathematically transform it from its 3-dimensional source, the Earth. The 3-dimensional source of spatial data is called the *geographic coordinate system*.

Each layer in your *Exercise_02.gdb* has been projected from the geographic coordinate system to a projected coordinate system. If each coordinate system is defined correctly, ArcGIS Pro will project all layers into the common coordinate system. The coordinate system from the first layer added will be used to project all other layers that are subsequently added to the *Contents pane*. This process is called on-the-fly projection. This on-the-fly projection is temporary, and the actual coordinate system stored in each layer's file structure will not be changed.

Oftentimes, however, it is necessary to have layers in the same coordinate system, especially if we want to conduct analysis and apply topology rules.

1. In the *Catalog pane*, expand the *Folders* and the *Chapter02* folders and the *Exercise_02.gdb* and then right-click each layer and select *Properties*.
2. Expand the *Spatial Reference* heading by clicking on the arrow to the left.
3. Scroll down and examine the *Projected Coordinate System* box to identify the projected coordinate system for each layer.

QUESTION 2.1

In the *Exercise_02.gdb*, which layer's projected coordinate system does not match the other three?

a. SC_Dtl_Counties
b. Sc_Gen_Counties
c. SC_MjrCities
d. SC_MjrRds

4. Click, hold, and drag each layer (starting with *SC_Dtl_Counties* first) from the *Catalog pane* to your *Contents pane*.
5. Press the *List By Editing* icon (highlighted in Figure 2.2).

FIGURE 2.2

6. Scroll over the triangles with the exclamation point and read the warning description. You should see three warning triangles.
7. On the *Contents pane*, right-click on *Map* and select *Properties*.
8. Click on the *Coordinate Systems* heading. The projected coordinate system of the first layer (*SC_Dtl_Counties*) added to the *Contents pane* is listed at the top. All of the other layers are projected on the fly to this projected coordinate system.
9. Select *NAD 1983 UTM Zone 17N* and click OK. You should now see one warning triangle in the *Contents pane*. In this case, *SC_Dtl_Counties* is now being projected on the fly to the projected coordinate system of the other three layers.

On-the-fly projection used by ArcGIS Pro permanently overwrites the coordinate system of a layer.

a. True
b. False

10. In the *Contents pane*, press the *List By Drawing Order* button.
11. Click and drag the layers as needed to reorder them within the *Map* in the following order: *SC_MjrCities* listed first, followed by *SC_MjrRds*, *SC_Dtl_Counties*, and finally *SC_Gen_Counties* (Figure 2.3)

FIGURE 2.3

Which layer in Figure 2.3 is drawn first?

a. SC_Dtl_Counties
b. Sc_Gen_Counties
c. SC_MjrCities
d. SC_MjrRds

Choosing Layers for Map Creation

Casual users of GIS tend to treat spatial data as scaleless because they can zoom in and out on the map. Zooming in or out does change the viewing scale of the map, but it does not change the level of detail that was captured when the layer was originally created. Today's spatial data are still very similar to traditional map outputs. They are compiled (often from paper maps) at a specific scale that limits their mapping applications to a range of scales around the original compilation scale. In this section, you will explore the metadata of each layer to see how their compilation scales relate to one another. More generalized layers are better suited for mapping small-scale projects (e.g., state or country level). More detailed layers are better suited for mapping large-scale projects (e.g., city boundaries or a small island along the coast). Remember, large-scale maps show smaller areas in more detail while small-scale maps show larger areas in less detail.

1. Make sure *SC_Dtl_Counties* and *SC_Gen_Counties* layers are turned on and *SC_MjrCities* and *SC_MjrRds* are turned off. Use the check boxes beside each layer to turn the layers on and off.
2. Zoom in on an area along the coastline of South Carolina to examine the differences in coastline detail as represented by each layer (Figure 2.4).
3. Check and uncheck the layer that is drawn on top to see the differences more clearly.

FIGURE 2.4

4. Click on your *Project* tab (upper left corner of your session).
5. Select *Options* and then *Metadata*.
6. Click on the arrow to expand the *Metadata style* heading and select *North American Profile of ISO19115 2003*. This sets the style template of ArcGIS Pro to match the style of the metadata text associated with the layers.
7. Click OK.
8. Click the *Back Arrow* (upper left corner of your session).
9. In the *Catalog pane*, right-click on *SC_Dtl_Counties* and select *View Metadata*. This will open the details of the metadata in the *Catalog View* window. Note: The *Catalog View* is a different component than the *Catalog pane*, and although they have similar capabilities, they are designed to do different tasks.
10. Scroll through the metadata description until you find the *Resource Details* heading. Under *Spatial resolution*, make a note of the *Scale denominator* (the scale at which the layer was compiled). 100,000
11. Make sure *SC_Dtl_Counties* is selected in the *Catalog View* (Figure 2.5).

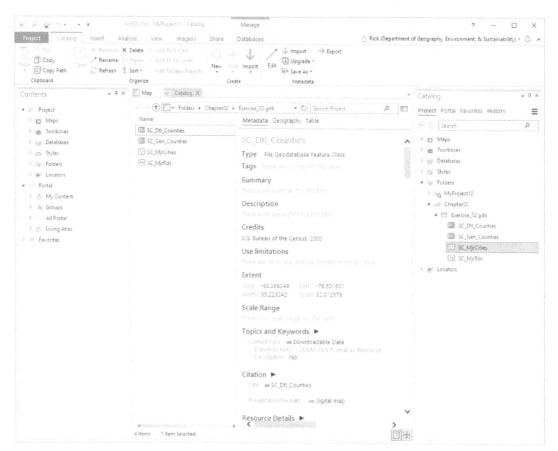

FIGURE 2.5

What is the compilation scale of *SC_Dtl_Counties*?

a. 1:1,000
b. 1:10,000
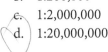
c. 1:100,000
d. 1:1,000,000

What is the compilation scale of *SC_Gen_Counties*?

a. 1:2,000
b. 1:200,000
c. 1:2,000,000

d. 1:20,000,000

Large-scale maps show larger areas in less detail while small-scale maps show smaller areas in more detail.

a. True
b. False

12. When you have finished answering the questions, close the *Catalog View* window by clicking on the X (highlighted in Figure 2.5).

Setting the Map Scale

Map scale in GIS is a very fluid parameter since you can zoom in and out on the map. When you are adding symbols and labels, however, or preparing a layout for printing, you will often want to have more control over how map scale behaves.

You can, for example, set a *reference scale* for your map, which will freeze symbol and text sizes so that they always match the scale, regardless of whether you zoom in or out. You might also want to set a *fixed scale* for your map. This setting keeps the map scale of your layout constant. In this section, you will set the *reference scale* for your map and the *fixed scale* in the *Layout*. The *Layout* is the place where you can create and design cartographic maps by adding a legend, north arrow, scale bar, title, and other items.

Reference Scale

1. Click the *Full Extent* button to reset the view of your map.

2. Remove the *SC_Dtl_Counties* layer by right-clicking on the layer and choosing *Remove*. You will be mapping at the state level, so we will use *SC_Gen_Counties* rather than the more detailed version of the state.

3. Check to make sure *SC_MjrCities* and *Sc_MjrRds* are turned off.

4. In the *Contents pane*, double-click on the rectangle symbol just under the *SC_Gen_Counties* layer name.

5. In the *Type here to search* box, type *Yellow* and press *Enter*.

6. Select *Yellow (Pastel)*.

7. Close the *Symbology* pane by pressing the X (upper right corner of the *Symbology* pane).

8. Right-click on *SC_Gen_Counties* layer and select *Label*.

9. Zoom in and out on your map in the *View*. The size of the labels should change as you change the scale. You will now set the reference scale that will fix the scale of the labels and symbology.

10. Right-click on *Map* in the *Contents pane* and select *Properties*.

11. In the *Map Properties* dialog box, select *General*. Change the *Name* from *Map* to *SC Reference* and set the *Reference scale* to 1:2,000,000, then press *Enter*.

12. Zoom in and out on your map in the *View* and observe how the labels behave now that you have set the reference scale. The size of the labels should remain constant in relation to the map since you set them to a specific scale.

Fixed Scale

1. Select the *Insert* tab and choose *New Layout* (Figure 2.6). The *New Layout* window shows a series of standardized page formats ranging from letter to poster sizes, and also allows you to create a custom page size, if necessary.

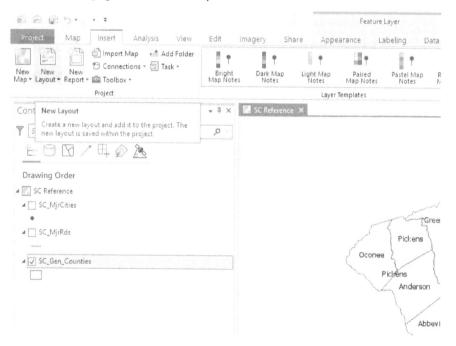

FIGURE 2.6

2. Select *ANSI-Landscape* > *Letter* (8.5" × 11"). A blank layout page should appear.

3. From the *Insert* tab, under the *Map Frames* tools group, press the *Map Frame* button. Under *SC Reference* select *Default Extent*.

4. Left-click, hold, and drag your cursor over the blank page to draw a box. This will insert your map into the layout.

5. Right-click on *Layout* in the *Contents pane* and select *Properties*.

6. Under *General*, change the *Name* to *MySCMap*.

7. Click *OK*.

8. In the *Contents pane*, click on *Map Frame*.

9. Roll your mouse cursor over each button icon in the *Element* dialog box to become familiar with their descriptions (highlighted in Figure 2.7).

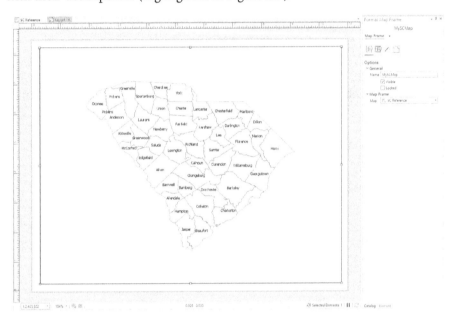

FIGURE 2.7

10. Press the *Display Options* button.

11. Under *Constraint*, select *Fixed Scale*.

12. Under *Scale*, type in 2,500,000 and press *Enter* on your keyboard. When you set your layout map to a *Fixed Scale*, it will not change even if you change scales in the *View*.

13. Now press the *Placement* button.

14. Under *Placement*, type 10.5 for the *Width* and 8 for the *Height*.

15. Right-click on the map, and select *Align* and then *Align to Page*.

16. Right-click on the map, and select *Align Center*.

17. Again, right-click on the map, and select *Align Middle*.

18. In the *Element* dialog box, expand the *General* heading and check the box next to *Locked*. This will lock the *Map Frame* so that it cannot be moved or changed unless the *Locked* box is unchecked. This makes it easier to add other elements to the map.

19. When finished, the size and position of your map should look like the one in Figure 2.7.

Creating Scale Representations

A map's scale is a *ratio* and is defined as *Map Distance/Ground Distance*. This ratio, when *Map Distance* is represented by a measurement of 1 and both map and ground distances use the same units of measurement, is called a *representative fraction (RF)*. Using conversions, we could change the units of measurement for the *Ground Distance* and create a *verbal statement* of scale. The ratio 1:24,000, for example, could be restated as "1 in. represents 2,000 feet". Another user-friendly format for scale is the *graphic scale*. A graphic scale is simply a line on the map that is subdivided into major units representing ground distances.

1.   In the *Map Surrounds* tools group, select the drop-down arrow for the button *Scale Bar*.
2.   Under the *Imperial* category, select *Alternating Scale Bar 1*.
3.   Left-click, hold, and drag your mouse cursor on your layout page to create a box. Your scale bar should appear.
4.   Resize the scale bar until the units start with 0 and end in 100 miles as shown in Figure 2.8 (you can adjust the size by clicking, holding, and dragging the edges).

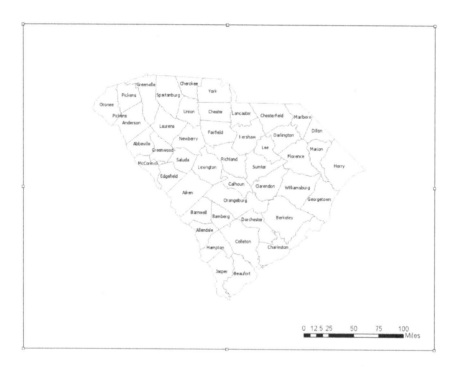

FIGURE 2.8

5.   Select *SC Reference* to return to the data *View* by pressing the tab highlighted in Figure 2.9.

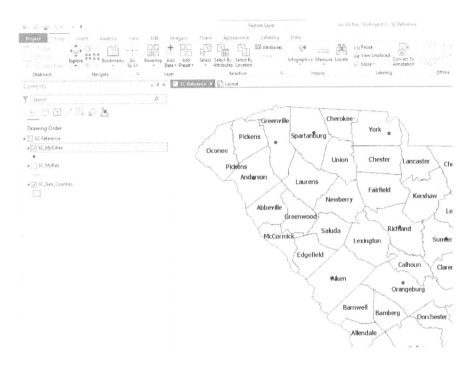

FIGURE 2.9

QUESTION 2.7

Convert the RF of 1:2,500,000 to a verbal statement where "1 in. represents approximately X miles." Which one of the following statements is correct?

a. 1 in. represents approximately 3.9 miles
b. 1 in. represents approximately 39 miles
c. 1 in. represents approximately 325 miles
d. 1 in. represents approximately 3,500 miles

Creating Effective Symbols

Usually, you are interested in a specific attribute attached to the real-world feature you are symbolizing. The way in which that attribute has been measured directly affects how we may visually present its variation on the map. In the context of levels of measurement, four measures affect how we may manipulate a symbol: *nominal*, *ordinal*, *interval*, or *ratio*.

Finding the most effective method of symbolizing this attribute requires that you know the *level of measurement* of the attribute so that you can choose the most appropriate *visual variable*. A symbol's dimension and its attribute's level of measurement affect which visual variable should be used in drawing the symbol. Bertin's six traditional visual variables are *shape*, *size*, *hue*, *value*, *orientation*, and *texture*.

Verifying an Attribute's Level of Measurement

1. Right-click *SC_Mjr_Cites* in the *Contents pane* and select *Attribute Table*.
2. Move the blue scroll bar (at the bottom of the table) to view all the attributes in the table.

Three of the attributes in this table include RANK_MAX, Capital, and GN_POP. RANK_MAX is used to record the ranking of each city within the state according to its metropolitan population. Capital is used to record whether the city is a state capital. GN_POP is used to record the urban population of each city.

QUESTION 2.8

Choose the most appropriate visual variable for GN_POP when using point symbols.

a. Size
b. Hue
c. Shape
d. Orientation

QUESTION 2.9

Choose the most appropriate visual variable for RANK_MAX when using point symbols.

a. Size
b. Hue
c. Shape
d. Orientation

QUESTION 2.10

Choose the most appropriate visual variable for Capital when using point symbols.

a. Size
b. Value
c. Shape
d. Texture

3. Close the attribute table by clicking the X next to the name (upper left corner of your attribute table).

4. Right-click *SC_Gen_Counties* and select *Label* to remove the labels.
5. Make sure *SC_Mjr_Cities* is visible by checking the box.
6. Right-click *SC_Mjr_Cities* and select *Symbology*.
7. Under *Primary symbology*, select *Graduated Symbols*.
8. Select *GN_POP* for the *Field*.
9. Choose 12 pt for the *Minimum size* and 36 pt for the *Maximum size*.
10. Leave *Normalization* and *Method* as default.
11. Change *Classes* to 5.
12. Press the point symbol next to *Template*.
13. Search for and select *Circle 1* in the *Type here to search* box.
14. Click on *Properties* (right next to *Gallery*)
15. Click the Color drop-down arrow. Hover your cursor over the color boxes to identify the color names.
16. Change the color of the symbol to *Mars Red* and press *Apply*.
17. Press the back arrow in the *Symbology* dialog box (your selections up to this point should look like those in Figure 2.10).
18. Press the *Advanced symbol options* icon highlighted in Figure 2.10.

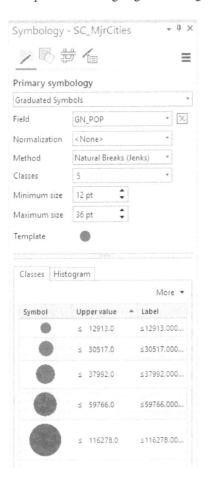

FIGURE 2.10

19. Expand *Format labels* and change the *Decimal places* to 0.
20. Right-click on *SC_Mjr_Cities* in the *Contents pane* and select *Label*.
21. Right-click again on *SC_Mjr_Cities* in the *Contents pane* and select *Labeling Properties*.
22. On the *Label Class* page, click on the *Symbol* option and expand *Appearance*.
23. Change the *Font Style* to Bold and *Size* to 14. Press *Apply*.
24. Close your *Label Class* page by pressing the X.

QUESTION 2.11

What visual variable do the graduated symbols use to display variation in city rankings on your map?

a. Size
b. Value
c. Shape
d. Texture

25. Click on the *Layout (MySCMap)* tab. The changes you made should show up on your map in the layout.
26. Select the drop-down menu for *North Arrow* in the *Map Surrounds* tool group.
27. Select a north arrow that you like and add it by drawing a box using your mouse in the layout canvas.
28. Resize and position the north arrow over the scale bar.
29. Press the *Legend* button in the *Map Surrounds* tool group and draw a box to add a legend.
30. Right-click on the newly inserted legend and select *Convert to Graphics*. This will allow for the modification of the legend so that it is more descriptive.
31. Again, right-click on your legend and select *Ungroup*.
32. Select and delete the legend symbol for *SC_Gen_Counties*.
33. Right-click and ungroup the remaining portion of your legend, and make it match the one in Figure 2.11.
34. On your own, add a title.

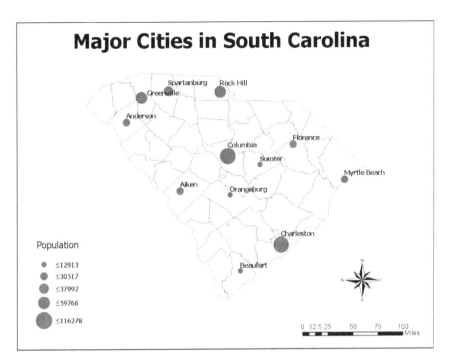

FIGURE 2.11

35. In your *Catalog pane*, expand the *Layouts* folder and right click on *Layout*. Export your map as a PDF into your class folder. Name the map *Ex02_yourlastname*. (Figure 2.12).

FIGURE 2.12

CHAPTER 3
The Geographic Coordinate System

The foundation upon which GIScience and its related technologies is built rests upon many of the initial ideas that were conceived by Greek scholars. We know this because *Strabo*, a Greek geographer born around 63 B.C., reported on these ideas and the people behind them. Strabo spent five years at the Library of Alexandria in Egypt studying these writings. His 17-volume *Geography* combined knowledge from mathematics, physics, politics, and history into a discourse on geography; it is one of the few writings to survive the Greek period (Brown, 1977). In his research for *Geography*, Strabo discovered that Greek philosophers began to influence geographic thought as early as 600 B.C. Of their many contributions, there are three key concepts we need to explore in this chapter: (1) the concept of the Earth as a sphere; (2) the determination of the circumference of the Earth; and (3) the origination of the **geographic coordinate system**, or **latitude** and **longitude**. Each of these ideas undergirds all of GIScience.

The Earth's Shape

We can find evidence through Strabo's writings that Pythagoras was one, if not the first, to contemplate both the shape and size of our planet. Certainly one of the more famous Greek philosophers, Pythagoras lived during the sixth century B.C. He founded a school of philosophy around 523 B.C., and proved several scientific hypotheses, including the Pythagorean Theorem. Of the hypotheses that Pythagoras put forth, potentially the most important one was his proposal that the *Earth is spherical in shape*.

Although it remains unclear exactly how he came to support this contention, *Aristotle* (384-322 B.C.), another of the founding figures in Western philosophy, later agreed with Pythagoras. More importantly, Aristotle used *celestial observations* to prove the idea that our planet was, indeed, spherical. For example, during a partial eclipse of the moon, he noted the curve of the Earth's outline on the moon. Since the alignment of the Moon, Earth, and Sun caused the eclipse, he argued that our planet must be spherical. He also observed that certain stars visible in Egypt and Cyprus were not visible at locations further north, and again attributed this to a curving, not straight, horizon (Brown, 1977).

The **spherocity** of the Earth can be observed when a ship moves out to sea from port, as described by Campbell (1998). As the ship increases its distance from us, it doesn't just appear then disappear, as it might if our planet was flat or disc-shaped. Rather, it first grows smaller, and then appears to sink, with the hull disappearing first and the top of the mast disappearing last. This phenomenon occurs uniformly over the planet, providing further evidence for a spherical shape. Finally, we in the twenty-first century have what is undoubtedly the most direct evidence—photographs of our planet by astronauts and satellites. One of the most famous is the "Blue Marble," taken by astronauts aboard *Apollo 17* in 1972 (Figure 3.1). This image shows a fully illuminated Earth; its name reflects the perception of the astronauts that the Earth looked like a glass marble.

Source: http://earthobservatory.nasa.gov/Features/BlueMarble/BlueMarble_history.php

FIGURE 3.1
NASA's 1972 Blue Marble image.

The Earth's Circumference

With Aristotle's observations to back up the theory of a spherical Earth, the general population soon came to accept the idea, and people began to wonder just how large a sphere Earth might be. Several made guesses, including Aristotle, but no one supplied any details on how they arrived at their estimates. The first person to lay out these ideas using a logical framework was the same man that coined geography: *Eratosthenes*. Eratosthenes' method and resulting accuracy in estimating the circumference of our planet is one of the great accomplishments of Greek science and a quite interesting story (Thrower, 1996).

Eratosthenes began by accepting the Earth as a sphere. He knew that if he were to "slice" this sphere in half, he would have a circle (Figure 3.2a). Using some basic geometry and a few facts about nearby locations, he proceeded to set up a method for estimating the circumference. First, he divided the circle, much the way you might section a grapefruit. At this point, he grappled with more questions: *How many sections comprised the circle, and what was the length of the arc for each section?*

To answer this question, Eratosthenes knew he needed real-world data. As luck would have it, at least according to one story, a caravan passed through Alexandria with a report about a well they saw in Aswan, Egypt (Laskey, 2001). According to the travelers, on June 21, at noon, the sun shone directly into the well—casting absolutely no shadows. Eratosthenes thought about this and realized that on that same day there *were* shadows cast at noon in Alexandria, Egypt. This seemed curious to him, and the more he thought about it, he realized—with a little help from the sun and a spherical Earth—he could set up a geometry problem to solve his puzzle.

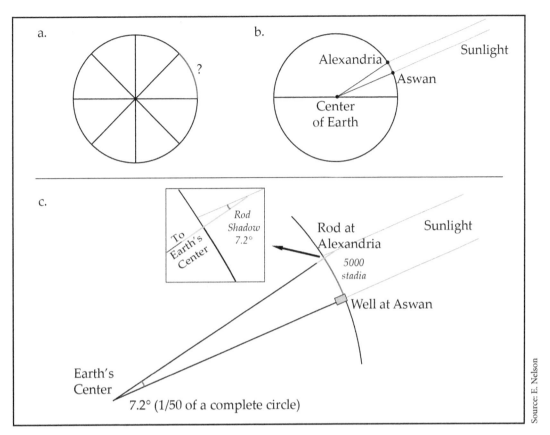

FIGURE 3.2
Eratosthenes's method for establishing the circumference of Earth.

He began by making two assumptions:

1. The rays coming from the sun were parallel as they struck the Earth.
2. Alexandria was directly north of Aswan—in other words they were both located on the same circle that would be created if the Earth were sliced in half along that route (Figure 3.2b).

The laws of geometry then say the angle at which the rays of light hit a straight line, such as a rod sticking straight up out of the ground, equals the alternating angle at the Earth's center whose two rays pass through the endpoints of the arc (in this case, between Alexandria and Aswan). When Eratosthenes measured the angle of the shadow cast by the sun in Alexandria, he discovered it was approximately 7.2° (Figure 3.2c). At this point, he had one part of his puzzle solved. It was about 7.2° from Alexandria to Aswan.

Now, he needed to convert that into a practical measurement, requiring him to make some additional assumptions. First, he needed to know what percentage of the circle 7.2° equaled. This was easy; he knew a circle was comprised of 360°, and by dividing that by 7.2, you would come up with about 1/50 of the complete circumference. His last missing piece was to come up with the actual distance from Alexandria to Aswan. He arranged to have surveyors trained to walk with equal steps walk the distance between these two cities; they estimated the distance to be 5,000 stadia (a stade was equivalent to the length of a Greek stadium). Today, scientists consider a stade about 1/10 of a mile, making the distance that they walked in our terms of measurement about 500 miles. If you multiply this distance of 500 miles by 50, since the distance is 1/50 of a complete circle, the answer is about 25,000 miles.

Considering our most recent measurements of the circumference of our planet is 24,906 miles long (Slocum, et al., 2005), Eratosthenes' estimate was pretty close. Of course, he was also a little lucky! In reality, Alexandria is not directly north of Aswan, but about 3° west. Furthermore, even though the caravan claimed the sun cast no shadow down the well in Aswan on June 21, Aswan is situated about 37 miles north of the point where that would be most accurate, as we will see shortly. In the end, the mistakes canceled each other out, giving the ancient Greeks an estimate that was close to the actual measurement.

The Geographic Coordinate System

Eratosthenes wasn't just interested in determining the circumference of the Earth as an academic exercise. He was actually working on a map of the habitable world and wanted to know the length of a degree to plot locations from the sphere to a flat piece of parchment with accuracy. To do that, he needed a systematic way of dividing the Earth that would also allow him to plot locations of places in two dimensions.

He began by following some of the work of earlier Greek scholars and divided his map into "…unequal, straight-sided geometrical figures compatible with the shapes of different countries" (Thrower, 1996, 22). This was largely unsuccessful, but it did prompt *Hipparchus* (190-120 B.C.), one of the best astronomers of the time, to propose a systematic grid of intersecting lines that eventually became our *geographic coordinate system* of today. As an astronomer, Hipparchus' idea was to project the grid lines on the sphere using the rotation of the Earth and the movement of the sun as a more scientific and rigorous underpinning.

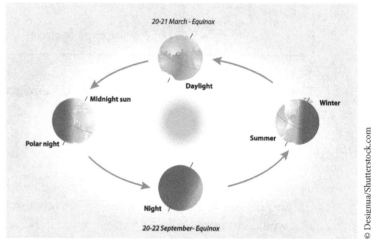

FIGURE 3.3
Plane of the ecliptic and the four seasons.

He started with a core concept in astronomical studies: **the plane of the ecliptic** (Figure 3.3). The plane of the ecliptic is the plane in which the Earth orbits the sun. As the Earth completes its annual orbit around the sun, it rotates on its polar axis. If this polar axis was perpendicular to the plane of the ecliptic, the sun's rays would always shine directly on the **equator**, which is an imaginary line established when you pass a plane through the surface of the Earth perpendicular to its axis of rotation. Imaginary lines such as the equator, which bisect the planet into two equal halves, are known as **great circles**. The equator bisects our planet into Northern and Southern Hemispheres. The equator provides us with the starting point for determining latitude, or position north or south on the globe. Other lines of latitude may also be plotted: They are known as **small circles**, since they do not bisect Earth. The key to locating these lines lies in the fact that the Earth's axis of rotation is not perpendicular to the plane of the ecliptic, but, in fact, is tilted approximately 23.5° relative to the perpendicular.

As Figure 3.3 shows, with the Earth's axis tilted relative to the plane of the ecliptic as it makes its orbit around the sun, the sun's rays do not always shine perpendicularly on the equator, but travel north and south throughout our year. Changes in the sun's position relative to the equator can be measured using the slant and length of shadows. This type of tracking by the Greeks led to the development of two further lines of latitude relative to the equator (Figure 3.4): the **Tropic of Cancer** (Summer Tropic, or Summer Solstice), at 23.5° north of the equator, and the **Tropic of Capricorn** (Winter Tropic, or Winter Solstice), at 23.5° south of the equator. These lines represent **solstices** or days on which the sun

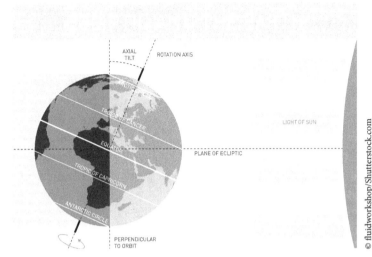

FIGURE 3.4
Framework for the system of latitude.

shines directly overhead at these locations, and provide the greatest number of hours of daylight. For the Tropic of Cancer, that day is June 21. For the Tropic of Capricorn, it is December 21. From a seasonal perspective, these are balanced by the **vernal** (March 20 or 21) and **autumnal** (September 20 or 21) **equinoxes**, which are points in the Earth's journey around the sun where the sun is directly overhead at the equator. The equinoxes are the midpoint between the northern and southern limits of the sun's travels due to the tilt of our planet's rotational axis. While earlier Greeks first established these lines through observation, Hipparchus instituted the precedent of measuring lines of attitude using the stars, which increases the accuracy of establishing latitudinal positions for locations.

LATITUDE

Latitude, then, represents a location on the Earth's surface between the equator and either the North or South Pole. Lines of latitude, or **parallels**, form when we imagine intersecting a plane perpendicular to the Earth's axis of rotation through the planet (Figure 3.5). The traditional measuring of the latitude of a location required determining the "...function of the angle between the horizon and North Star (or some other fixed star)" (Dent, et al., 2009, 28).

In the Northern Hemisphere, Polaris, the North Star, is our fixed star. If you were standing at the North Pole, this star would appear directly overhead, or 90° above the horizon. As you travel south from the North Pole, this star will appear lower and lower in the sky until it reaches 0° at the equator.

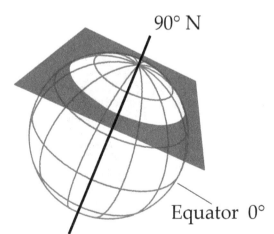

FIGURE 3.5
Visualizing lines of latitude.

To determine the angle of latitude for any given position in the Northern Hemisphere, we can use the position of the North Star in the sky at our location and geometry (Muerchke, et al., 2001, 288). The proof requires that you assume the line of sight from the center of the Earth to the North Star is parallel to the line of sight from your position on the planet to the North Star (Figure 3.6). Once this is accepted, the laws of geometry state that a straight line drawn from your position on Earth through the Earth's center will intersect those parallel lines of sight at the same angles (55°). Because of this, the adjacent angles (35°) must also be equal, since the sum of adjacent angles in both cases must equal 90°. Thirty-five degrees represent your latitude, which can also be measured via surveying or GPS technology today.

The range of latitude varies from 0° at the equator to 90° at each pole, with the parallels marking the change of degree as you approach either pole from the equator. For example, Cairo, Egypt and New Orleans, Louisiana are both located at approximately 30° north. If we wanted, however, we could be even more accurate by measuring parts of a degree, that is, using minutes (60 in a degree) and seconds (60 in a minute). In this case, Cairo's latitudinal coordinate would be 30° 03' 53" N and New Orleans would be 29° 57' 15" N. This unit of measurement is derived from the **sexagesimal** *system* of dividing a circle into 360° and is frequently denoted as *DMS format* (degrees, minutes, seconds) in GIS.

LONGITUDE

Of course, just knowing the latitude of a location is only part of the equation for specifying position on our planet. If we know that both Cairo and New Orleans are at 30° north, but don't know where they are positioned on the globe east or west, we have no idea where along that line of latitude the cities actually exist. To pinpoint the exact location on the globe, we also need to know each location's *longitude*. We create lines of longitude by passing a plane through the center of the Earth so the plane intersects the Earth's axis of rotation and bisects the planet into Eastern and Western Hemispheres. Because lines of longitude bisect the Earth, they, like the equator, also form great circles (Figure 3.7). You should note that lines of longitude are fundamentally different from lines of latitude. Lines of latitude are parallel to one

FIGURE 3.6
Measuring Latitude.

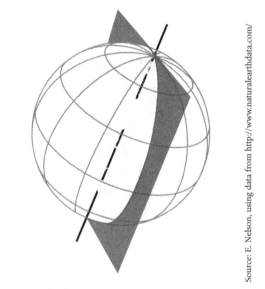

FIGURE 3.7
Visualizing lines of longitude.

another and are spaced at equal intervals on the globe. Lines of longitude, on the other hand, are equally spaced around the Earth at the equator, but the distance between them decreases as you move north or south because they intersect the axis of rotation, converging at the poles. This difference creates a dilemma—if all lines of longitude are great circles, *which circle do you use as a starting point for measuring location east and west?* The answer is not an easy one. Early on, each country tended to have their own **Prime Meridian**—the line of longitude from which they measured distance in degrees from east and west—and typically, it ran through their capital city. That was fine when mapping occurred in their own country, but as you might imagine, it created quite the mess when countries wanted to communicate locations with each other. The other issue with longitude was how, precisely, to measure it from any given starting point. From a conceptual standpoint, the Greeks were able to reason it out quickly, but the actual ability to technically measure it eluded them; the problem wasn't actually solved with any degree of accuracy until well into the 1700s.

At its root, longitude is really a time problem; the Greeks knew the Earth rotates west to east, and that a full revolution took approximately 24 hours. By dividing the 360° of the sphere by 24 hours, they knew that positions east or west of any meridian changed by 15° every hour. In other words, for every 15° you travel westward, the local time moves back one hour. If you know the local times, then at two different points, you can use the different times between them to determine your position longitudinally.

Unfortunately, the Greeks didn't have a mechanism sturdy or accurate enough to measure time from one location to the next. Over the centuries, many people worked at developing a timepiece. It wasn't until 1773 that a **marine chronometer**, a timepiece developed by *John Harrison*, was accurate enough to be acceptable for navigation (Brown, 1977). After that, it was another century or so, in 1884, before the international community would formally designate a world Prime Meridian. In that year, the International Meridian Conference chose the meridian (1/2 a line of longitude, from the North Pole to the South Pole) that ran through **Greenwich, England** to be the world's standard from which to measure longitude.

By setting the chronometer to the time in Greenwich, England, and then comparing the time on the chronometer to local high noon, mariners could use the difference between the times at the two locations to determine the ship's longitude. Thus, as you move west, longitude values run from 0° to 180° west from the Prime Meridian, with the other half of the line of longitude being designated as the **International Date Line** (Figure 3.8). This line separates consecutive calendar days, with the Eastern Hemisphere always being one day ahead of the Western Hemisphere. With the other half of the coordinate system in place, we can now fully distinguish between the locations of Cairo (30° N, 31° E) and New Orleans (30° N, 90° W). This spherical coordinate system of latitude and longitude is known as the *geographic coordinate system.*

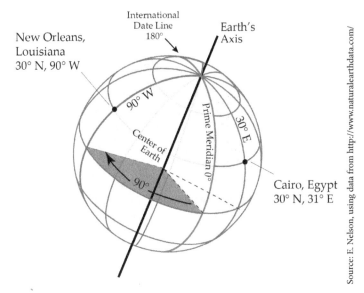

FIGURE 3.8
Measuring Longitude.

Key Terms

Geographic coordinate system
Spherocity
Plane of the ecliptic
Great circle
Equator
Small circle
Equinox
Vernal equinox
Autumnal equinox
Solstice

Tropic of Cancer
Tropic of Capricorn
Latitude
Parallels
Longitude
Sexagesimal
Prime Meridian
Marine chronometer
Greenwich, England
International Date Line

Questions

1. Who was Strabo, and why was he important to Geography?

2. What are some phenomena that support the concept that Earth is a sphere?

3. How did Eratosthenes calculate the circumference of the Earth?

4. What is the plane of the ecliptic?

5. What is Earth's axial tilt, and why is it important?

6. What is the difference between a great circle and a small circle?

7. What is the difference between a solstice and an equinox?

8. How many seconds are in a degree?

9. Why is the North Star important?

10. Why was John Harrison important?

11. What do latitude and longitude measure, and how are they different?

Bibliography

Brown, L.A. 1977. *The Story of Maps*. New York, NY: Dover Publications, Inc.

Campbell, J. 1984. *Introductory Cartography*. Englewood Cliffs, NJ: Prentice-Hall, Inc.

Campbell, J. 1998. *Map Use & Analysis*. 3rd ed. Boston, MA: WCB McGraw-Hill.

Crane, G.R. 2009. *Perseus Digital Library Project*. Tufts University Last accessed January 5, 2019 http://www.perseus.tufts.edu.

Dent, B.D., Torguson, J.S., and T.W. Hodler. 2009. *Cartography: Thematic Map Design*. 6th ed. New York, NY: McGraw-Hill.

Laskey, K. 2001. *The Librarian Who Measured the Earth*. Morris Plains, NJ: Houghton Mifflin.

Muehrcke, P.C., Muehrcke, J.O., and A. J. Kimerling. 2001. *Map Use: Reading, Analysis, Interpretation*. 4th ed. Madison, WI: JP Publications.

NASA-Johnson Space Center. 2009. "The Gateway to Astronaut Photography of Earth." Last accessed September 16, 2018. https://www.nasa.gov/image-feature/apollo-17-blue-marble

Raisz, E. 1948. *General Cartography*. New York, NY: McGraw-Hill Book Company, Inc.:.

Robinson, A.H., Morrison, J.L., Muehrcke, P.C., Kimerling, A.J., and S.C. Guptill. 1995. *Elements of Cartography*. 6th ed. New York, NY: John Wiley & Sons, Inc.

Slocum T.A., McMaster, R.B., Kessler, F.C., and H.H. Howard. 2005. *Thematic Cartography and Geographic Visualization*. 2nd ed. Upper Saddle River, NJ: Pearson Education, Inc.

Thrower, N.J.N. 1996. *Maps and Civilization: Cartography in Culture and Society*. Chicago, IL: University of Chicago Press.

Latitude and Longitude

In this exercise, you will explore how latitude and longitude coordinates are used in a GIS.

OBJECTIVES

- Explore the system of latitude and longitude
- Estimate how latitudinal and longitudinal distances vary over our planet
- Create a layer from a table of latitude and longitude coordinates

SOFTWARE

This exercise uses ESRI's ArcGIS Pro 2.3.2.

DATA

The data for this exercise are available from the Kendall Hunt Student Ancillary site. See the inside front cover for access information. You may also be directed to download the data from a different location by your instructor.

1. Download the data as directed by your instructor
2. Save the file to a location where you have read/write privileges

The files are compressed and must be decompressed prior to use.

Add Spatial Data to the Map Document

You will be creating a project rather than opening an existing one, and setting the properties of the *Map* and layers.

1. Start ArcGIS Pro.
2. Select *Map* under the *New > Blank Templates* in the dialog box.
3. Leave the defaults for *Name* and *Location*. Click OK. ArcGIS Pro creates a default folder to store all components of a project, but, for this lab, we will use the folder provided in the class data.
4. Right-click on the *Topographic* layer in the *Contents pane* and select *Remove*. This base map automatically loads anytime you start a new project. We do not need the base map for this exercise.
5. In the *Catalog pane*, right-click the *Folders* icon and select *Add Folder Connection*.
6. Navigate to and select your *Chapter03* class folder.
7. Click OK
8. Expand your *Folders* and *Chapter03* folders and your *Exercise_03.gdb* by clicking on the arrow to the left of each icon to view the contents (Figure 3.1).

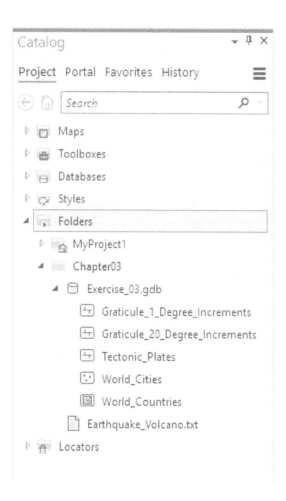

FIGURE 3.1

9. Click on *Project* (upper left corner of your session) and select *Save As*.
10. Navigate to your *Chapter03* class folder and save the project as *Ex03_yourlastname*.
11. In the *Catalog pane*, click and drag each layer from your *Exercise_03.gdb* into the *Contents pane*. Hint: You can click the first layer and hold the shift key while selecting the last layer to select them all at once.
12. In the *Contents pane*, make *Graticule_1_Degree_Increments*, *World_Cities*, and *Tectonic_Plates* invisible by unchecking their check box.
13. In the *Contents pane*, right-click on *Map*, and select *Properties*.
14. Change the *Name* to *World* and click OK.
15. Right-click on *Graticule_20_Degree_Increments* layer and select *Labeling Properties*.
16. Delete the text in the *Expression* box by selecting it and then pressing *Delete* on your keyboard.
17. Double-click on degrees in the *Fields* box and press *Apply*. This will assign the label text property to the field in the attribute table containing the degrees for the graticule (Figure 3.2).
18. Close the *Label Class* pop-up box by clicking on the X.

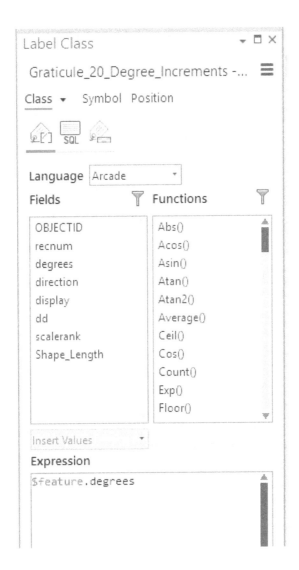

FIGURE 3.2

19. Right-click on the *Graticule_20_Degree_Increments* layer and select *Label*. The labels showing the degrees for each line in the graticule will appear.

Latitude and Longitude

We specify feature locations on Earth by latitude and longitude, which forms a network of intersecting lines called a *graticule*. Latitude is expressed as 0° at the Equator and runs 90° to the North Pole (90° N) and 90° to the South Pole (90° S). Longitude is 0° at the Prime Meridian and runs 180° to the west and 180° to the east, meeting at the International Date Line. Since the computer doesn't know N, S, or E, W, we code points north of the Equator positive and points south of the Equator as negative. Points east of the Prime Meridian are positive, and points to the west are negative. A location north of the Equator and to the west of the Prime Meridian might have a latitude and longitude of 36° N, 79.8° W, or 36°, −79.8°.

1. In the *View*, move your cursor over the map and watch the latitude values track in the lower right middle portion of your *View*.
2. Click on the check box next to *World_Cities* to make the layer visible.

QUESTION 3.1

Zoom and pan to find the location listed below. When you have found the location, click on the country to determine its name.

Which country is 30° north, 30° east?

    a. Egypt
    b. Afghanistan
    c. Nigeria
    d. Somalia

QUESTION 3.2

Zoom and pan to find the location listed below. When you have found the location, click on the country to determine its name.

Which country is 20° south, 60° west?

    a. Peru
    b. Chile
    c. South Africa
    d. Paraguay

QUESTION 3.3

Zoom and pan to find the location listed below (or use the *Go to XY* tool). When you have found the location, click on the city to determine its name.

Which city is located at 50.83° north, 4.33° east?

    a. Brussels, Belgium
    b. Paris, France
    c. Bern, Switzerland
    d. Vaduz, Austria

Zoom and pan to find the location listed below (or use the *Go to XY* tool). When you have found the location, click on the city to determine its name.

Which city is located at 39.74° north, 104.98° west?

a. Houston, Texas
b. Paris, France
c. Bern, Switzerland
d. Denver, Colorado

The Geographic Coordinate System (GCS)

In a GIS, latitude and longitude coordinates are part of the geographic coordinate system, or GCS. The GCS specifies the other parameters necessary for latitude and longitude coordinates to be used with maximum accuracy when locating features and calculating distances and directions. These parameters include the measurement framework, its 3D unit of measurement, its Prime Meridian, and its reference ellipsoid and datum.

1. Right-click the *World* map frame in your *Contents pane*.
2. Select *Properties > Coordinate Systems*.

What is the name of the current XY system assigned to your world map frame?

a. GCS WGS 1984
b. GCS NAD 1983
c. GCS Sphere
d. GCS Clarke 1866

Exploring the Graticule's Geometric Properties

There are four geometric properties of the graticule that you should be able to recognize, so that you can assess how transforming 3D coordinates to a 2D map alters them: These are *distance*, *shape or angle*, *area*, and *direction*. In this section, we will focus on distance and area. First, let's view the graticule as it would look on the globe.

1. Right-click on the *World* map frame and select *Properties* and then *Coordinate Systems*.
2. Scroll down until you see *Projected coordinate system* and click the arrow to expand the listing.

3. Scroll down, expand *World*, and search for *Vertical Perspective (world)*.
4. Right-click on *Vertical Perspective (world)* and select *Copy and Modify*.
5. Select the value for *Latitude of Center* and change it to 45.
6. Click *Save* and then *OK*.
7. Zoom in to the intersection of the Equator and the Prime Meridian (a scale of around 1:20,000,000.
8. In the scale box (lower left corner of your *View*), choose the 1:1,000,000 scale.
9. In your *Contents pane*, click on *Graticule_1_Degree_Increments* to make it visible.
10. From the *Map* tab, press the arrow underneath the *Measure* tool button in the *Inquiry* tool group and select *Measure Distance*.
11. Set the measuring distance to *Miles*.
12. Hover your mouse to find the *Mode* icon (next to the box where you changed the distance to miles), click it, then select *Geodesic* to measure in 3D.

QUESTION 3.6

Click on the Equator (0°) and then double-click on a line of latitude 1° away.

What is the approximate distance between these two lines of latitude?

a. 69 miles
b. 102 miles
c. 129 miles
d. 150 miles

QUESTION 3.7

Measure the distance between two lines of longitude near the Equator (hint: You can clear the previous measurements by pressing the *Clear Results* eraser icon in the *Measure Distance* box).

What is the approximate distance between these two lines of longitude near the Equator?

a. 69 miles
b. 102 miles
c. 129 miles
d. 150 miles

QUESTION 3.8

Zoom out and pan to 60° latitude at a scale of about 1:10,000,000 and re-measure the distance between two adjacent lines of latitude (hint: Close the *Measure* tool to pan and reopen it when you need it again. Double check to make sure you are measuring in miles and geodesic).

What is the approximate distance between two lines of latitude at 60° latitude?

a. 69 miles
b. 102 miles
c. 129 miles
d. 150 miles

Zoom out and pan to 60° latitude at a scale of about 1:10,000,000 and re-measure the distance between two adjacent lines of longitude (hint: Close the *Measure* tool to pan and reopen it when you need it again. Double check to make sure you are measuring in miles and geodesic).

What is the approximate distance between two lines of longitude at 60° latitude?

a. 3 miles
b. 35 miles
c. 75 miles
d. 107 miles

Mapping Earthquakes and Volcanoes

What types of spatial relationships exist between earthquakes and volcanoes? Mapping them is a good way to begin investigating the relationships between the two. A subset of earthquake and volcano locations is found in the *Earthquake_Volcano.txt* file located in your *Chapter03* folder. This file is not a spatial data file. It is a listing of latitude and longitude values for several volcano and earthquake locations saved in a spreadsheet format. To plot these locations in the display window, you must display them as XY coordinate data.

1. Click and drag the *Earthquake_Volcano.txt* file from the *Chapter03* folder in the *Catalog pane* to the *Contents pane*
2. Right-click on the *Earthquake_Volcano.txt* file and select *Open* to explore the attributes. Use the values contained in the fields of *Latitude* and *Longitude* to help answer the following questions. Close the table when you are finished.

When the latitude value is specified as a negative number, then the point's location is north of the Equator.

a. True
b. False

When the longitude value is specified as a positive number, then the point's location is:

a. North of the Equator
b. East of the Prime Meridian
c. West of the Prime Meridian
d. South of the Equator

Creating Geographic Features from Coordinate Listings

1. Right-click the *Earthquake_Volcano.txt* file in the *Contents pane* and select *Display XY Data*.
2. Make sure the *X Field* is *Longitude* and the *Y Field* is *Latitude*. The *Coordinate System* should be *GCS_WGS_1984*.
3. Click on the folder for *Output Feature Class* and navigate to your *Exercise_03.gdb*.
4. Name your feature class table *MyEarthquake_Volcano* and press *Save* and then *Run*.
5. Close the *Geoprocessing* dialog box by clicking on the X.

Visualizing Categories of Point Features

1. Right-click on your *MyEarthquake_Volcano* layer in the *Contents pane* and select *Symbology*
2. Under *Primary symbology*, click on the drop-down arrow and select *Unique Values*.
3. Next to *Field 1*, choose *Point_Type*.
4. Click on the *Format symbol* for earthquake and choose a red circle (Circle 5).
5. Press the back arrow.
6. Click on the *Format symbol* for volcano and choose the black square (Square 1).
7. Close the *Symbology* dialog box by clicking on the X. The locations of the earthquakes and volcanoes will appear as red circles and black squares on your map.

Visualizing Relationships: Earthquakes, Volcanoes, and Plate Boundaries

Your map is a representation of the physical world and is a great way to begin exploring the spatial relationships between earthquakes, volcanoes, and tectonic plate boundaries. Earthquakes and volcanoes are familiar features of our planet, but what is a plate boundary and why is it important?

Plate boundaries are physical features and are described in the theory of plate tectonics, a concept from geology that explains most of our planet's major surface features and associated activities. According to plate tectonic theory, our planet's outer layer is composed of fragmented slabs of rock. These slabs overlay molten material that allows them to move relative to each other. The movements, in turn, create features like mountains, earthquakes, and volcanoes. Most maps of tectonic plates show only the major plates. There are many smaller plates as well.

Maps like the one you have just created can be read just like you might read a statistical graph. Typically, you look for where features exist, how they cluster, and whether other features tend to cluster with them. From these insights, you might develop hypotheses about the relationships that can be statistically tested if you are working in a research context.

1. Turn off the *Graticule_1_Degree_Increments*, *Graticule_20_Degree_Increments*, and *World_Cities* by checking the box next to the layer names.
2. In the *Contents pane*, click the check box next to *Tectonic_Plates* to make it visible.
3. Click the line symbol under *Tectonic_Plates* and change the line width and color to make it more visible.
4. Right-click on the *World* map frame and select *Properties*.
5. Select *Coordinate Systems*.
6. Expand *Layers* by clicking on the arrow and select *GCS WGS 1984*. This resets your *World* map frame to this coordinate system.
7. Press the *Full Extent* button to zoom to your entire map. The *Full Extent* button is in the *Navigate* group of tools in the *Ribbon* (highlighted in Figure 3.3)

FIGURE 3.3

8. Your map should look similar to the one in Figure 3.4.

FIGURE 3.4

Our sample data include earthquakes and volcanoes in the region of East Africa, where there is no volcano within 1,000 miles of a plate boundary (hint: Use the measure tool to estimate distances between volcano locations and the plate boundary along East Africa).

a. True
b. False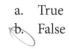

One result of plate tectonics is the Ring of Fire, an arc of volcanic and seismic activity that stretches around the edges of the Pacific Ocean (Figure 3.5). Similar in shape to a horseshoe, it arcs up from New Zealand into Japan and along the eastern edge of Asia, then across the Aleutian Islands of Alaska before heading south along the coasts of North and South America. This is an area where several tectonic plates meet the Pacific Plate.

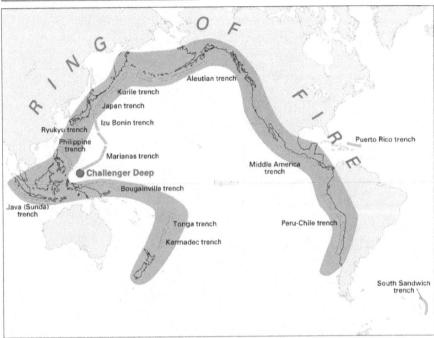

FIGURE 3.5

To center your view of the world on the Ring of Fire, complete the following steps.

1. Right-click on the *World* map frame and select *Properties*.
2. Select *Coordinate Systems*.
3. Under *XY Coordinate Systems Available*, expand *Projected coordinate system*.
4. Navigate to *World* and expand the selection.
5. Scroll to find *Robinson (world)*, right-click on the name, and choose *Copy and Modify*.
6. Click in the *Central Meridian* value box and type in the value of 180 to change the center of the display.
7. Press *Save* and then *OK*.
8. Press the *Full Extent* button to view the Ring of Fire. The *Full Extent* button is in the *Navigate* group of tools.

QUESTION 3.13

Our sample data along the boundaries of the Ring of Fire show only volcanoes but no earthquakes.

a. True
b. False

1. Press the *Full Extent* button and save your project.
2. In the *Catalog pane*, export your map as a PDF to your *Chapter03* class folder by expanding the *Maps* folder, and then right-clicking on *World* and choosing *Export to File* (Figure 3.6). Name the file *MyWorld_yourlastname.pdf.*

FIGURE 3.6

CHAPTER 4
Projected Coordinate Systems

The geographic coordinate system pinpoints any location on the planet using its spherical system of latitude and longitude. It does this by creating a **graticule**, or network of intersecting meridians and parallels over the sphere. With this system in place, it was only natural to want to put it down on paper—a flat surface—to make it easier to carry while traveling. Systematically transferring these to a flat surface (a plane) using planar coordinates produces a *map projection*. When we transfer the locations from a sphere to a flat surface, however, we distort key properties of the original coordinate system. Because these properties are compromised, this affects how you might use any given map most accurately. To understand this process more clearly, let's examine one of the earlier map projections on record.

Moving from Sphere to Map

Maps, of course, existed in various forms long before the development of latitude and longitude. It was only as commerce with other nations began to increase that the demand for more accurate maps soared. At this point, the use of latitude and longitude, along with accompanying methods of transforming this coordinate system to a flat map, became critical.

THE PLANE CHART

While Hipparchus provided us with the conceptual framework for the geographic coordinate system, it was a man by the name of Claudius Ptolemy who laid the groundwork for transforming these coordinates using map projections. Ptolemy (90-168 A.D.) published several writings on the subject; some of these were descriptive, while others, such as *Geographia*, outlined methods of mapping that would eventually contribute to the foundation of modern cartography (Brown, 1977). Even though the world was still awaiting the marine chronometer to measure longitude accurately, Ptolemy devised several projections using the concepts of latitude and longitude. He accomplished this by refining a nautical chart of the habitable world that a contemporary named *Marinus* had previously created around 120 A.D.

Marinus was a Greek geographer and mathematician. One of his contributions to geography was the development of a system of nautical charts that used latitude and longitude to map location over small areas. The result was a simple, rectangular, plane chart, known today as the **equirectangular projection** or, sometimes, the **Plate Carrée projection** (Figure 4.1). The chart was composed of a grid of equidistant straight lines of latitude that were crossed at right angles by equidistant straight lines of longitude. It is a

FIGURE 4.1

The Plane Chart, also known as the Equirectangular projection or the Plate Carrée projection.

simple transformation, but, in the end, quite unsatisfactory. To understand why, however, you must compare the characteristics of the graticule on the sphere to what happens to those characteristics after Marinus transformed it to paper.

CHARACTERISTICS OF THE GRATICULE

Four key geometric properties of the sphere—properties that we do not typically want our maps to distort relative to the original coordinate system of latitude and longitude—are *distances*, *shapes (local angles)*, *areas*, and *directions*. To recognize their distortion on a map, you must first recognize what these properties look like on the sphere. Dent and colleagues (2009) provide a good description of these properties; the following basics are derived from their discussion and are visualized in Figure 4.2:

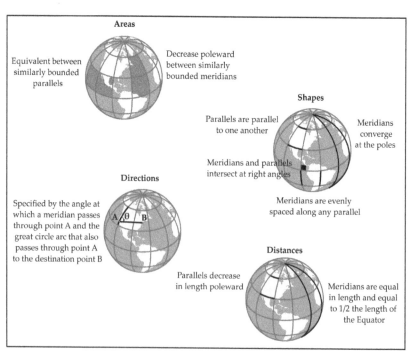

FIGURE 4.2

Key geometric properties of the sphere.

1. Parallels and meridians have a fixed-distance relationship on the sphere. All meridians, for example, are the same length, and they are all equal to 1/2 the length of the equator. Parallels of latitude, on the other hand, decrease in length as you move from the equator to either pole, and this change can be modeled mathematically.

2. Meridians and parallels intersect at fixed angles. Parallels are always parallel to one another, and they are evenly spaced along meridians. Meridians are evenly spaced along parallels, but they converge at both poles and diverge as you move toward the equator. When a parallel and meridian intersect, it always forms a right angle.

3. Intersecting parallels and meridians form quadrilaterals, which have the property of area. Areas are equal for all quadrilaterals that lie between two parallels, as long as they have the same longitudinal extent. On the other hand, areas of quadrilaterals between any two meridians vary with latitudinal extent.

4. Direction is specified by the angle formed from a meridian passing through a point and the great circle arc (the shortest distance between two locations on the sphere) also passing through that point to the destination point. This direction is traditionally reported as the angle clockwise from geographic north.

With these characteristics in mind, let's look at the graticule characteristics of the equirectangular or Plate Carrée projection (Figure 4.3). First, since the lines of latitude are all equidistant, you should note that distances become stretched east to west as you move north and south of the equator. The lines of longitude are

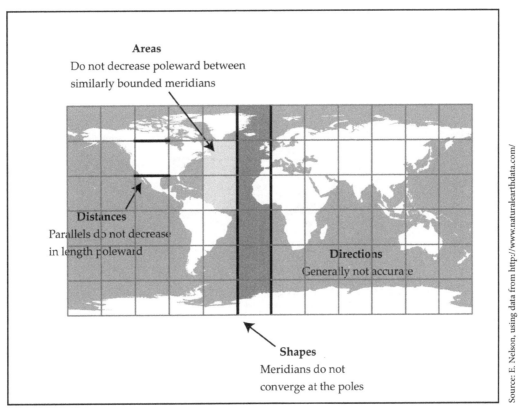

Source: E. Nelson, using data from http://www.naturalearthdata.com/

FIGURE 4.3
Distortion of key geometric properties: the Equirectangular or Plate Carrée projection.

also straight and equidistant; distances along them, thus, remain correct, but the lack of convergence at the poles distorts the areas and shapes of quadrilaterals as you move poleward from the equator. General directions are also distorted in this transformation. In other words, this projection preserves none of the basic geometric properties over an entire map. Because mapmakers typically are looking to preserve one or more of these properties, this limits the usefulness of the projection for most mapping applications.

TRANSFORMING DEGREES, MINUTES, SECONDS TO DECIMAL DEGREES

Despite these limitations, many geographic information systems use the Plate Carrée projection as a "default" projection when initially displaying spatial data. From a software perspective, this is not unusual. It is a simple projection to program, and the result is a familiar Cartesian grid. The grid uses the equator as the x-axis and the prime meridian as the y-axis, subdividing the world into four quadrants and using positive and negative signs in place of directional designations, a format more suitable to the computer world (Figure 4.4). Note that when projected into the digital realm the familiar (latitude, longitude) description found in a typical atlas changes (longitude, latitude); we determine our east-west position by moving along the x-axis, which, paradoxically, is the equator, a line of latitude. This transformation in coordinate specification moves us from the traditional degrees, minutes, seconds (DMS) to decimal degrees (DD). So, the Plate Carrée projection finds a "home" for initial GIS computations, but it is critical for a GIS user to recognize the limitations of the projection from a map-use perspective.

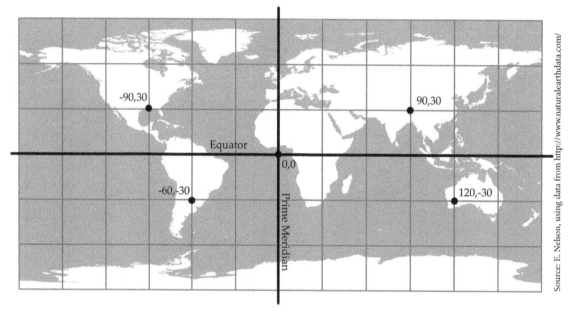

FIGURE 4.4
Latitude and longitude expressed as decimal degrees.

Classes of Map Projections

Marinus' plane chart may have been the dominant projection inherited from the Greek period, but Ptolemy also described others. He actually created two compromises of the Plate Carrée that he believed retained spherical relationships more accurately. His first projection also had meridians drawn as straight lines, but instead of being parallel straight lines, they converged at the North Pole. From this projection, he then outlined another in which he curved the meridians. The curved meridians provided a better visual representation, but were much more difficult to construct by hand, so it saw less use than the one with straight, converging meridians.

Ptolemy's *Geographia* is critical to further innovations not only for map projections but also for general cartographic principles; it is the starting point for measuring all progress in Western cartography (Thrower, 1996). With the fall of Rome, Europe entered a period in which theology overshadowed scientific interest, and works such as Ptolemy's, based heavily on mathematics, were largely forgotten or hidden. Because of this, his ideas weren't improved upon until *Geographia* was rediscovered by Europe at the beginning of the Renaissance in the 1300s. Many of the maps of the Middle Ages were more philosophical than scientific, and with the new push to explore the world, explorers and cartographers needed a mathematical basis to map coastlines more accurately. Ptolemy's work fit the bill nicely.

DEVELOPABLE SURFACES

Marinus' plane chart and Ptolemy's revised projections served as the prototypes for developing modern map projections. A **developable surface**, which is a surface that can be flattened into a plane without tearing, stretching, or compressing that surface, forms the foundation for discussing the basics of projection development. There are three

FIGURE 4.5
Developable surfaces and the reference globe.

developable surfaces used to create map projections: cylinders, cones, and planes (Figure 4.5). Although current projections are mathematically derived using computers, examining how these surfaces can be used conceptually to create a map can help us understand the limitations of any particular projection.

We begin with one these surfaces and a *reference globe*, which is a "…reduced model of reality" (Dent, et al., 2009). The size of the reference globe depends on the size of the final map. Ideally, once you have the reference globe, you would simply peel the surface off and lay it flat to produce your map. Unfortunately, making a spherical surface lie flat without tearing, stretching, or compressing is impossible (Figure 4.6), which leaves us to figure out how to transfer the features of the reference globe to either a cylinder, cone, or plane.

Take Marinus' equirectangular projection, for example. This projection is a prototype of the cylindrical class of projections. In this instance, a cylinder is placed over the reference globe so that its long axis is parallel to the Earth's axis. As the cylinder is placed over the globe, it touches or is *tangent* along the equator. If you were to imagine a light inside the globe projecting its graticule to the surface of the cylinder, you could trace the graticule, and then simply unroll the cylinder to lay the map flat. Cylindrical projections typically produce straight, equally spaced, parallel lines of longitude and straight, parallel, equidistant lines of latitude. The lines of latitude and longitude meet at right angles (Figure 4.7a).

FIGURE 4.6
Making a spherical surface lie flat requires tearing, shearing, and compressing it.

While cartographers traditionally used cylinders to map the entire world, they found that cones and planes handled regions more accurately. Ptolemy's first compromise of Marinus' projection is an example of a simple conic projection (Figure 4.7b). A cone wrapped around the reference globe will become tangent to a mid-latitude parallel rather than the equator; while it cannot transfer information from the entire reference globe, it might be better relaying information about the middle latitude regions. Transferring the

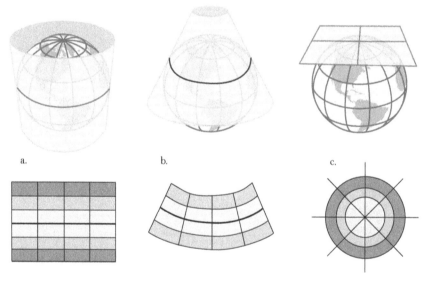

FIGURE 4.7
Distortion patterns associated with developable surfaces projected using a normal aspect.

information needed using this surface, and then unrolling it produces a conic projection. The resulting transformation is wedge-like, where meridians are straight lines radiating from a central point, such as the North Pole, and lines of latitude are concentric arcs of small circles.

Our third surface, the plane, has actually been in existence as a projection longer than either the cylinder or cone, but the Greeks primarily used it to map the heavens, not our planet. Placing a plane against the reference globe means that the surface is tangent to a point, not a line. A common point of tangency in this instance is the North Pole. Like the cone, cartographers cannot use the plane to map the entire Earth, but rather use it for mapping smaller regions of our planet. Planes also produce distinctive graticule patterns; here, the results are straight meridians radiating from the center of the projection, or **standard point**, and parallels that are equally spaced concentric circles centered on the standard point (Figure 4.7c).

Key Projection Characteristics

STANDARD POINTS AND LINES

Regardless of which developable surface the cartographer uses, one of the most important characteristics of the final projection is the line or point at which the projection surface touches the reference globe. Known as the **standard line** (or standard parallel, if it is a parallel) or standard point, these key features mark the line or point along the map where the transfer of information from reference globe to map is made without distorting geographic features. Map distortion patterns, then, are related to the standard line or point of the map, with the least distortion occurring around the line, then increasing as you move away from that line. In the case of the Plate Carrée or equirectangular projection, for example, distortion is least at the equator and increases as you move toward either pole (the lightest gray in Figure 4.7a represents less overall distortion). For the typical conic projection, distortion is least along the standard parallel and increases as you move away from it in either direction (Figure 4.7b). In the instance of the planar surface, distortion increases in concentric rings that radiate outward from the standard point as you move away from the point (Figure 4.7c).

In the typical GIS, these standard lines and points may sometimes be manipulated to help control distortion in the region to be mapped. Take the typical conic projection. This surface is most useful for regional maps in the mid-latitudes because the surface contacts the globe along a standard parallel as opposed to the equator (Figure 4.7b). In many of the conic projections, the user can specify the exact parallel to better control the overall distortion for the region of interest. For example, if we were to map the United States using a conic projection, we might specify the standard parallel at 40° north, but if we wanted to map Brazil, a better choice for a standard parallel might be 15° south.

PROJECTION CASE

So far, we have confined ourselves to projections with only one standard line, but mathematically, you can create projections that have multiple standard lines. Many conic projections, for example, are based on two standard lines, which are formed when the developable surface is conceptually pushed "through" the reference globe (Figure 4.8). These projections are more complicated, of course, but their

FIGURE 4.8
Conic secant case projection.

advantage is that they provide even tighter control over distortion. Whether you have one standard line or multiple ones defines the *case* of your projection. A projection with one standard line produces a *tangent* case; the *secant* case has more than one standard line. Although more complicated, secant cases are important as they are widely used in today's software packages. We'll look at some specific examples in the following section.

ASPECT

Aspect refers to how the projection surface is positioned relative to the reference globe. When the surface's axis of symmetry aligns with the axis of the reference globe, the aspect of the projection is called *normal*; this class of aspect produces the simplest graticules (see Figure 4.7). For the cylinder, the equator or equatorial aspect is the normal aspect. A cone, on the other hand, uses a mid-latitude parallel to produce its normal aspect, while the normal aspect of a plane is the polar aspect. You can also specify a *transverse* aspect, which rotates the projection surface 90° from normal. Both transverse and *oblique* aspects produce complex graticules and are used primarily to better center the projection surface over an area to be mapped (Figure 4.9).

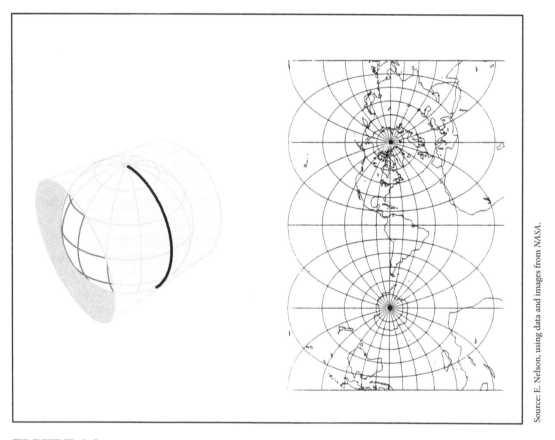

Source: E. Nelson, using data and images from NASA.

FIGURE 4.9
Example of a transverse aspect, resulting in a complex graticule: Transverse Mercator projection.

The concept of aspect categories is somewhat dated in the digital environment, where aspect is expressed and manipulated numerically (Strebe, 2009). In the world of GIScience, it is easier to think of aspect as a centering process, which involves precisely specifying a central meridian and standard parallels or points for a chosen projection (Figure 4.10). The central meridian is a specified meridian that is central to the area you are mapping. Specifying standard parallels as well helps minimize distortion

Coordinate System Details	✕
Projected Coordinate System	North America Lambert Conformal Conic
Projection	Lambert Conformal Conic
WKID	102009
Authority	Esri
Linear Unit	Meters (1.0)
False Easting	0.0
False Northing	0.0
Central Meridian	-96.0
Standard Parallel 1	20.0
Standard Parallel 2	60.0
Latitude Of Origin	40.0

Source: ESRI

FIGURE 4.10
Centering a map projection in a GIS.

within the mapped region. For example, if you were to make a map of the contiguous United States, you could minimize distortion by specifying a central meridian of 96° west and standard parallels at 20° north and 60° north.

Preserving Key Geometric Properties

One of the goals of map projections is reducing the overall distortion in the area mapped; another, equally important goal, is preserving key geometric properties, depending on the application for which the map is being made. The four key properties, which we mentioned earlier, are shape or local angles, area, distance, and direction. No map projection can preserve all four; at best, we might preserve one or two key properties. One of the primary ways of manipulating these properties, across all projection surfaces, is to vary the spacing of the parallels. In the following section, we look at each geometric property using specific projection examples.

SHAPE

We've talked a lot about the Greek influence on cartography and have highlighted some of the prototypical projections developed by key scholars of that era. We have also noted that this period of scientific advancement ended with the fall of the Roman Empire and did not resurface until travel and exploration began to demand a need for more accurate map projections. At that point in time, navigators began to call for a map projection on which constant compass directions could be drawn with a straight line. Sailors had found it was one thing to sail within sight of land, and quite another to try to navigate over larger stretches of ocean, where land was not visible.

To create a map where lines of constant compass direction plot as straight lines requires preserving shapes or local angular relationships (**property of conformality**) across the map.

On the globe, meridians and parallels intersect at fixed angles, and direction is specified by the angle formed from a meridian passing through a point and the great circle arc also passing through that point to the destination point. Lines of constant compass direction, known as **loxodromes** or **rhumb lines**, then are complex curves on the globe—they spiral toward the poles in order to cross each meridian at the same angle (Figure 4.11). To create a map on which rhumb lines plot as straight lines means preserving these angular relationships; the first person to achieve this was Gerardus Mercator, who produced one of the most famous projections of all—the **Mercator Projection**—in 1569.

The Mercator projection (Figure 4.12) is a cylindrical, conformal projection that uses the equator as its standard line. On this projection, parallels and meridians intersect at right angles just as they do on the globe, providing our cardinal directions of north, south, east, and west. To compensate for angular distortions caused by non-intersecting meridians, Mercator graphically expanded the spacing of the parallels so that they became progressively further apart as the poles were approached. The rate at which he spaced them matched the rate at which the meridians were expanded. Today, we call this the *principle of equal stretching*; it corrects the initial angular distortion caused by the projection, but greatly exaggerates distances and areas in doing so.

While rhumb lines may now be drawn as straight lines, the use of this projection for other purposes is quite limited. To see what we mean, compare Greenland to the continent of South America. On the globe, Greenland is about 1/8 the size of South America, but on the Mercator projection, the relationship is different, with Greenland appearing to be much larger. In fact, as you approach the

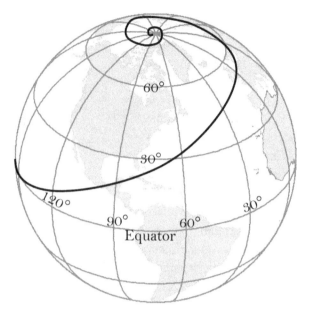

FIGURE 4.11
Loxodrome or rhumb line as seen on a sphere.

FIGURE 4.12
Mercator projection.

poles, distortion becomes increasingly worse. At 60° north, for example, the parallel is 1/2 the length of the equator on the globe, but on the Mercator projection, the same parallel is twice its original length. When you match that with an equal stretching of length between the meridians, the result is a fourfold increase in areas at that latitude. The Mercator projection, then, is most useful for navigation, and for mapping regions near its standard line, the equator (within about 35° of the equator), where distortion in geometric properties is minimal.

Two other conformal projections that you will run across quite frequently are the **Lambert Conformal Conic projection** and the **Transverse Mercator projection**, both invented by Johann Lambert in the late 1700s. Each was developed because the mapping community needed more precise projections on which to plot countrywide surveys and newly discovered coastlines. With the development of calculus in the field of mathematics, Lambert was able to harness new ideas that allowed for more precision in projection development. The Lambert Conformal Conic projection, for example, was designed to provide more accurate mapping for mid-latitude regions; not only was the standard line a mid-latitude parallel of choice, but with this revision of conic projections, cartographers could now specify two standard lines, effectively reducing distortion even more than a simple conic projection (Figure 4.13).

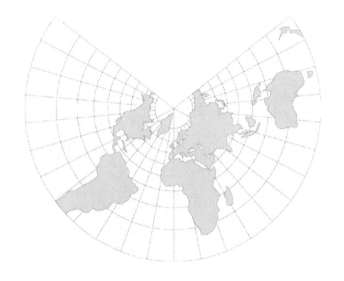

FIGURE 4.13
Lambert Conformal Conic projection.

The Transverse Mercator projection was developed by conceptually rotating the cylindrical surface 90° with respect to the globe. In using the transverse aspect, the long axis of the cylinder becomes perpendicular to the Earth's axis, and the surface is now tangent to the globe along a meridian of choice rather than the equator. While the world graticule is much more complex, this effectively makes the mappings of regions with a long north-south extent more accurate than if we were forced to map them using a parallel as a standard line (see Figure 4.9). Furthermore, since we confine ourselves to a smaller part of the graticule, we don't notice the complexity of it.

AREA

In our examination of the Mercator projection, we saw that to maintain angular relationships required exaggerating both distances and areas. Here, we will see that maintaining areal relationships requires exaggerating angular relationships; the two properties are *mutually exclusive*—you can never have both on the same map. Lambert, after having conquered conformality, was the first to manipulate the graticule deliberately to achieve equal areas or equivalence (Snyder, 1993). Beginning with a simple cylindrical projection, he had already determined that conformality was achieved by the principle of equal stretching and noticed that this process deliberately distorted areas. To maintain areal relationships, then, he concluded that he would need to decrease the spacing of the parallels relative to the meridians of this projection (Figure 4.14). This narrowing of parallel spacing, creating the **Lambert Cylindrical Equal Area projection**, is based on the sines of the latitudes, and the result is a distortion of angular, distance, and directional relationships to maintain areal relationships. This type of map, while not particularly useful for basic reference mapping, is the best choice for thematic maps, whose primary purpose is to compare spatial distributions between one or more regions.

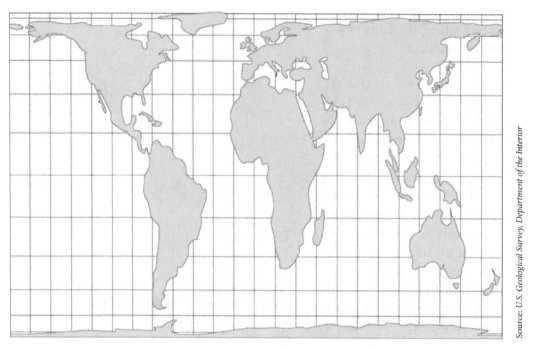

Source: U.S. Geological Survey, Department of the Interior

FIGURE 4.14
Lambert Equal Area Cylindrical projection.

The **Lambert Azimuthal Equal Area projection** and **Albers Conical Equal Area projection** are two examples of equivalent projections that are commonly used in today's mapping. The Lambert Azimuthal Equal Area is an equivalent projection based on a plane surface (Figure 4.15). Producing a circular graticule centered on the North Pole, the parallels of latitude are concentric circular arcs that are centered on the pole, and the meridians are straight lines that intersect at the pole. Equivalency is preserved by spacing the lines of latitude closer together as you move away from the pole, similar to the spacing of the cylindrical equal-area projection. As you might expect, this projection is used to map polar areas; it is also useful, however, as a

Source: U.S. Geological Survey, Department of the Interior

FIGURE 4.15
Lambert Azimuthal Equal Area projection.

surface on which to map hemispheres, continents, and countries if you manipulate the aspect of the projection from normal (polar) to oblique or transverse.

The *Albers Conical Equal Area* (Figure 4.16) is a special case of the Lambert Conical Equal Area, where the secant case of a conic surface is used, resulting in two standard parallels instead of the tangent case used by Lambert. Developed in 1805 by Heinrich Albers, it is the last of the basic conic projections developed (Snyder, 1987). As with the other conic projections, this projection has been widely used to map regions in the mid-latitudes, particularly those like the United States, which are wider in east-west extent than north-south extent.

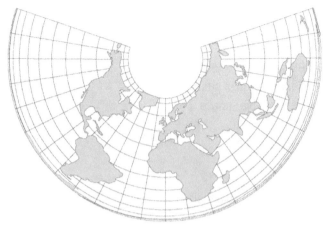

Source: U.S. Geological Survey, Department of the Interior

FIGURE 4.16
Albers Equal Area Conic projection.

DISTANCE AND DIRECTION

Unlike angles (conformality) and areas (equivalency), which are considered global properties that can be preserved over an entire map, preservation of distances and directions are limited to only certain areas of a map due to the transformation process. Because of this, these two properties are being considered together as local properties. Examples of projections that you might run across or want to use that preserve these properties are the *Lambert Azimuthal Equal Area Projection* (Figure 4.15) and the **Azimuthal Equidistant projection** (Figure 4.17). Both of these are developed on a plane surface—we just discussed the equal-area property of Lambert's projection above—and both preserve directions from the standard point to all other points on the map. The Azimuthal Equidistant projection also preserves distances from the center point to all other points, making it useful for mapping purposes such as airport traffic and missile launch sites.

Source: U.S. Geological Survey, Department of the Interior

FIGURE 4.17
Azimuthal Equidistant projection.

Key Terms

Graticule

Plate Carrée projection

Equirectangular projection

Developable surface

Standard point

Standard line

Case

Aspect

Property of conformality

Loxodrome

Rhumb line

Mercator projection

Lambert Conformal Conic projection

Transverse Mercator projection

Lambert Cylindrical Equal Area projection

Lambert Azimuthal Equal Area projection

Albers conical equal area projection

Azimuthal equidistant projection

Questions

1. What is a graticule?

2. Who was Marinus, and why was he important?

3. What are the four geometric properties of the sphere that we do not want to distort on a map?

4. What is a developable surface, and what types are used to create map projections?

5. What is a standard point, and what type of developable surface is it usually associated with?

6. What is a standard line, and what type of developable surface is it usually associated with?

7. What is the property of conformality, and why would you want to use a conformal map?

8. What is the principle of equal stretching? Give an example of one of the problems it creates.

9. Why was the Lambert Conformal Conic projection an important breakthrough?

10. When would it be most appropriate to use the Transverse Mercator projection, and why?

11. When discussing geometric properties, which two properties are mutually exclusive?

12. What type of projection is best for thematic mapping, and why?

Bibliography

American Cartographic Association. 1988. *Choosing a World Map*. Falls Church, VI: American Congress on Surveying and Mapping.

American Cartographic Association. 1991. *Matching the Map Projection to the Need*. Bethesda, MD: American Congress on Surveying and Mapping.

Brown, L.A. 1977. *The Story of Maps*. New York, NY: Dover Publications, Inc.

Dent, B.D., Torguson, J.S., and T.W. Hodler. 2009. *Cartography: Thematic Map Design*. 6th ed. New York, NY: McGraw-Hill.

Robinson, A.H., Morrison, J.L., Muehrcke, P.C., Kimerling, A.J., and S.C. Guptill. 1995. *Elements of Cartography*. 6th ed. New York, NY: John Wiley & Sons, Inc.

Slocum, T. A., McMaster, R. B., Kessler, F.C., and H.H. Howard. 2005. *Thematic Cartography and Geographic Visualization*. 2nd ed. Pearson Education, Inc.: Upper Saddle River, New Jersey.

Snyder, J. 1987. *Map Projections: A Working Manual*. Washington, DC: U.S. Geological Survey Professional Paper 1395.

Snyder, J. 1993. *Flattening the Earth*. Chicago, IL: University of Chicago Press.

Strebe, D. 2009. "Map Projection Essentials." Accessed September 24, 2019. http://www.mapthematics.Com/Essentials.php

Thrower, N.J.N. 1996. *Maps and Civilization: Cartography in Culture and Society*. Chicago, IL: University of Chicago Press.

Map Projection Basics

In this exercise, you will examine the foundations of map projections, manipulate their characteristics, and explore several specific projections that are popular for different applications.

OBJECTIVES

- Examine the characteristics of the *Plate Carrée* projection
- Set a projected coordinate system
- Examine the differences between projected coordinate systems
- Explore projection classes, characteristics, and distortions

SOFTWARE

This exercise uses ESRI's ArcGIS Pro 2.3.2.

DATA

The data for this exercise are available from the Kendall Hunt Student Ancillary site. See the inside front cover for access information. You may also be directed to download the data from a different location by your instructor.

1. Download the data as directed by your instructor
2. Save the file to a location where you have read/write privileges

The files are compressed and must be decompressed prior to use.

The Plate Carrée

One of the earliest projections on record is the equirectangular, or *Plate Carrée*, projection. This projection produces a simple, rectangular chart composed of a grid of equidistant straight lines of latitude that are crossed at right angles by equidistant straight lines of longitude.

It is a simple transformation, but the resulting map preserves none of the basic geometric properties most cartographers require. Despite these limitations, it is easy to implement and store the spatial coordinates in their original 3D form, which enhances analytical accuracy.

1. Start ArcGIS Pro.
2. Select *Map* under the *New > Blank Templates* in the dialog box.
3. Leave the defaults for *Name* and *Location*. Click OK. ArcGIS Pro creates a default folder to store all components of a project, but, for this lab, we will use the data provided in the class folder.

4. Right-click on the *Topographic* layer in the *Contents pane* and select *Remove*. This base map automatically loads anytime you start a new project. We do not need the base map for this exercise.
5. In the *Catalog pane*, right-click the *Folders* icon and select *Add Folder Connection*.
6. Navigate to and select your *Chapter04* class folder.
7. Click *OK*.
8. Expand your *Folders* and *Chapter04* folders and your *Exercise_04.gdb* by clicking on the arrow to the left of each icon to view the contents (Figure 4.1).

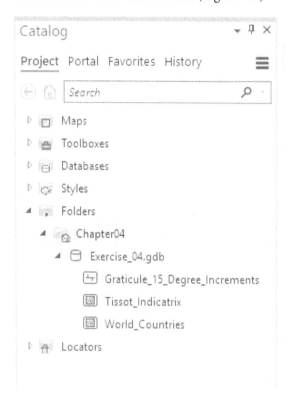

FIGURE 4.1

9. Click and drag all layers from the *Catalog pane* to your *Contents pane*.
10. In your *Contents pane*, press the *List By Drawing Order* icon.
11. Reorder your layers so that *Tissot_Indicatrix* is listed first followed by *Graticule_15_Degree_Increments* and *World_Countries*.
12. Uncheck the *Tissot_Indicatrix* to make it invisible.
13. Right-click on your *Map* frame and select *Properties*.
14. Click on *Coordinate Systems* in the list on the left side of the *Map Properties* dialog box.
15. Click on *Details* (top middle portion of the dialog box).

What is the name of the geographic coordinate system listed for the Map frame?

a. NAD 1983
b. GCS WGS 1984
c. NAD 1927
d. Clarke 1966

What is the name of the spheroid used in the coordinate system?

a. NAD 1983
b. WGS 1984
c. NAD 1927
d. Clarke 1966

1. Click *Cancel*.
2. Right-click the *Graticule_15_Degree_Increments* layer in the *Contents pane* and select *Label*.
3. Zoom in to North America.
4. Set the scale to 1:15,000,000 by typing the value in the *Map Scale* box located on the lower bottom portion of the *View*.
5. Pan and navigate to 60° north and between 75° and 90° west.
6. Select the *Measure Distance* tool under the *Inquiry* tool group in the *Ribbon*.
7. Change the units to *Miles* and the *Mode* to *Geodesic* to measure in 3D. The *Mode* icon is to the right of the word "Miles" in your *Measure Distance* box.
8. Measure the longitudinal distance between the 75° west and 90° west longitudinal lines along the 60° north latitudinal line.

Which of the following measurements most closely approximates the distance between the two longitudinal lines at 60° north latitude?

a. 52 miles
b. 2,500 miles
c. 519 miles
d. 250 miles

9. Repeat the process to measure the longitudinal distance between 75° west and 90° west along the 30° north latitudinal line. Make sure you are in *Geodesic* mode.

Which of the following measurements most closely approximates the distance between the two longitudinal lines at 30° north latitude?

    a. 52 miles
    b. 380 miles
    c. 89 miles
    d. 899 miles

10. Repeat the process to measure the longitudinal distance between 75° west and 90° west along the 0° latitudinal line.

Which of the following measurements most closely approximates the distance between the two longitudinal lines at 0° latitude?

    a. 103 miles
    b. 3,800 miles
    c. 890 miles
    d. 1,038 miles

11. In your *Measure Distance* tool, change *Mode* to *Planar* to measure in 2D.
12. Repeat the measurement between the 75th and 90th west longitudinal lines at 60° north latitude and 30° north latitude that you made in the previous section.
13. Note the differences in the measurements obtained using *Geodesic* mode versus *Planar* mode. *Geodesic* mode considers the Earth's curvature while the *Planar* mode distorts these distances.
14. Close the *Measure* tool.

Classes of Map Projections

While all map projections are mathematical transformations, the foundation of many of them is a *developable surface*, or geometric shape, that can be flattened onto a surface where features are mapped. Common developable surfaces include the *cylinder*, *cone*, and *plane*.

The Cylinder

The *Plate Carrèe*, which was a prototype for developing modern map projections, is based on the cylindrical model. With this model, a cylinder is wrapped (theoretically) around the globe, features are transferred from the globe to its surface, and then the surface is unwrapped and laid flat to produce maps.

1. Zoom to full extent by pressing the *Full Extent* button in the *Navigate* tool group.
2. Right-click on your *Map* frame and select *Properties*.
3. Select *General* from the list of options to the left of the dialog box.
4. Rename your *Map* to *Cylindrical* and press *OK*.

QUESTION 4.6

In a simple cylindrical projection, like the *Plate Carrée*, which of the following is NOT TRUE regarding the appearance of the graticule.

a. The lines of longitude are straight lines
b. The lines of longitude are equally spaced along the lines of latitude
c. The lines of longitude are drawn at right angles to the lines of latitude
d. The lines of longitude converge at the poles.

The Cone

One of the first modifications proposed for the *Plate Carrée* projection was to make the meridians behave more like they do on the globe. Using a conic surface forces the meridians to converge toward one pole because the cone, when wrapped around the globe, sits on the globe like a hat. The features are transferred to the cone, and then the conic surface is unwrapped and laid flat. The result is a map with a distinctly different graticule from the cylindrical model.

1. Select the *Insert* tab in your *Ribbon*.
2. Press the *New Map* icon. A new map should appear.
3. Remove the *Topographic* layer by right-clicking on it and selecting *Remove*.
4. Select your *Cylindrical* map by clicking on the tab at the top of your *View*.
5. Select all three layers by clicking on the first one, holding down the shift key, and then selecting the last one.
6. Right-click and select *Copy*.
7. Select the tab where you created a new *Map*.
8. Right-click on *Map* in your *Contents* pane and select *Paste*.
9. Right-click again on *Map* and select *Properties*.
10. Select *General* from the list and rename your new map *Cone*. You should now have two maps with the same data—one named *Cylinder* and another named *Cone* (Figure 4.2).

FIGURE 4.2

16. In the *Contents pane*, right-click on the *Cone* map frame and select *Properties*.
17. Select *Coordinate Systems* from the list to the left of the dialog box.
18. Scroll to and expand the *Projected coordinate system* option.
19. Expand *Continental* and then *North America*.
20. Scroll down to *WGS 1984 Canada Atlas LCC* (LCC stands for Lambert Conformal Conic projection) and select it.
21. Click *OK*.

QUESTION 4.7

Which of the following best depicts the appearance of the simple conic graticule applied to your Cone map?

a.

c.

 b.

d.

The Plane

The third developable surface is the plane. Unlike the cylinder and the cone, the plane is not wrapped around the globe. It is pinned to a point, usually a pole. When features are transferred from the globe to the plane, a third unique graticule is created.

1. Select the *Insert* tab in your *Ribbon*.
2. Press the *New Map* icon. A new map should appear.
3. Remove the *Topographic* layer by right-clicking on it and selecting *Remove*.
4. Select your *Cylindrical* map by clicking on the tab.
5. Select all three layers by clicking on the first one, holding down the shift key, and then selecting the last one.
6. Right-click and select *Copy*.
7. Select the tab where you created a new *Map*.
8. Right-click on *Map* in your *Contents pane* and select *Paste*.
9. Right-click again on *Map* and select *Properties*.
10. Select *General* from the list and rename your new map *Plane*. You should now have three maps with the same data—one named *Cylinder*, one named *Cone*, and another named *Plane*.
11. In the *Contents pane*, right-click on the *Plane* map frame and select *Properties*.
12. Select *Coordinate Systems* from the list to the left of the dialog box.
13. Scroll to and expand the *Projected coordinate system* option.
14. Expand *Polar*.
15. Scroll down to *North Pole Lambert Azimuthal Equal Area* and select it.
16. Click OK.

QUESTION 4.8

Which of the following best depicts the appearance of the simple planar graticule applied to your Plane map?

 a.

c.

b.

d.

Projection Distortion

The projection surface, in conjunction with other projection characteristics, will influence how the geometric properties of area, shape, distance, and direction are specifically distorted.

Preserving Geometric Properties

While reducing overall distortion for a mapped area is a key component driving the choice of a projection, equally important is preserving one or more key geometric properties. No map projection can preserve all four; at best, we might preserve one or two for any given application.

Shape. To create a map for traveling or for use as a basic reference that might be used to estimate distance and direction over a limited area requires preserving the shapes of local features. This property is called conformality, and projections that preserve conformality are known as conformal projections.

Area. Preserving the areas of different features relative to one another is not particularly useful for navigation, but it is the best choice for thematic maps, whose primary purpose is to compare spatial distributions between one or more regions. This property is called equivalency, and projections that preserve area are known as equivalent or equal-area projections.

Distance and direction. Unlike conformality and equivalency, which can be held across an entire map, preserving distances and directions is only possible for certain areas of a map. Typically, both properties are preserved only from the map's standard point to all other points on the map. Projections that preserve distance are termed equidistant, and projections preserving directions are called azimuthal.

The *Tissot_Indicatrix* layer consists of a set of *ellipses of distortion* that can be used to visually characterize projection distortion (Figure 4.3). Each ellipse describes the distortion occurring at a single point on the map and is the result of projecting a circle of infinitesimal radius from a globe onto the map. By studying how each circle is deformed, distortions in feature areas and shapes, as well as the distances between features, can be described:

- The smallest circles indicate areas on the projection that have minimal distortion
- Circles that change size indicate a deformation in the areal extent of a feature
- Circles that change shape indicate a deformation in feature shape
- Circles in which the semi-major and/or semi-minor axes change length in relation to the smallest circles indicate a distortion in distance
- Direction cannot be evaluated with this tool

FIGURE 4.3

1. Select your *Cylindrical* map by pressing the tab.
2. Order your layers so that the *Tissot_Indicatrix* is listed first followed by *Graticule_15_Degree_Increments* and *World_Countries*.
3. Click the check box to make *Tissot_Indicatrix* visible and make sure it's the only layer that is highlighted.

Using what you know about changes in the Tissot Indicatrix when map projections are modified (reread the beginning of this section), answer the following questions.

The *Plate Carrée* distorts the area and shapes of map features.

    a. True
    b. False

The *Plate Carrée* has minimal distortion along which line of latitude?

    a. 0° (Equator)
    b. 30°
    c. 60°
    d. 90°

Projection Characteristics

Regardless of which developable surface the cartographer uses, the first step in projecting features from the reference globe to a surface is to establish either a *point* or *line of contact* between the two models. These contacts, where the surface touches the globe during the transfer of features, are known as *standard lines* and *standard points*, or *lines and points of tangency*. Like the smallest circles plotted when using a Tissot's Indicatrix of distortion, this characteristic is significant because it marks locations on the map where there is minimal distortion in the transfer of geographic features.

    1. Select your *Cone* map by clicking on the tab.
    2. Right-click on the *Cone* map frame and choose *Properties* and then *Coordinate Systems*.
    3. Click on *Details* and answer the following questions.
    4. Close the *Map Properties* dialog box when you are finished.

What are the standard lines or standard parallels for the WGS 1984 Canada Atlas LCC?

    a. 0° N
    b. 29° N and 45° N
    c. 49° N and 77° N
    d. 90° N and 90° S

Centering

Overall distortion is also minimized by centering the projection. When you center a projection, you customize its standard parallel(s) and central meridian to correlate with the area of the world you are mapping. We could, for instance, use the *WGS 1984 Canada Atlas LCC* to make a map of Brazil if we re-centered the projection.

1. In the *Contents pane*, right-click on the *Cone* map frame and select *Properties*.
2. Select *Coordinate Systems* from the list to the left of the dialog box.
3. Select *Projected coordinate system* from the option list.
4. Right-click on *WGS 1984 Canada Atlas LCC* and select *Copy and Modify*.
5. Change the *Central Meridian* to −52, the *Standard Parallel 1* to 0, and the *Standard Parallel 2* to −30.
6. Change the *Name* to *WGS 1984 Brazil LCC*.
7. Click *Save* and then *OK*.
8. Press the *Zoom to Full Extent* button.
9. Check the box next to *Tissot_Indicatrix* to make it visible.

QUESTION 4.12

The modified *WGS 1984 Canada Atlas LCC* projection now called *WGS 1984 Brazil LCC* shows the most distorted Tissot circles in which country on your map?

a. Brazil
b. Mexico
c. Canada
d. South Africa

10. Save your project to your class folder as *Ex04_yourlastname*.

CHAPTER 5
Mapping Location

As the race for developing an accurate navigational timepiece raged, cartographers were also calling for improvement of land surveys. Governments wanted better documentation of the lay of the land within their borders; although earlier surveys of relatively small land areas existed, the standards used in creating them were not rigorous enough to map larger areas at the same scale. Information on such topics as elevation change and river flows, in particular, was sorely needed. The first country to respond to this call was France, where the Académie Royale des Sciences was formed in 1666. This society consisted of a distinguished group of scientists whose purpose was to inspire and improve scientific research in France. Funded by King Louis XIV, one of their first missions was to increase the accuracy of French land surveys. They began work when the Académie brought Jean-Dominique Cassini, an astronomer from Italy, onboard in 1669 (Brown, 1977).

Earth Models and the Survey of France

REESTABLISHING THE EARTH'S CIRCUMFERENCE

After much discussion, the Académie's scientists decided the first step in increasing the accuracy of these survey maps would be to re-determine the length of one degree of latitude. This meant beginning the survey by reestablishing the circumference of the Earth. Ultimately, they decided to use a variant of Eratosthenes's method (see Chapter 2), with the primary difference being that the French had access to better measuring methods and equipment to carry out the task (Brown, 1977). Jean Picard, a French astronomer, directed this aspect of the survey while Cassini oversaw the larger operation. **Triangulation** was Picard's method of choice for solving the problem because it replaced the need to measure the distances between every pair of locations comprising the survey. Instead, his team calculated one distance measurement between two known locations to form a baseline and then they applied trigonometric principles and angle measurements from each end of that baseline to a third location to determine the distances to that point (Figure 5.1). From this first triangle, the other two sides were then used as baselines to extend the network to other locations.

The distance of the final meridian line, which ran north from Paris, was approximately 77.8 miles in modern-day units of measurements. With the length of that line established, Picard's surveyors then made astronomical observations at both of its endpoints to determine the length of the line in degrees, with the result being approximately 1° 11' 57" (1.2°). Multiplying the 77.8 miles by the number of 1.2° segments it takes to produce 360° (300) gives us an estimated circumference of 23,340 miles for our planet, which is quite close to today's measurement of 24,906 miles (Slocum et al., 2005). Finished in 1670, Picard's meridian line, along with a topographic survey of Paris, formed the foundation for what would soon be the first large-scale survey of an entire country (Brown, 1977).

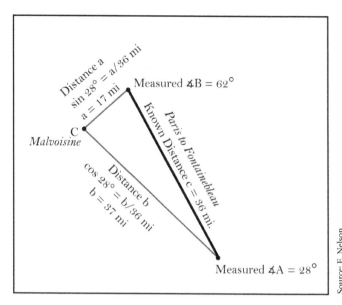

FIGURE 5.1
Triangulation Example.

VARYING LATITUDE MEASUREMENTS CREATE CONTROVERSY

Following this initial survey and Picard's death in 1682, Jacques Cassini, son of Jean-Dominique Cassini, took over and extended Picard's work. He surveyed one arc northward to Dunkirk, and another southward toward the boundary with Spain. When he calculated the length of a degree of latitude in both arcs, however, he discovered a difference, which cast doubt on the accepted convention of the Earth being spherical in

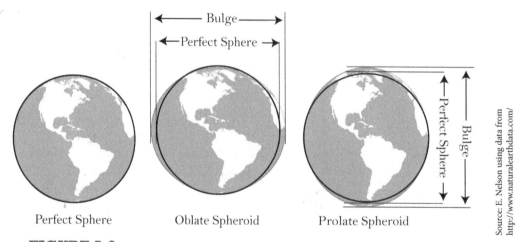

FIGURE 5.2
Proposed shapes for Earth: Aristotle's sphere (l), Newton's oblate spheroid (m) and Cassini's prolate spheroid (r).

GEOGRAPHIC INFORMATION SCIENCE

shape. By his calculations, the length of a degree in the northern arc was shorter than the one in the southern arc, suggesting that the Earth might actually be a **prolate spheroid** (Figure 5.2), or, in more descriptive terms, egg-shaped (O'Connor and Robertson, 2008).

Such results presented a dilemma. First, although the differences were small, they couldn't be easily dismissed. Isaac Newton's theory of universal gravitation also proposed that the Earth, due to centrifugal forces from rotating on its axis, was not spherical. Interestingly enough, however, Newton believed the Earth's shape was more like an **oblate spheroid**—flatter at the poles and slightly bulging at the equator (an egg on its side, if you will). Second, if Cassini were correct, and the lengths did differ, then the whole area would have to be resurveyed and surveying methods refined to produce a truly accurate map.

To put this controversy to rest, the Académie sponsored two expeditions to widely separated latitudinal regions to find a definitive answer. They sent one team of surveyors to equatorial South America and another to the Arctic Circle. It took ten years, but in the end, both teams confirmed Newton's hypothesis: The Earth was not spherical after all, but really an oblate spheroid, with the poles slightly flattened in comparison to the equator. The difference is actually small (Figure 5.2 is exaggerated) and can usually be ignored when mapping at small scales. For example, one Earth model widely used in mapping (the World Geodetic System) is a spheroid with only 21-km difference between the radius at the equator (6,378.137 km) and the radius at the poles (6,356.752 km). Of course, 21 km makes a big difference when the map you are making is a larger-scaled map to be used by others to calculate distances and directions.

With this new knowledge, the Académie had the Paris meridian resurveyed. Although Jean-Dominque Cassini passed away in 1712 before the entire country could be surveyed, his son, Jacques Cassini, continued the project. In the late 1700s his grandson, Cesar-Francois Cassini de Thury, completed it. Known as the *Carte de Cassini*, the methods by which it was created became the standard in surveying techniques, and other countries later adopted them in the creation of their own surveys (Thrower, 1996).

Topographic Mapping and the United States Geological Survey

Between roughly 1500 and 1800, thousands of maps of the United States were produced; they ranged from crude sketches to surveys of limited scope (Brown, 1977). It wasn't until 1878, however, that Congress requested the *National Academy of Sciences* to devise a plan for surveying the territories of the United States. The result of this request was the formation of the *United States Geological Survey (USGS)* in 1879, whose initial purpose was to classify public lands and study the geologic structures and economic resources of the country (USGS, 2000). Under its first director, Clarence King, exploration of the West became much more of an exact science than any previous survey attempts. By 1882, as they worked to produce the first geologic map of the country, the USGS program added **topographic mapping** as one of its primary functions. This type of mapping remains central to the USGS today, as one of the organization's goals is to provide complete and up-to-date coverage of the United States. The term *topographic* is derived from the Greek *topographos*, which means "to describe a place." USGS topographic maps do just that (Figure 5.3). They describe prominent natural and cultural features using a cartographic symbol set on a backdrop of one or more *planar coordinate systems*, which allows you to locate the positions of represented features on the Earth's surface.

FIGURE 5.3
Example of USGS topographic map.

Source: U.S. Geological Survey, Department of the Interior

DATUMS AND THE GEOGRAPHIC COORDINATE SYSTEM

A planar coordinate system requires a three-dimensional surface that approximates the size and shape of our planet as its foundation. As we have seen, the Earth's surface more closely approximates an oblate spheroid than a true sphere. Mathematically, an oblate spheroid is an ellipse that is rotated on its shorter, semi-minor axis—the polar axis in Earth's case (Figure 5.4). The resulting three-dimensional surface often goes by the term **reference ellipsoid**. Its final shape is determined by (1) the length of the equatorial (or semi-major) axis *a* and (2) the length of the polar (semi-minor) axis *b*. Geodesists also specify reference ellipsoids by their inverse *flattening* $(1/f)$, where $f = ((a-b)/a)$, the proportion of difference between the equatorial and polar axes relative to the equatorial axis in length. When the difference in axis lengths is small, say 21 km, the flattening that occurs is also very small (1/300), although still significant for large-scale mapping.

By the time the USGS began their topographic program, survey measurements had been recorded in several locations, with the length of a degree of latitude varying slightly from place to place. This is interesting, because it implies that a standard ellipsoid tied to a specific point on the Earth's surface varies in fit as you map different locations. Depending on the local area being mapped, the ellipsoid's axis lengths and their proportion to one another must be modified to create a best-fit and to determine the most accurate coordinates. What might cause this? As it turns out, when surveyors were pinpointing these locations, the traditional equipment they used was oriented using the pull of gravity. This pull varies from place to place due to the Earth's rotation and the variation in composition and density of its crust—among other things. In other words, the Earth is not really an ellipsoid, either. Its true nature is rather lumpy, and goes by the name **geoid** (Figure 5.5).

The geoid, however, is mathematically complex and cumbersome to use as a model for most surveys. Instead, different countries choose to use different "best-fit" ellipsoids when conducting local surveys. In North America, for example, surveyors chose the **Clarke 1866 Ellipsoid**. They established a ground zero, or starting point, for measuring the locations of features, by tying the ellipsoid to the Earth's surface at **Meades Ranch, Kansas**. Using latitude, longitude, and the process of triangulation, they were then able to work outward from that location and measure a set of locations called **geodetic control points**. These points were located using benchmarks; they form a **geodetic datum** from which all other features can be located. This datum (Figure 5.6), known as the **North American Datum of 1927** (*NAD27*), consists of the ellipsoid, the origin of the coordinate system, and some 26,000 surveyed points in the United States and Canada (Bolstad, 2005). Its purpose is to describe locational, directional, and scale relationships to Meades Ranch. Most large-scale maps of areas in the United States produced from the late 1800s through the late 1900s

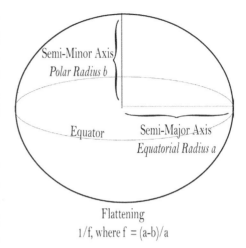

Source: E. Nelson

FIGURE 5.4
Parameters for specifying a reference ellipsoid.

Source: NASA

FIGURE 5.5
A depiction of the Earth's geoid using gravity field anomalies.

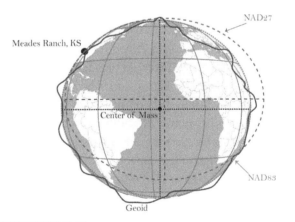

Source: E. Nelson, using data from http://www.naturalearthdata.com/

FIGURE 5.6
North American Datum of 1927, showing how the Clarke 1886 reference ellipsoid was tied to Meades Ranch, Kansas to create a 'best-fit' scenario for U.S. topographic mapping.

use this datum as the foundation for locating features within the country.

As you might suspect, when you change the shape of the model you use to represent the Earth, you also change the absolute positions of features to a certain extent. Different Datums use different models to approximate the shape of the Earth. The **North American Datum of 1983** *(NAD83)*, for instance, was the successor to NAD27; as technology improved and more locations were surveyed, the National Coast and Geodetic Survey was assigned the task of updating our national maps. Instead of using Clarke 1866 as the ellipsoidal reference, they chose the **Geodetic Reference System 1980** *(GRS80)* ellipsoid because technology had improved to the point that the local, fixed-station approach of NAD27 was outdated. With NAD27, the ellipsoidal surface was tied to the Earth at one point, Meades Ranch, Kansas; thus, it was of limited use to anyone outside of North America.

FIGURE 5.7

NAD27 tic marks on an updated USGS topographic quadrangle.

NAD83 ties the GRS80 ellipsoid to the center of the Earth's mass, making it a datum that is global in use, as opposed to local (Figure 5.6). The result? Some locations in North America shifted by up to 1,312.3 ft., requiring the publication of new latitude and longitude values for some 250,000 control points. Of course, the features themselves did not really change location; rather, by moving to an updated datum, their locations in the new system are more precisely defined. This change is shown on older topographic maps by a dashed plus sign in the upper and lower left boundaries of the quadrangle, which indicates the map corner's position for the older NAD27 coordinates (Figure 5.7).

What does this mean for us, as users of these products and of other technological services? Take as an example, a parcels layer created from a survey that used the NAD27 datum as its basis for recording the parcel locations (Figure 5.8). This layer has been overlaid on an aerial photograph of the same area, only the two layers do not align. The problem is that the aerial photograph is based on the NAD83 datum, so when the two are overlaid, you get a shift in feature positions, which, at times, can be on the order of 200 m (about 656 ft.). Discrepancies such as this are quite common when compiling GIS projects, and the solution lies in using the correct software transformations to bring one layer into alignment with another by making sure all geographic coordinate systems match in the reference ellipsoid they use as their foundation for specifying latitude and longitude positions.

Measurements from Topographic Maps

SPECIFYING LOCATIONS

The USGS produces topographic maps at a variety of scales, with the 1:24,000 (or 7.5 minutes) mapped series being the most popular. The 7.5-minute series comprises 57,000

FIGURE 5.8
Misalignment of spatial data due to datum shifts.

maps, where each map, or quadrangle, is bounded on the east and west by meridians that are 7.5 minutes apart, and bounded on the north and south by parallels that are 7.5 minutes apart. Each sheet is named in the upper right corner after a prominent city or landscape feature on the map. The Philpott Lake Quadrangle in southern Virginia, for example, spans from 80° 00' 00" W to 80° 07' 30" W and from 36° 45' 00" N to 36° 52' 30" N.

There are multiple methods for specifying locations using a topographic quadrangle. Latitude and longitude, marked by graticules and/or tic marks along the edges of the map, is the traditional system. Latitude and longitude, however, can be cumbersome for humans to manipulate. As a sexagesimal system designed to work with a spherical surface, we find it awkward to compute changes in degrees, minutes, and seconds for location features, and even more awkward to convert changes in locations to linear distances quickly. If the location being specified happens to be located at the intersection of a meridian or parallel, it may be justified, but if the location requires that we estimate between known lines of latitude and longitude, it may cause problems. This is especially true when distances and directions are involved, as we will see shortly. Fortunately, there are other means of specifying locations and measuring distances and directions when using a topographic quadrangle. These systems are based on the idea of **Cartesian coordinates**, developed by a French philosopher/mathematician named René Descartes. Descartes used two perpendicular axes that cross at a central point as the basis of his plane. The central point, called the *origin*, along with the two axes, divides the plane into four quadrants, much like we saw when we transformed our geographic coordinate system to a plane using the Plate Carrée projection (Figure 5.9). Object positions can be determined east or west of the origin along the *x*-axis (the **easting coordinate**) and north or south of the origin along the y-axis (the **northing coordinate**). In GIScience, when working with navigational tasks, we are only interested in working in Quadrant I. This is because it is quicker and less error-prone to calculate positions, distances, and directions by working solely with positive numbers. How can we make this work, though, for any location on the planet? The answer lies in manipulating the coordinate system to create a customized system for navigational tasks.

FIGURE 5.9
Latitude and longitude expressed as a planar coordinate system.

State Plane Coordinate System. Developed in the 1930s, the State Plane Coordinate System (SPCS) is a customized grid system used at the state level in the United States to record locations using Cartesian coordinates. The system was a boon for surveyors and engineers who could now complete their work without the need of spherical trigonometry. One key to the development of the system, however, was the need to minimize scale distortion; remember that as larger and larger areas are mapped, more distortion creeps in due to transforming our curved surface to a flat plane. To minimize the interference of curvature, it was decided to divide each state into one or more zones and then create a separate coordinate system for each of these smaller regions (Figure 5.10).

Within each of these regions, positioning using this coordinate system is quite accurate, but outside each zone, accuracy declines. As a coordinate system, the SPCS is not useful for national mapping applications. Each zone also has its own projection surface to minimize distortion even further. For example, the Lambert Conformal Conic is used for zone shapes that have a predominant east-west extent like Tennessee, and the Transverse Mercator is used for zone shapes that have a predominant north-south extent, such as Georgia.

North Carolina's SPCS, for instance, is based on the Lambert Conformal Conic Projection (Figure 5.11). This projection has two standard parallels that help control distortion within the state. These parallels are specified so that they lay one-sixth of the zone width from the northern and southern zone boundaries of the state. A central meridian that is near the center of the zone is also specified. The central meridian serves as the starting point for a y-axis in this modified Cartesian system. Remember, however, that in GIScience, practitioners only want to deal with Quadrant I, where all coordinates are positive numbers. To make this work on SPCS, GIScientists use a **false origin**, which is established west of the central meridian (2,000,000 ft. for zones using the Lambert Conformal Conic projection and 500,000 ft. for those using the Transverse Mercator projection). The modified starting point for the *x-axis* is just south of the zone boundary and is called the **latitude of origin**.

False origins, then, are created by adding numbers to the original origin of the projection. In doing so, the new origin is repositioned to the west and south of the original so that all coordinates within the mapped area

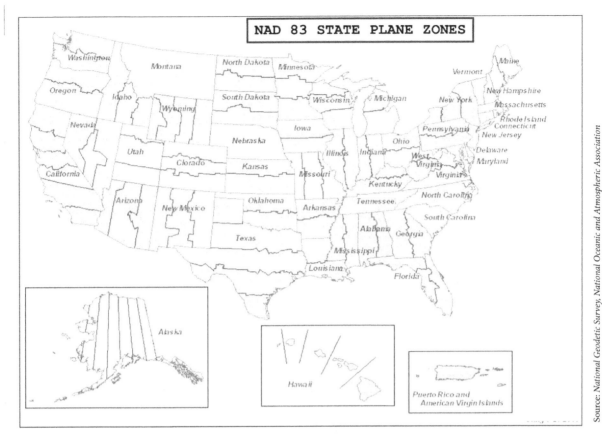

FIGURE 5.10
State Plane Coordinate System.

Source: National Geodetic Survey, National Oceanic and Atmospheric Association

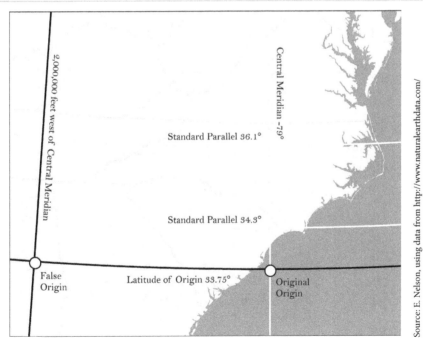

FIGURE 5.11
North Carolina's State Plane Coordinate System.

Source: E. Nelson, using data from http://www.naturalearthdata.com/

become positive coordinates. To specify the location of a feature using the SPCS, you measure the distance in feet east and north of the false origin, and specify the location using that *easting* and *northing*—which act like an (*x*, *y*) coordinate—also noting the state and zone for the coordinate. As the *x*-coordinate, the easting gives the distance east from the false origin, while the northing (or *y*-coordinate) gives the distance north of it. Since you are only working with mapped features within that zone, recalibrating the coordinates to account for the false origin doesn't affect measurements. Instead, it makes them easier to calculate. On the topographic quadrangles, grid lines for the SPCS are marked using black tics along the edges of the map.

If the feature you are locating lies on one of the intersections of these gridlines, the easting and northing coordinate can be specified with little extra work. If, however, the point of interest is located somewhere between gridlines, as the Lewis and Clark school is in Figure 5.12, then approximating the location requires using methods of interpolation. To locate the school, for example, you would:

1. Find the nearest gridlines that are south and west of the feature
    Northing and easting values are posted at one tic along each side of the topographic quadrangle. Additional unlabeled tic marks are posted for every 10,000 ft. for the 1:24,000 series.
2. Using a strip of paper, measure the distance from each gridline to the point by making a tic mark on the strip at each point

FIGURE 5.12
Locating a feature using the SPCS.

3. Align the strip along the map's scale bar to determine the ground distance between each gridline and the feature
4. Add the gridline values to each measured distance to determine the easting and northing coordinate for your point

For the Lewis and Clark school, this would result in a coordinate location of approximately: (1,154,752' E, 924,541' N, OR), with the final accuracy influenced by measuring accuracy.

Universal Transverse Mercator (UTM) System. While the SPCS were defined only for the United States, the introduction of more modern technology allowed us to create a worldwide grid coordinate system. The *Universal Transverse Mercator (UTM) System* is one such system (Figure 5.13). It works by dividing the Earth into 60 north-south zones, each of which extends from 84° north to 80° south. Each zone, numbered 1 to 60 beginning at the International Date Line and moving east, is based on a transverse Mercator projection with its own specified central meridian that acts as a standard line. Because each zone is only 6° wide, the projected data have a high degree of accuracy. The Polar Regions are covered by their own complementary grid coordinate system, called the **Universal Polar Stereographic System**. Both systems measure distances in meters north and east of a zone origin.

Each UTM zone has a separate false origin for its Northern and Southern Hemisphere components. The false easting for these origins is defined similarly—it is always 500,000 m west of the central meridian for

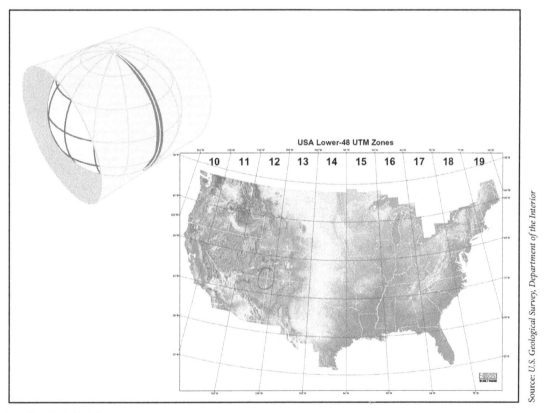

FIGURE 5.13
Universal Transverse Mercator Coordinate System.

the zone in question. Thus, the central meridian in each of the 60 zones is marked 500,000 m, and locations west of that meridian range from 0 to 500,000 m. Those locations east of the central meridian have eastings greater than 5,000,000 m. The false northing is hemisphere-dependent. In the Northern Hemisphere, the northing origin (0 m) is the equator, so that all northing coordinates are greater than 0 m. A location is specified by giving the false easting coordinate, the false northing coordinate, the zone, and the hemisphere (Figure 5.14). When working in the Southern Hemisphere, the equator is assigned the value of 10,000,000 m, displacing the false origin to the southern polar region, so that all coordinates may be reported as positive numbers.

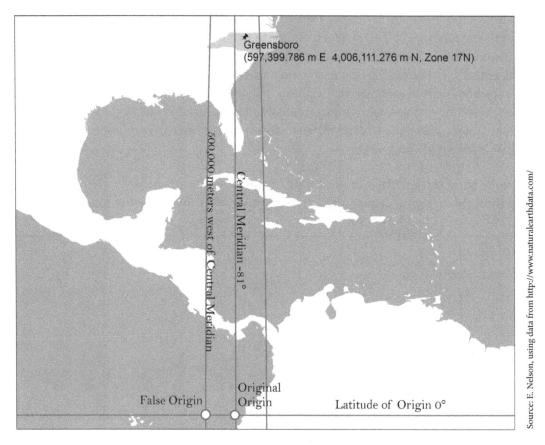

FIGURE 5.14
Feature location using the UTM coordinate system.

Each zone can then be mapped using multiple map sheets, depending on the scale needed. Specifying the location of a feature on the map using UTM follows the same procedures as those outlined for the SPCS, but the measurements are metric and the grid interval, using 7.5-minute series (1:24,000) map, is 1,000 m. It is worth noting that most UTM grid designations are abbreviated, with the last three zeros omitted. Designations of 100,000 or more may also be shown in smaller type. A reading of [6]**69**, for example, would be reported as 669,000 m. When working with these coordinates, trailing zeroes can be dropped in computations, simplifying calculations, but must be added back in when reporting locations.

Determining the coordinates for features of interest is a primary task when working with topographic quadrangles. Another is determining the physical distance between two features. If you are hiking in an area, for example, you might be interested in knowing the distance between waypoints along your trail. On large-scale maps, where the Earth's curvature is accounted for using conformal map projections and ellipsoidal datums, there are several ways to estimate these distances. In Chapter 2, we examined the representative fraction, the verbal statement, and the bar scale as different ways of accomplishing this task.

Another, perhaps more precise, way to do this, would be to use the **Distance Theorem** in conjunction with the planar coordinates of the two features of interest. This is the process that a **Global Positioning System** (**GPS**, which is discussed later) and a GIS use to calculate distances. The Distance Theorem is a derivation of the familiar **Pythagorean Theorem**, which concerns itself with right triangles, and is expressed as $a^2 + b^2 = c^2$. If c is the hypotenuse of this triangle, then its length will be $\sqrt{a^2 + b^2}$. Figure 5.15 shows how this would work if we wanted to find the distance between the Lewis and Clark School and the Navy Radio Station.

If we make the distance between these two locations the hypotenuse (c), we can create a right triangle by connecting the easting coordinates of the two locations and the northing coordinates of the two locations ($x_2 - x_1$). The difference between the easting coordinates of these two locations is one known leg of the triangle (a); the difference between the northing coordinates of the two locations ($y_2 - y_1$) gives you the length of the second leg of the triangle (b). When we substitute these distances in the original Pythagorean Theorem, the Distance Theorem results in this equation: $d = \sqrt{(x_2 - x_1)^2 + (y_2 - y_1)^2}$ where (d) is used in place of (c) to denote distance. You can use any planar coordinate system, and you should get very similar results.

FIGURE 5.15
Determining the distance between two features using the UTM coordinate system.

While this is a relatively straightforward process, it should only be used when your locations are within the same zone. Once you involve more than one zone in your calculations, you increase your chances of measurement errors, because the size of the region (and its associated curvature) grows beyond what can be handled accurately with planar coordinates.

DETERMINING DIRECTION

Geographic north. Most map users working with distances between locations will also want to know the direction they need to travel from their starting location to their destination. To determine that direction, a frame of reference is needed. Geographically, that reference is typically a north-south baseline that is oriented to true, or geographical, north. A **true north** reference line points to the north pole of the Earth's axis of rotation. A meridian on a globe, then, from any point on the planet to the North Pole is a true north reference line.

North is one of the four **cardinal directions** used to orient yourself geographically on Earth. Together, north, south, east, and west are called *cardinal directions*, and are possibly the primary type of direction with which you are familiar. The geometric foundation (our north-south baseline) of this system, however, allows us to specify direction more precisely as an angular deviation from that reference line. As you face north, you can determine the direction to any other point by extending an imaginary line from you to that point, then measuring the angle made by the intersection of that direction line with the baseline. This form of direction is known as **azimuth** and it is measured in angular degrees clockwise from *true north* (Figure 5.16). Thus, as you move clockwise from true north, east is at a right angle and is designated as 90°, south is 180°, and west is designated as 270°.

On maps, true north is either assumed to point to the top of the map, or it is indicated by a north arrow. On a topographic quadrangle, it is indicated by a north arrow marked with a star (Figure 5.16). If you are trying to find true north while navigating the environment, you have several options, from using astronomical observations to observing shadows or the sun's location in the sky. By far the easiest in today's world, however, is to use a system of satellites popularly known as GPS or *Global Positioning System*. This network of satellites was developed by the U.S. Department of Defense and was deployed in the 1990s. Containing some 32 satellites orbiting the Earth, each satellite transmits a radio signal to Earth that can be read by a GPS re-

FIGURE 5.16
Determining the azimuth between two features.

ceiver to calculate not only your position on the planet but also distances and directions to distant locations. Once you have established your location, calculating distances and directions to another feature requires you only to input the location of that feature—the GPS does the remaining mathematical work.

Grid north. Since our goal is to familiarize ourselves with how maps work, we will focus here on determining directions using topographic maps. True north is actually just one of three north-south baselines you will find on a topographic quadrangle (Figure 5.16). More commonly used in map work are both **grid north** (the north arrow marked with GN) and **magnetic north** (the north arrow marked with MN). Grid north is used in conjunction with grid coordinates, such as UTM and SPCS. Planar coordinate systems are artificial, though; thus, working with grid north will be artificial as well. This means that the directions measured will only be useful in the context of the map sheet with which you are working. Grid north is the direction of a grid line that is parallel to the central meridian of the map's projected coordinate system. Typically, this line won't align with true north because it ignores the fact that meridians actually curve and converge at the poles. It is, however, a useful designation for measuring and computing directions from maps and is the way that many GIS calculate azimuth readings.

Figure 5.17 shows an example of determining this type of direction from Moore's Knob at Hanging Rock State Park to Danbury, North Carolina. First, the grid coordinate of each feature is determined by following the same steps outlined earlier in this chapter. Once these are known, a right triangle can be formed by connecting the two locations with a straight line and using the easting and northing coordinates to determine the distances of the other two legs of the triangle. Right triangles, in addition to being associated with the Pythagorean Theorem, are also linked to several trigonometric functions useful for calculating angles from distance ratios.

In this case, the *tangent* function is used to calculate the **grid azimuth** between Moore's Knob and Danbury. Measuring from a horizontal baseline, the tangent function computes an angle from the ratio of the length

FIGURE 5.17
Determining a grid direction between two features in Quadrant I.

of the triangle's side opposite of the angle in question to the side of the triangle adjacent to the same angle. It is determined by using this formula:

$$Tan\ (a) = |y_1 - y_2|/|x_1 - x_2|$$

Once the ratio is determined, the associated angle (*a*) is calculated by taking the inverse tangent function.

Since the grid azimuth should be measured from a line pointing north as the starting point instead of the horizontal baseline from which you calculated your angle, we must make one final modification. This modification must always be made, but it is slightly different depending on which quadrant your feature is in. To convert the angle to a grid azimuth in this example, we must subtract the angle from 90° since we're working in Quadrant I. Moving clockwise from our north-pointing line, if our feature was in Quadrant IV, we would need to add the calculated angle to 90°; if our feature was in Quadrant III, we would need to subtract our calculated angle from 270°; if our feature was in Quadrant II we would need to add our calculated angle to 270°.

As a second example, suppose we were asked to determine the azimuth from Moore's Knob to Flat Shoals (Figure 5.18), which is in Quadrant IV. We would need to add 90° to the initial angle to account for moving from the north-south baseline through Quadrant I to Quadrant IV.

The angular difference between grid north and true north, as shown in the declination diagram on the topographic quadrangle (Figure 5.16), is called the *grid declination*. The grid declination can be used to convert a grid azimuth to a true azimuth or a magnetic azimuth. If the grid declination is east of true north, for example, then you would subtract the grid declination from the grid azimuth to arrive at the true north azimuth. Likewise, if the grid declination is west of true north, you would add the grid declination to the grid azimuth to reach a true north azimuth. In Figure 5.17, the grid declination is 18' E of true north. If our grid azimuth

FIGURE 5.18
Determining a grid direction between two features in Quadrant IV.

from Moore's Knob to Danbury is 83°, then to convert that azimuth to a true north reading, we would need to subtract 18' from the number; thus 82° 42' would be the true north azimuth.

Magnetic north. True north and grid north are the two primary forms of north-south reference lines used in determining directions. There is also a third that bears mentioning: *magnetic north.* Used in conjunction with magnetic compasses, magnetic north points to the Earth's magnetic pole, which is aligned north and south, but does not align with true north. On top of not aligning with true north is the fact that the magnetic north pole actually shifts or changes position through time. Currently, it is located in Canada, some 800 miles south of the true North Pole. The difference between the location of true north and magnetic north is called the *magnetic declination* and is noted on USGS maps with a MN at the top of the north arrow in the declination diagram (Figure 5.16). Because the magnetic pole shifts over time, the date a map is produced is critical to relying on the magnetic declination information posted. There are maps designed to show magnetic declination over large areas, such as the United States; they display variations in angular difference between true and magnetic north using **isogonic lines**, or lines of equal declination angles (Figure 5.19). It is interesting to note that there is a line of no angular difference, the **agonic line**, which is currently in the east central part of the United States. In other words, navigating with a magnetic compass in this part of the United States is relatively problem-free, compared to the northwest or northeast, where magnetic declination is more substantial, requiring navigators to compensate when trying to plot a course for true north.

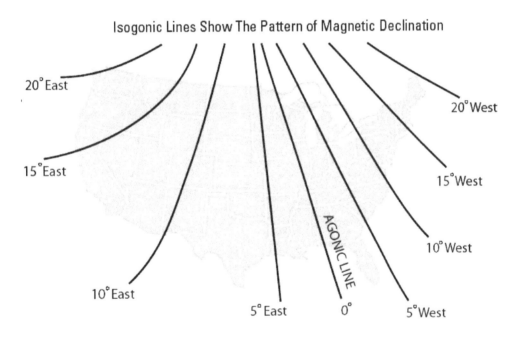

Source: U.S. Geological Survey, Department of the Interior

FIGURE 5.19
Isogonic lines showing the degree of variation from magnetic north for the contiguous United States.

Symbology and Topographic Maps

Like reading a page of text, you must be familiar with the meanings of the "letters, words, and punctuation" of the cartographic alphabet to read and understand a map (Miller and Westerback, 1989). The map features that are typically noticed at first glance on a topographic quadrangle are areal, and symbolized by variation in *color hue*. Areas of vegetation, for example, are visualized using a green hue, whereas water features are associated with blues, and built environments with reds. In some instances, changes to the original topographic sheet, which were derived from interpreting aerial photographs, are visualized using a purple hue. There are also point features, such as buildings, campgrounds, schools, and churches; these are typically differentiated by changing the *shape* of the symbols. Linear features, like areas, are categorized by color hues: Roads are red or black (double lines), railroads and political boundaries are black (single lines), and streams and rivers are blue.

The symbol that differentiates the topographic map from most others, however, is the **contour** (Figure 5.20). Brown in color, the contour is an imaginary line that represents a "...narrow band of places sharing roughly the same elevation above a datum, or fixed reference elevation, usually mean sea level" (Monmonier and

FIGURE 5.20
Example of contour lines on a topographic quadrangle.

Schnell, 1984, 75). The contour adds a third, vertical dimension to the topographic map that is not present on the traditional planimetric map, which does not attempt to show elevational changes. Where the purpose of the planimetric map is to show where geographic features are and what their relationships are to one another, the topographic map not only accomplishes this but also provides symbology for visualizing 3D changes in terrain via *contour shapes* and *spacings*.

VISUALIZING TERRAIN

Vertical datums. Similar to the horizontal datums used to pinpoint coordinate locations on the planet, there are also **vertical datums** that we use to measure elevation, or height above mean sea level. One way to think of mean sea level is as the average height of the ocean's surface when all high and low tides are taken into account. Many world maps use a mean-sea-level datum tied to the global geoid as their reference datum, but there are also other, local datums in use. For example, on some USGS topographic sheets you might see a reference to the **National Geodetic Vertical Datum of 1929** *(NGVD29)* or to the **North American Vertical Datum of 1988** *(NAVD88)*. Elevations made from these datums, which are based on local measures of mean sea level, will naturally vary not only between the two datums but also from those mapped using a global geoid. GPS adds yet another option, as it calculates ellipsoidal heights above and below the WGS84 ellipsoid surface it uses. These measurements, however, should not be confused with elevations because they are not measured relative to mean sea level. To use these measurements as elevation values requires a conversion process. Like the choice of horizontal datum, then, the choice of vertical datum used in mapping is also important in defining what level of accuracy you can expect to obtain from your maps and mapping projects.

The contour line. Contours are used to mentally visualize the three-dimensional terrain that has been mapped, but the symbology and how to use it for that purpose may not be readily apparent to someone unfamiliar with it. Contours are probably best understood when connected to an actual three-dimensional model of the surface that was mapped (Figure 5.21). Theoretically, a contour line is simply the trace outline of a plane, horizontal to mean sea level, that passes through that surface. This trace represents all those locations that have approximately the same elevation. Since any one location can only have one elevation, contour lines will never cross one another. The increment between any two adjacent contour lines is called a **contour interval**, and it represents the vertical change in elevation between the lines. For the purposes of the mapping technique, the change in elevation is assumed to be linear and uniform from one contour to the next. The contour interval is stated on USGS topographic maps, but you can also determine the interval on your own by locat-

Source: U.S. Geological Survey, Department of the Interior

FIGURE 5.21
Concept behind contour lines.

ing two **index contours**, which are labeled, and subtracting the difference in elevation, then dividing that difference by the number of "bands" created by the intermediate contours running between them (number of intermediate contours + 1).

This idea is easily seen in Figure 5.22. The index contours of 500 and 650 ft. have 2 intermediate contours (3 bands) between them. Subtracting 500 from 650 leaves 150; 150 divided by 3 gives the map a contour interval of 50 ft. Index contours typically occur every fifth contour; they are the only labeled contours, a practice aimed at reducing map clutter. These labeled contours are also drawn using a slightly wider line so that is stands out relative to the other contours. Examples of other contour designs are shown in Figure 5.23. All provide additional information about the landscape, although some may be more commonly seen than others. **Supplementary contours**, for example, are used in areas where there are only slight changes in elevation to provide the map user with more detail in that particular area of the map. On USGS topographic maps, these lines are similar to intermediate or unlabeled contours, only lighter in value. Also fairly common are **depression contours**, which have tic marks added to the contours. These tics are drawn at right angles to the contour and point downhill, indicating that the area is a depression instead of a hill. Note that the outer depression contour (the first one marking the depression) will have the same elevation as its adjacent intermediate or index contour (Kimerling et al., 2009).

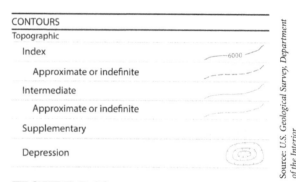

FIGURE 5.22
Determining the contour interval.

CONTOURS

Topographic

Index ——————6000

Approximate or indefinite

Intermediate

Approximate or indefinite

Supplementary

Depression

FIGURE 5.23
Types of contour lines.

Interpreting contours. The shapes of contours and their spacings relative to one another are keys to visualizing the changing terrain (Figure 5.24). Contours that form closed loops, for example, indicate either a summit (hill) or a depression, depending on the type of contour line marking the area. The smaller loops representing a summit, then, will have the higher elevations; the larger loops are lower in elevation and are, thus, downhill. Depressions, on the other hand, have smaller loops that are lower in elevation and downhill from the larger loops.

If you see contours that form v's, then you are in a valley with a stream. The v shows where the contour crosses the stream, and the tip of the v points upstream toward the headwaters or uphill. The open end of the v points downstream or downhill. V's can occur whether or not the stream is actually mapped. Saddles are low points, or dips in a ridge, which is a linear range of high elevations with little variation.

The spacing of contours in an area also provides information. Closely spaced contours, for example, are indicative of steep hills or rugged terrain; change in elevation is occurring rapidly over a small horizontal distance. If the contours are uniformly spaced, then the change in slope over that area will also be uniform.

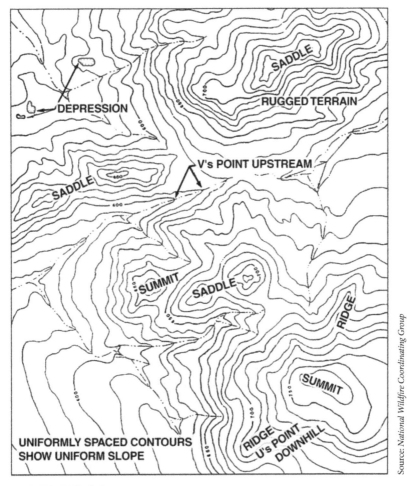

FIGURE 5.24
Interpreting contour shapes and spaces.

Slope is the term for the change in elevation that occurs over a given horizontal distance. You can infer slope, as we have been discussing, by visually interpreting contour spacings. You can also estimate it numerically between two given points. To estimate it, use the following five steps (National Wildfire Coordinating Group, 2007):

1. Determine the contour interval of the map
2. Determine the elevation of the two points in question
3. Subtract the lower elevation from the higher elevation to determine the *rise* or vertical distance between the points
4. Measure the *run* (horizontal) map distance between the two points
5. Use the formula ($\frac{\text{Rise}}{\text{Run}} \times 100$) to determine the slope percentages

Key Terms

Triangulation
Prolate spheroid
Oblate spheroid
Topographic mapping
Reference ellipsoid
Geoid
Clarke 1866 ellipsoid
Meades Ranch, Kansas
Geodetic control points
Geodetic datum
North American Datum of 1927
North American Datum of 1983
Geodetic Reference System 1980
Cartesian coordinates
Easting coordinate
Northing coordinate
State Plane Coordinate System
False origin
Latitude of origin
Universal Transverse Mercator System
Universal Polar Stereographic system

Distance Theorem
Global Positioning System
Pythagorean Theorem
Geographic north
True north
Cardinal directions
Azimuth
GPS
Magnetic north
Grid azimuth
Isogonic lines
Agonic line
Contour
Vertical datum
National Geodetic Vertical Datum of 1929
North American Vertical Datum of 1988
Contour interval
Index contour
Supplementary contour
Depression contour

Questions

1. Why do the positions of features on the Earth's surface change if you use NAD83 instead of NAD27?

2. Why does the State Plane Coordinate System use a false origin?

3. From which cardinal direction are grid azimuths measured?

4. How do you calculate a grid azimuth for point *b*, from point *a*?

5. When calculating a grid azimuth, what final calculation needs to be made when your point falls in each of the four quadrants?

6. When looking at contours on a topographic map, how can you tell if you're looking at a hill or a depression?

7. What do contour lines that are closely spaced signify?

8. How do you estimate slope from a contour map?

Bibliography

Alder, K. 2002. *The Measure of All Things: The Seven-Year Odyssey and Hidden Error That Transformed the World*. New York, NY: Free Press.

Bogens, M., Durfee, M., Gardner, L., and R. Streeper. 2007. *Basic Land Navigation*. Boise, ID: National Wildfire Coordinating Group.

Bolstad, P. 2005. *GIS Fundamentals*. 2nd ed. White Bear Lake, MN: Eider Press.

Brown, L.A. 1977. *The Story of Maps*. New York, NY: Dover Publications, Inc.

Campbell, J.C. 1984. *Introductory Cartography*. Englewood Cliffs, NJ: Prentice-Hall, Inc.

Dent, B.D., Torguson, J.S., and T.W. Hodler. 2009. *Cartography: Thematic Map Design*. 6th ed. New York, NY: McGraw-Hill.

Faul, S. 2019. *Triangulation*. Accessed September 20, 2019. https://mappa.mundi.net/locus/locus_008/index.html.

Harvey, F. 2008. *A Primer of GIS: Fundamental Geographic and Cartographic Concepts*. New York, NY: The Guilford Press.

Kimerling, A.J., Buckley, A.R., Muehrcke, P.C., and J.O. Muehrcke. 2009. *Map Use: Reading and Analysis*. 6th ed. Redlands, CA: ESRI Press.

Miller, V.C., and M.E. Westerback. 1989. *Interpretation of Topographic Maps*. Columbus, OH: Merrill Publishing Co.

Monmonier, M. and G.A. Schnell, 1984. *Map Appreciation*. Prentice-Hall, Inc.: Englewood Cliffs, New Jersey.

National Academy of Sciences. 2010. "Founding of the National Academy of Sciences." *The National Academies*. Accessed September 20, 2019. http://www.nationalacademies.org/archives/nasfounding.html.

National Wildfire Coordinating Group. 2007. *Basic Land Navigation*. Boise, ID: NWGS.

O'Connor, J.J., and E.F. Robertson. 2008. "Jean Picard." *The MacTutor History of Mathematics Archive*. Accessed September20, 2019. http://www-history.mcs.st-andrews.ac.uk/Biographies/Picard_Jean.html.

Robinson, A.H., Morrison, J.L., Muehrcke, P.C., Kimerling, A.J., and S.C. Guptill. 1995. *Elements of Cartography*. 6th ed. New York, NY: John Wiley & Sons, Inc.

Sickle, J.V. 2004. *Basic GIS Coordinates*. Boca Raton, FL: CRC Press.

Shodor. 2010. "Cartesian Coordinate System." Accessed September 20, 2019. http://www.shodor.org/interactivate/lessons/CartesianCoordinate.

Slocum, T. A., McMaster, R. B., Kessler, F.C., and H.H. Howard. 2005. *Thematic Cartography and Geographic Visualization*. 2nd ed. Upper Saddle River, NJ: Pearson Education, Inc.

Snyder, J. 1993. *Flattening the Earth*. Chicago, IL: University of Chicago Press.

Taylor, L.H. "Navigation: Near Shore Mapping: Adding Underwater Objects to the Contour." Accessed September 20, 2019. http://www-personal.umich.edu/~lpt/mapping2.htm.

Thrower, N.J.N. 1996. *Maps and Civilization: Cartography in Culture and Society*. Chicago, IL: University of Chicago Press.

USGS. 2000. "Geological Surveys Before the Civil War." *US Geological Survey Circular 1050*. Accessed September 20, 2019. http://pubs.usgs.gov/circ/c1050/before.htm.

Digital Topographic Mapping

In this exercise, you will use topographic maps and elevation data to work with planar coordinate systems and explore the visualization of elevation.

OBJECTIVES

- Identify map collar information on a topographic quadrangle
- Specify feature locations using 2D coordinate systems
- Estimate distances between geographic features
- Interpret elevation changes between contour lines

SOFTWARE

This exercise uses ESRI's ArcGIS Pro 2.3.2 and Adobe's Acrobat Reader DC.

DATA

The data for this exercise are available from the Kendall Hunt Student Ancillary site. See the inside front cover for access information. You may also be directed to download the data from a different location by your instructor.

1. Download the data as directed by your instructor
2. Save the file to a location where you have read/write privileges

The files are compressed and must be decompressed prior to use.

Open the Project

1. Start ArcGIS Pro.
2. In the dialog box, select *Open another project*. The option is in the lower left corner of the dialog screen (Figure 5.1).

 Open another project

 Settings

FIGURE 5.1

3. Navigate to the *Chapter05* folder in the provided class folder and select *Exercise_05.aprx*.
4. You should see the topographic map (Figure 5.2).
5. Change your X, Y coordinate units to Degrees, Minutes, Seconds by selecting the arrow next to the coordinate display located at the bottom middle portion of the *View*.

FIGURE 5.2

Identify Map Collar Information

USGS topographic quadrangles are composed of the map and the map collar. The map collar is the border that surrounds the map. It includes supplementary information crucial to working with the map. Lines of latitude and longitude bound the sides of the USGS quadrangle. Using this information and your suite of *Navigate* tools, answer the following questions about these boundaries.

QUESTION 5.1

The latitudinal line that forms the northern boundary of the quadrangle is 36° 52' 30" N.

    a.   True
    b.   False

The longitudinal line that forms the eastern boundary of the quadrangle is 109° 00' 00" W.

a. True
b. False

The quadrangle is part of which map series?

a. 30-minute topographic series
b. 15-minute topographic series
c. 7.5-minute topographic series
d. 1-minute topographic series

The quadrangle located directly north of this quadrangle is:

a. Aneth SE
b. Cow Butte
c. Pastora Peak
d. Rocky Point

The quadrangle is part of which UTM zone?

a. 11
b. 12
c. 13
d. 14

The grid lines shown on this quadrangle are for the UTM grid system. What is the ground distance between adjacent grid lines in this system?

a. 100 ft.
b. 1000 m
c. 100,000 m
d. 100,000 ft.

Coordinate Systems and Feature Locations

The numbers running along the boundaries of the map refer to three different coordinate systems: Latitude and Longitude, the Universal Transverse Mercator System (UTM), and the State Plane Coordinate System (SPCS).

Latitude and longitude coordinates are printed every 2'30" between the map boundaries. They are marked with black tic marks that are plotted on the inside edge of the map boundaries.

UTM coordinates, on this quadrangle, are marked by the grid. They represent distances in meters and usually are listed using two font sizes, with the trailing 000s in a smaller size. Often, the trailing zeros are omitted. When specified this way, there is an assumed 000 that should be added after the numbers to arrive at the correct coordinate specification. A reading of 669, for example, would be reported as 669,000 m.

The SPCS measures distances in feet and are readings marked with solid black tic marks that are plotted outside the map boundaries. In this section, we will explore coordinate locations for the Four Corners Monument, a marker pinpointing the only U.S. location where the corners of four states—Colorado, New Mexico, Arizona, and Utah—meet.

1. Scroll along the top of the map to find the Four Corners Monument—it will be at the top, toward the middle of the quadrangle, where the four states meet, marked by a small symbol at the end of a road as indicated by the red arrow (Figure 5.3).

FIGURE 5.3

GEOGRAPHIC INFORMATION SCIENCE

2. Roll the mouse cursor over the location of the monument and note the coordinate locations that are displayed on the bottom middle of the *View.*

Which of the following coordinates best approximates the actual location of the monument?

a. 79° 45' 03" E, 36° 04' 21" N
b. 79° 45' 03" W, 36° 04' 21" N
c. 36° 59' 57" E, 109° 02' 43" N
d. 109° 02' 43" W, 36° 59' 57" N

Establishing the Estimated Location of the Four Corners Monument

When first establishing the monument, Congress stated that the monument should be placed at 37° 00' N latitude and at the 32nd meridian of longitude west of the Washington, DC, meridian. Using the best available surveying methods and technology in the 1800s, the location of the monument was estimated to be at 37° 00' N, 109°03' W. However, the monument's actual location versus the location originally surveyed in the 1800s is off by a small distance.

How far is the actual location off the estimated location? Let us explore to find out.

1. Zoom in to the area of the actual and estimated locations of the Four Corners Monument.
2. Use the Measure tool to calculate the distances between the estimated location and the actual location of the Four Corners Monument.

What is the approximate distance between the actual and estimated locations of the Four Corners Monument?

a. 1,630 ft.
b. 2,100 ft.
c. 2,500 ft.
d. 5,000 ft.

UTM Coordinates

You may not always be in a digital environment that has software tools to automate measurement tasks. In that case, it becomes important to have a planar coordinate system, like the UTM system, at your disposal to enhance your ability to complete these tasks manually. Latitude and longitude are a 3D system with coordinates that are measured in angles; in addition, the distance covered by a degree of longitude changes as you move from the equator and toward the poles. The UTM system eliminates these complexities—it is a 2D linear system where distance relationships are constant across the map, making it easier and quicker than latitude and longitude when it comes to calculating distances and directions in the field.

In this section, you will change the display units to UTM coordinates and calculate the distance between the estimated and actual locations of the Four Corners Monument once again, except you will be using the *Distance Formula* rather than the *Measure* tool.

1. Change your *X*, *Y* coordinate units to UTM by selecting the arrow next to the coordinate display located at the bottom middle portion of the *View*.
2. Use the mouse cursor and the *X*, *Y* coordinate display to answer the following questions.

QUESTION 5.9

Which of the following UTM coordinates best represents the estimated location of the monument?

 a. 650,276 m E; 4,996,428 m N
 b. 673,516 m E; 4,096,443 m N
 c. 4,896,428 m E; 673,566 m N
 d. 4,096,456 m E; 650,276 m N

QUESTION 5.10

Which of the following UTM coordinates best represents the actual location of the monument?

 a. 674,004 m E; 4,096,336 m N
 b. 603,516 m E; 4,287,118 m N
 c. 4,287,118 m E; 603,516 m N
 d. 4,096,347 m E; 674,004 m N

3. Close ArcGIS Pro. You do not need to save the changes.

Calculating Distance

With the UTM coordinates we have specified for both the estimated location and the actual map location of the monument, we can assess the actual extent of the displacement by hand to determine the distance between the two locations.

To compute distances, the Distance Formula can be used in conjunction with the planar coordinates of the two features of interest. The Distance Formula is a derivation of the familiar Pythagorean Theorem, where easting (x) and northing (y) coordinates of the two features are used to determine the distance between them.

Using the UTM coordinates previously identified (Questions 5.9 and 5.10) and the Distance Formula, calculate how far apart the two locations are in meters.

The formula is:

where: $$d = \sqrt{(x_2 - x_1)^2 + (y_2 - y_1)^2}$$

x_2 = Easting UTM coordinate for the estimated monument location

x_1 = Easting UTM coordinate for the actual monument location

y_2 = Northing UTM coordinate for the estimated monument location

y_1 = Northing UTM coordinate for the actual monument location

QUESTION 5.11

Using the Distance Formula, find out what is the approximate distance between the actual and estimated locations.

a. 120.13 m
b. 306.17 m
c. 499.59 m
d. 700.15 m

Contour Lines

The symbol that sets topographic maps apart from all others is the contour. Brown in color, the contour is an imaginary line that represents locations on a map that share the same elevation value. These lines provide symbology for visualizing 3D changes in terrain by visually interpreting *contour shapes* and *spacings*. Contours that form closed loops, for example, indicate either a summit (hill) or a depression, depending on the type of contour line marking the area. If you see contours that form V's, then you are in a valley with a stream. Closely spaced contours are indicative of steep hills or rugged terrain where change in elevation is occurring rapidly over a small horizontal distance.

The contour interval of the topographic map in Figure 5.4 is 40 ft. It may be difficult to see the details of the map in the book. For a better version, use the map named **Contour_Map.pdf** in your *Chapter05* folder to answer the following questions. Open the file with Adobe's Acrobat Reader DC.

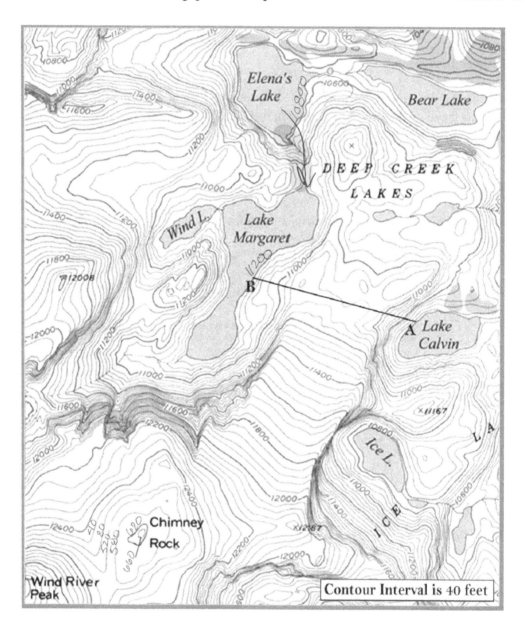

FIGURE 5.4

Ice L. is lower in elevation than *Lake Calvin.*

    a. True
    b. False

If you hiked from *Lake Calvin* to *Lake Margaret* along the A-B transect (traveling from A to B), or cut line, the steepest part of your hike would be the first half.

    a. True
    b. False

What is the elevation of the highest contour at the summit of Chimney Rock?

    a. 11,960
    b. 12,160
    c. 12,200
    d. 12,640

The stream connecting Lake Margaret and Elena's Lake is running from Lake Margaret to Elena's Lake (the stream is highlighted on the topographic map).

    a. True
    b. False

CHAPTER 6
Thematic Mapping

The same technological innovations that helped drive changes in the accuracy of large-scale topographic mapping also broadened the role of maps in portraying spatial features. The data that explorers collected during their forays in the seventeenth and eighteenth centuries included not only locational information but also information about the characteristics of those locations. Once most of the locational information was ensconced in map form, cartographers and other scientists turned their attention to these characteristics. Their interest in these data was initially driven by a desire to "see" the natural history of the places they had mapped. The realization that the *space* of location could be mapped as well as its *place* gave us a new method known as **thematic mapping**.

Because of this focus on space, thematic maps are quite different from general reference and topographic maps. Where the general reference map focuses on accurately locating multiple features within a region, the thematic map pushes the locational framework into the background of the map to serve as context, focusing instead on a specific theme or attribute distribution. Early thematic maps focused on portraying the physical characteristics of a place, such as its terrain, vegetation, or climate. With the development of statistics as a discipline in the early 1800s, interest in social or cultural characteristics like population change and incidences of crime and disease also began to be mapped. The point of this new form of mapping was to "…discover the geographical structure of the subject" (Robinson, 1982, 16). Today, the themes thematic maps undertake to portray are practically unlimited; they include the traditional physical and population characteristics as well as economic and other social attributes (i.e., religion, income, poverty). Displaying all this information using location as the context required the development of several new mapping techniques, most of which were developed during the early 1800s. These are still widely used today and include such forms as the isoline, the choropleth, the dot, and the proportional symbol.

The Isoline Map

Isoline maps depict changes in continuous surfaces, such as elevation, temperature, and precipitation, by using line symbols that connect data points with equal values (Figure 6.1). Whereas isoline maps is a generic term covering all forms of **isarithms**, many of these lines also have specific names, depending on the topic mapped. *Iso-* is Greek for *equal*, so an isoline of temperature is called an **isotherm**. **Isobars** are lines of equal barometric pressure, and **isohyets** are lines depicting equal amounts of rainfall. Probably the best known isoline is the one we explored in Chapter 5, the contour, or **isohypse**, which is a line of equal elevation.

The isoline map was the first thematic technique developed. Although used earlier, it was first published as a technique by Edmond Halley in 1701. He used the technique to produce a chart of magnetic variation of the Atlantic Ocean. Lines of equal magnetic variation are called *isogons*; they are sometimes called *Halleyan lines*, in honor of Halley's part in their development. A British scientist perhaps best known for determining the orbit of Halley's Comet, Halley was also the first to bear the title of *thematic cartographer* (Robinson, 1982). His isoline concept was expanded upon in 1817 when Alexander von Humboldt, a Prussian geographer famous for his work in establishing the foundations of biogeography, produced the first isothermal map showing lines of equal temperatures in the Northern Hemisphere.

Today, isolines are used to map a wide variety of topics. These include not only the traditional physical geography topics, but also cultural and social subjects, like infant mortality rates, disease incidences, and even ancestry patterns inferred from genetic studies. Unlike the more traditional subjects of elevation, tempera-

Source: South Carolina Department of Natural Resources, State Climatology Office

FIGURE 6.1
Mapping barometric pressure using isobars.

ture, and precipitation, which are portrayed using values that are measured at points across a surface, cultural and social subjects are conceptual and are typically visualized by using data values collected over discrete areas, which decreases the level of accuracy associated with their interpretation. In cartography, these types of maps are termed **isoplethic** (Figure 6.2), as opposed to **isometric**, which denotes those isolines constructed the traditional way.

FIGURE 6.2
Using isopleths to map malaria areas and risks.

Regardless of the underlying form, both isoplethic and isometric maps are interpreted in the same manner. The purpose of the display technique is to portray patterns in the data. The distance between two adjacent lines is termed the **isoline interval**: The rate of change between the lines is assumed to be even. Because lines connect points of equal value, each line can have only one value. On one side of the line, data values will be higher; on the other side, they will be lower, and the closer the lines are, the more rapidly the area changes in value.

The Choropleth Map

While the isometric map design led the way in visualizing distributions of continuous, physical data sets, it was the **choropleth map**, defined as "A method of cartographic representation which employs distinctive shading applied to areas other than those bounded by isolines" (Dent et al., 2009), that became the standard for mapping data values aggregated over administrative or political regions (Figure 6.3). Baron Charles Dupin, a French mathematician, developed the initial prototype in 1827. Dupin published in several venues, including education and economics, as well as mathematics. One of his many interests was the education of French workers and its relationship to the economy (Delamarre, 1909). He invented

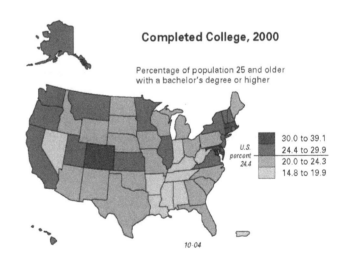

FIGURE 6.3
The choropleth map.

the choropleth map to visualize the level of educational instruction in France by shading the different districts of the country according to the number of people per male child in school (Robinson, 1982). Lighter shades represented lower rates of illiteracy (less people per male student) and darker shades represented higher rates of illiteracy.

The importance of Dupin's map cannot be understated; the "…visual impact opened the eyes of scholars" (Robinson, 1982, 199) as to the potential of thematic mapping techniques for making visible "landscapes" that are typically invisible due to the conceptual abstractness. As the data are aggregated, the choropleth map assumes the distribution of whatever is being mapped is fairly even over each region, which presents a more generalized picture of the larger administrative unit. More detail, for example, would be available from a county map of the United States showing variation in some subject than a state-level map of the subject covering the same area; compare Figure 6.4 with Figure 6.3, for example. Whether or not the data are classified prior to symbolization also affects how much detail is embedded in the map. Dupin's prototype did not classify the data but showed each department's level of illiteracy with a unique shade graded according to its value.

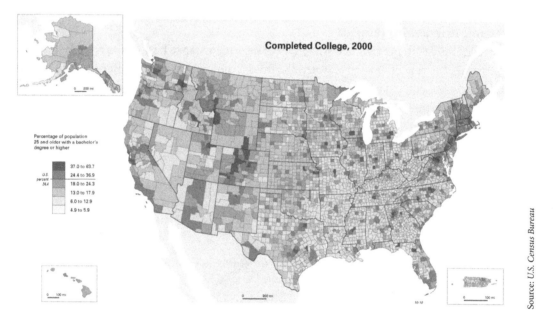

FIGURE 6.4
Smaller administrative units give a more detailed view of patterns in choropleth mapping.

Data Classification Methods

The modern choropleth map, due to perceptual limitations in our ability to discriminate between multiple levels of shading, typically uses classified data sets. The first choropleth map to attempt classification was produced in 1828; it was a Prussian map of population density, but little is known about the designer of its thematic component (Robinson, 1982). Because the choropleth map is one, if not the most, popular thematic mapping technique, researchers have put a great deal of effort into perfecting its design. As a part of that work, different data classification methods have been developed and studied. The objectives of these methods are to create a classification that (1) is understandable to the map user, and (2) minimizes cartographic bias. Different methods can produce wildly different interpretations of the same data set, which affects the information a map user receives when using the map. GIS will vary in how many, and which methods are offered, but almost all will provide these: **Natural Breaks**, **Quantile**, and **Equal Interval**.

Natural breaks. Part of minimizing bias in the map means that from a classification perspective, the least biased interpretation will (1) maximize the numerical differences between class groups, and at the same time, (2) minimize the numerical differences within each of those groups. Of the three methods mentioned, *Natural Breaks* comes the closest to achieving this for any given data set (Figure 6.5). Traditionally, this method works by sorting the data values in the set in ascending order and then identifying the largest gaps between data values. The gaps become the locations where the class breaks are placed. In most GIS, the manual implementation of this method is called **Manual Breaks**; the Natural Breaks option is automated using the **Jenks Optimization Algorithm**, leaving the cartographer only with the decision of how many classes to use.

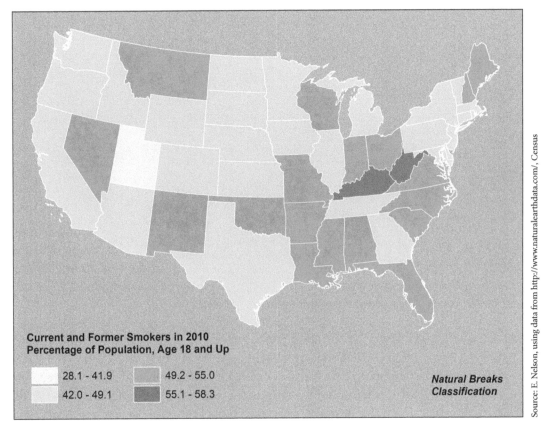

Current and Former Smokers in 2010
Percentage of Population, Age 18 and Up

| 28.1 - 41.9 | 49.2 - 55.0 |
| 42.0 - 49.1 | 55.1 - 58.3 |

Natural Breaks Classification

Source: E. Nelson, using data from http://www.naturalearthdata.com/, Census

FIGURE 6.5
Percent of Smokers and Ex-smokers age 18 and up, 2010. Distribution classed using Natural Breaks with four classes.

The gaps in a data set are also visible when it is graphed using a **histogram** (Figure 6.6). The histogram visually presents the statistical distribution, or underlying form, of the data set by plotting the data values from low to high along the x-axis of the graph and their frequency along the y-axis; it is often used in GIS to explore the data set prior to mapping it. For example, if there are three large gaps in a data set when viewed using a histogram, this information might be used to break the data into four classes when choosing the parameters for the final classification method.

FIGURE 6.6
Histogram of Smoking dataset showing Natural Breaks class limits.

In addition to Natural Breaks, the other two most popular classification methods are *Equal Intervals* and *Quantiles*. Both are *blind classification* methods, meaning that they mathematically subdivide the data set into classes without regard to the form of the underlying data. Because of this limitation, they are typically used effectively only with uniform distributions, when making comparisons among multiple data sets, or when required for adhering to special rules aiding interpretation.

Equal intervals. The Equal Interval classification method divides a data set into equivalent ranges of data values (Figure 6.7). These ranges are identified by following a series of steps. First, the range of the entire data set (maximum data value—minimum data value) is divided by the number of classes desired. The result is the *numerical width of the range*, which is used to define each individual class range. The lowest-class range is then found by adding this number to the lowest data value in the data set to determine the first class break or limit. In Figure 6.7, the numerical width is 7.5, and when this is added to the lowest data value, gives a class break of 35.6 for the lowest data class. As can be seen from the histogram in Figure 6.8, adding 7.5 to 35.6 gives an upper range of 43.1 to the second class; its lower range is the next data value up from 35.6 (35.7). The process continues until all the classes have been defined. If the data are uniformly distributed, then this is an appropriate choice for classification. Unfortunately, most geographical data sets are not uniform distributions, but skewed. When used with these types of statistical distributions, it is important to realize that interpretation can be biased. Because Equal Intervals blindly classifies the data, it is quite possible to have

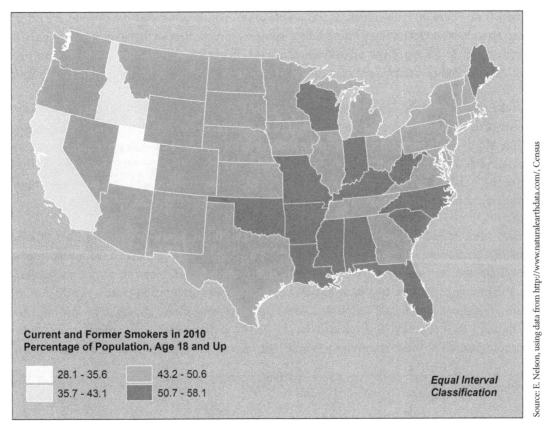

Source: E. Nelson, using data from http://www.naturalearthdata.com/, Census

FIGURE 6.7
Percent of Smokers and Ex-smokers age 18 and up, 2010. Distribution classed using Equal
Intervals with four classes.

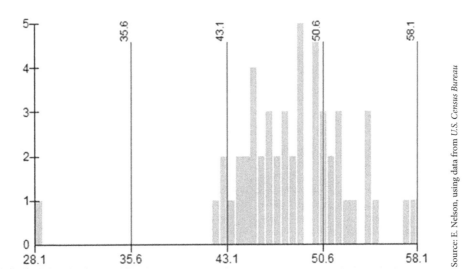

Source: E. Nelson, using data from *U.S. Census Bureau*

FIGURE 6.8
Histogram of Smoking dataset showing Equal Intervals class limits.

classes in which there are no data values, as well as classes in which dissimilar data values are grouped. On the plus side, this algorithm treats every data set the same way, regardless of distribution, so it is useful when asking the map user to compare two spatial distributions. It is also useful when working with percentage data, as the class widths are always some proportion of 100 percent, which most map users can easily grasp.

Quantiles. Like Equal Intervals, Quantiles also divides the range of data indiscriminately, only is assigns an equal number of data values to each class as opposed to an equal range of data values (Figure 6.9). Class breaks are determined by dividing the total number of data values in the data set by the desired number of classes. The result is the number of data values that should be placed in each class. In Figure 6.9, for example, the data set has 48 values and 4 classes, so there should be 12 values in each class. Starting with the lowest data value of 28.1 and counting off the first 12 data values, the first class break will be the 12th data value of 45.5.

The next data value marks the beginning of the second class break, and the same number of data values are counted off, continuing the process until all of the classes have been created. Like Equal Intervals, this is an appropriate choice if the data set is uniformly distributed. If not, bias can occur, particularly if two similar data values are split into two different classes or if classes are created from very dissimilar values. Traditionally considered significant limitations, these potential biases have shown to be less important than originally thought in one study (Brewer and Pickle, 2002). Using a series of general map reading tasks and epidemiological data, these researchers found that Quantiles outperformed even Natural Breaks for

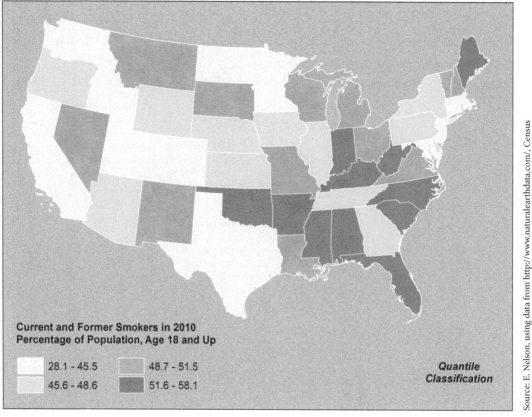

FIGURE 6.9
Percent of Smokers and Ex-smokers age 18 and up, 2010. Distribution classed using Quantiles with four classes.

successfully completing tasks. Brewer and Pickle speculate that this is the result of the median value of the data set consistently falling in the middle class, allowing data classes to be approached as ordinal rankings above and below that value; this perspective negates the problem of relative differences in data values within classes. Quantiles also offers one of the most pleasing visualizations, as each class shade is used an equal number of times on the map.

Color Schemes

Once the data set is classified, it is ready to be symbolized and displayed on the map base. For quantitative data sets (ordinal, interval, and ratio levels of data), the tradition is to shade the classes from light to dark, with the lighter shades representing lower data values and darker shades representing higher data values. The idea is to create a visualization that is intuitive, and cartographers have found that most people associate darker, richer colors with "more" and lighter, less saturated colors with "less." The easiest way to implement this is to choose one hue, such as blue, and vary its value from one class to the next to create the shading. This type of color scheme is called the **sequential single hue scheme**.

Sequential multi-hued schemes are also available; these are composed of a transition of adjacent hues from the visible spectrum of light energy. The visible spectrum is the region of light energy that the human eye can process and "see" as color. The different wavelengths form the rainbow and are ordered according to the acronym ROY G. BIV (red, orange, yellow, green, blue, indigo, violet). The key to creating a successful multi-hued scheme is to start with a light hue, such as yellow, and transition through one or two adjacent and increasingly darker hues, like orange and red, such that the light-to-dark look of the map takes visual precedence over the use of the multiple hues. These schemes, when well designed, offer the advantage of being able to produce more discriminable classes than the sequential single hue scheme. Generally, the sequential single hue scheme can support up to six classes before it becomes difficult to tell the shades of a hue apart. Because the sequential multi-hued scheme has two or three hues, the number of classes can be extended to somewhere in the range of eight to ten classes. Increasing the number of classes allows the cartographer to offer more detail about the subject being mapped; as the number of classes decreases, data values are grouped into larger and larger chunks, which obscures some of the finer variations occurring in the data. Many cartographers use a lower limit of four classes because of this, except for special circumstances.

Diverging color schemes are also popular. In these schemes, a light hue represents the middle of the color scheme, with each end diverging into a separate hue to highlight values above and below the midpoint of the data set. A data set, for example, might be represented using white for the class with the midpoint, diverging into shades of red for values above the midpoint and shades of blue for values below the midpoint. This scheme is more specialized; it is typically used with data sets that have been classified around the mean of the data set. It may also be useful for interpreting data classified as quantiles, if the emphasis is placed on the rankings of classes above and below the median value.

Unique Data Requirements

While the choropleth map is the most popular technique for mapping in a GIS, it is not as simple a choice as the default parameters make it appear. Since this technique uses the administrative areas of the base map as the actual symbols of the map, there is no standard size associated with the symbolization; thus, when interpreting the patterns of variation caused by shading them, this lack of consistency can impart misleading information depending on the type of data being mapped. The attribute data symbolized in thematic maps can be grouped into two basic types: *total values* or *derived (ratio) values*. Total values are counts associated with a topic of interest, such as total population or number of influenza cases. These types of data are often significantly influenced by the size of the administrative area from which they are collected, with larger areas home to greater numbers of people. This correlation makes the interpretation of total number patterns difficult when mapped using the choropleth technique. When examining population data for the United States, as in Figure 6.10, bigger states will often have more people than smaller states; here, two out of the top ten largest states in area are in the top class: California and Texas. What most people are associating with a map like this is not the total number of people in a particular location, but how crowded the location is; the only way to get around this interpretation is to process out, or *standardize* or *normalize*, the symbol areas so they do not affect the information being communicated.

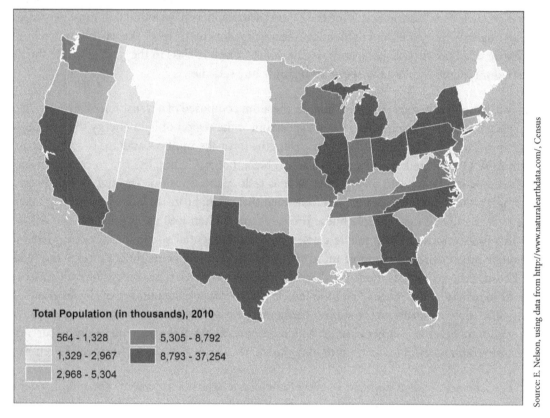

FIGURE 6.10
Total Population in the United States, 2010.

The most popular way of standardizing total values for choropleth mapping is to divide each attribute value by the area of the administrative unit; this results in a *density* value; for example, population data might be *population per square kilometer* (Figure 6.11). When treated this way, these data are not visually affected by the different sizes of the areal units. California, for example, is much more densely populated than Texas, but this does not show when mapping total numbers of people. There is also a larger block of more sparsely populated states to the west (Idaho, Montana, Nevada, Utah, the Dakotas, Nebraska, and Kansas) than the map of total population suggests. The data mapped using the choropleth technique, then, should always fall into the *derived values* category. Density measures are the most common, but areas can also be standardized

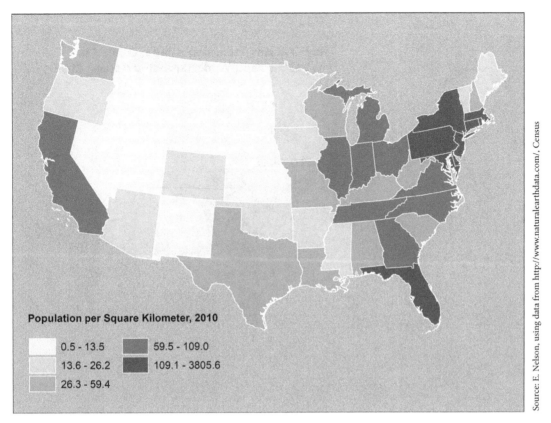

Source: E. Nelson, using data from http://www.naturalearthdata.com/, Census

Population per Square Kilometer, 2010

	0.5 - 13.5		59.5 - 109.0
	13.6 - 26.2		109.1 - 3805.6
	26.3 - 59.4		

FIGURE 6.11
Population per Square Kilometer, 2010.

in other ways. For crime data, for example, total values for each area could be divided by the total number of crimes in the country to arrive at a percentage of total crimes for each areal unit. A crime rate could also be created to standardize the data by dividing the total crime data for each area by the total population for each area. If it's total data that you need to map, there are other, more appropriate mapping techniques.

The Dot Density Map

Perhaps the purest form for mapping total values is the **dot density map**. Dot density maps show the presence of features by mapping them with dot symbols. Like the choropleth map type, the dot map was also first produced in France, where Frère de Montizon used the technique to show France's distribution of population by department. This prototype was developed in 1830, but did not pick up in popularity as quickly as Dupin's choropleth; the next person believed to have produced a map using a similar technique was Alexander von Mentzer, who used it to map the population distribution of the Scandinavian Peninsula.

The modern dot map technique uses dot symbols to represent the location of a cluster of features, where the actual number of features it represents is established by the cartographer (Figure 6.12). Locations, then, are not actual locations, but locations placed in the vicinity of the cluster using other ancillary data, such as

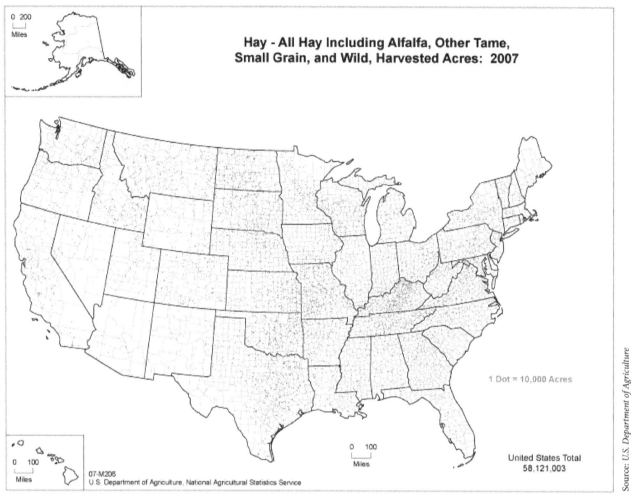

FIGURE 6.12
Dot map showing harvested acres of hay in 2007.

the location of water bodies or different land uses, to refine placements further. Dots, for example, are not placed in water bodies when mapping population distributions, as people would not be found there. The dot mapping technique is typically difficult to implement accurately in a GIS because of this constraint. Instead, most GIS opt to randomly place dots, leaving this to be a less-than-desired technique without careful modifications implemented by the person creating the display. The spatial pattern produced by the dots can also be affected by both the unit value assigned to the dot and the size of the dot chosen to create the map; if the dots are too numerous or too large, the pattern can look denser than it actually is. On the other hand, dots that are too few or too small may give the inappropriate impression of sparseness.

Proportional and Graduated Symbol Maps

PROPORTIONAL SYMBOL MAPS

Proportional symbol and graduated symbol maps are two other techniques used to map total values, as well as some types of derived values. Cartographic historians believe the first use of these symbols occurred in 1837, when Henry Drury Harness used them to create a map of city populations for the Irish Railway Commission (MacEachren, 1979). In this map, the symbols can be used to symbolize both discrete point data, like cities, and attribute values aggregated by the administrative area, such as county population (Figure 6.13). The technique supports the mapping of total data values, as well as percentages, averages, and rates. Density values, like population per square mile, are traditionally avoided, as the choropleth technique is particularly suited for mapping these types of data.

The symbols representing a data set are scaled relative to an *anchor value*. Usually this value is either the smallest or largest data value in the set. A circle size is chosen to represent this data value and then all other

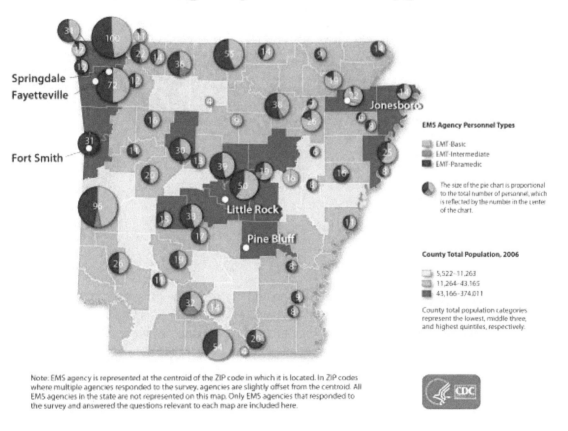

Source: *Centers for Disease Control, https://www.cdc.gov/dhdsp/data_statistics/ems/fs_ems_ar.htm*

FIGURE 6.13
Proportional symbol map of EMS personnel types in Arkansas.

circles are scaled in proportion relative to this value; it is important that the smallest circles be clearly visible, while at the same time the largest circles are not too dominant visually.

Because of this, one of the more vexing issues with **proportional symbols** is dealing with the range of the data values in a data set. If the range is too narrow, the scaled symbol sizes will appear too similar, making the final display of patterns uninteresting (Figure 6.14). On the other hand, if the range is too large, the largest symbols will be too large to be accommodated by the map if the smallest circle is visible (Figure 6.15). In this case, the total values are often converted to derived values to pull the range in a bit.

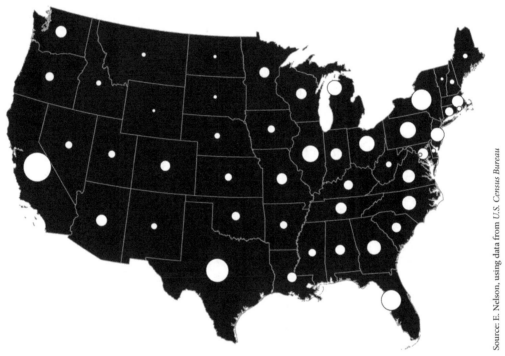

Source: E. Nelson, using data from *U.S. Census Bureau*

FIGURE 6.14
Proportional symbol map with symbol size range too small.

Research has shown that map users have a tendency to underestimate the sizes of the larger symbols in map reading tasks. This is a perceptual limitation on our part; as the dimensions by which a symbol is scaled (length, area, volume, etc.) gets larger, we become increasingly poorer at judging absolute size or relative changes in the symbols. Circles are often the symbol of choice because (1) they "grow" in size more slowly than changes in length, as the growth is spread over two dimensions, (2) they are more easily assessed than changes in volume (3D), and (3) they are a visually pleasing symbol lacking harsh lines that might clash with the base data. Some GIS do offer *perceptual scaling* options that, when checked, will rescale the larger symbols to compensate for our perceptual limitations.

Graduated symbol maps are a variant of proportional symbols in which the attribute data are classified prior to symbolization. Once the data are aggregated into a set number of classes, a symbol size is assigned to each class of data values (Figure 6.16). These symbols can be scaled proportionally to the mean of each class or they can be chosen so that each size is easily discriminable on the map. Classifying the data prior to symbol assignment reduces the number of differently sized symbols the map user has to process when interpreting spatial patterns. This simplifies the patterns in the data, although the generalization does mean some detail in the data will be lost. This variant of the **proportional symbol map** also helps control issues with data ranges that are too narrow or too wide by allowing the cartographer more leeway in size choices.

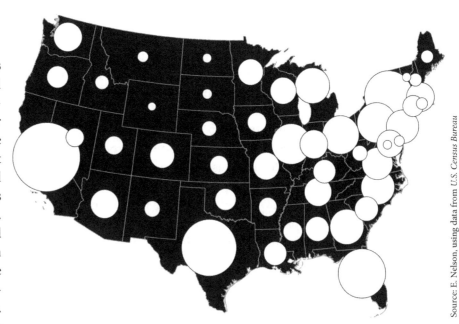

FIGURE 6.15
Proportional symbol map with symbol size range too large.

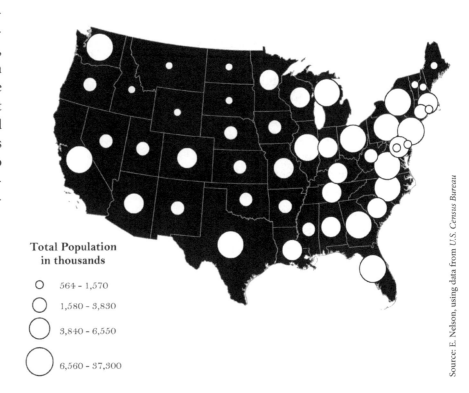

**Total Population
in thousands**

○ 564 – 1,570

○ 1,580 – 3,830

○ 3,840 – 6,550

○ 6,560 – 37,300

FIGURE 6.16
Graduated symbol map.

Source: E. Nelson, using data from U.S. Census Bureau

Map Design

The map itself, although by far the most important, is just one of many elements in a final cartographic layout. Without surrounding elements, like a title and a legend, to provide additional context, it can be difficult to understand the message the map is trying to communicate. In addition to interpretive difficulties, an "...ugly map, with crude colors, careless linework, and disagreeable, poorly arranged lettering may be intrinsically as accurate as a beautiful map, but it is less likely to inspire confidence" (Wright, 1942, 23). Map design addresses these issues and more; it is a complex process involving a series of decisions, each influencing the other. There are guidelines to assist the cartographer—Dent et al. (2009) lists simplicity, functional appropriateness, pleasing appearance, and economic considerations as some of the primary principles under which cartographers operate. One way to approach map design and implement these principles is to identify the major elements of most maps and then discuss how they are most effectively used in the layout process by dividing the design structure of the map into issues of **visual balance** and issues of **visual hierarchy**.

Map Elements

Foote and Crum (2000), writing for *The Geographer's Craft*, divide **map elements** (excluding the mapped area itself) into three basic groups: Those found on most, if not all maps, those that are essential but sensitive to context, and those used to enhance communication. Essential elements that tend to be context-sensitive include the map title, date of map production, and cartographer credits. Of the essential items, the map title is ranked the most important; it describes the theme of the map and orients the map user. Its content can be affected by other map elements, such as the legend title, which is used to expand upon the map title, but generally the map title should give the "big picture" to prevent it from overwhelming the map user; the details of the data should be left to the legend title. Production dates are time-sensitive, as are the dates of data collection. Both are needed by the map user to assess the currency of the map's subject. Knowing the producer of the map imparts the level of authority associated with map quality. Figure 6.17 is a map of population density of

FIGURE 6.17
Map elements.

Source: E. Nelson, using image from U.S. Central Intelligence Agency

Poland made by the CIA using data collected in 1987. The title is short and informative and is expanded upon by the legend title. The date associated with the data is listed underneath the legend in a secondary location; the cartographic agency is not credited, but this is not unusual for CIA products.

Also essential across almost all maps, but not as context-sensitive, are the map scale, north arrow, legend, and source statement. A map's scale tells the map user about distance relationships among features. Unless the map is of such a small scale that distance is a secondary relationship, a scale, whether it is a representative fraction, verbal statement, or more likely, a scale bar, should be included. The north arrow is required if the map is not oriented to true north; otherwise, on thematic maps, it is optional. In Figure 6.17, it has been omitted. The legend describes all of the most important symbols on the map and provides additional detail about the mapped data.

The symbols in the legend should match those on the map exactly and should be described clearly and accurately for the map user. The source statement tells the map user where your data originated and in what form, so they can backtrack and verify your interpretation of the data if so desired. The source in Figure 6.17 is alluded to, but not specified.

Although not specifically mentioned by Foote and Crum, it would be remiss not to at least mention the importance of labels/text for providing context and additional detail. Many of the elements listed so far do fall under this category, but text and labels comprise much more, from identifying components of the mapped area, like cities, rivers, and countries, to providing interpretive details in block form. Text is such an integral part of mapping that cartographers treat it as a cartographic symbol, using variations in typeface, type size, and type form to create differences among mapped features. Typefaces are families of fonts, and they come in two broad categories. *Serif* faces have small finishing strokes on the ends of the letters (like Harrington or Times New Roman). Sans serif fonts (like Arial and Verdana) do not have finishing strokes. This characteristic of type is often used to make qualitative distinctions between mapped features, such as physical versus cultural on reference maps. Type form includes variations in weight (**bold**) and style (*italic*) and type size (how large the font is). Weight and size are often used to emphasize important features; style is another qualitative differentiator. There are a variety of additional guidelines that can be found in cartography texts regarding the placement of lettering for different mapping situations.

Enhancing communication is the job of locator maps, inset maps, and neat lines. For maps of areas that are likely not to be well known by the map user, adding a smaller locator map places the main map in a broader, more recognizable geographical context. If Figure 6.17 would have been meant for a broader audience with less specialized knowledge, a locator map would have enhanced its design. Inset maps, on the other hand, provide a more detailed view of an area of the map in which the symbols obscure some of the additional map details. Last, but certainly not least, the neat line defines the space in which all the map elements should reside and helps focus the map user's attention on the map elements.

VISUAL BALANCE

Visual balance is the concept of arranging map elements within the neat line so that the structure of the final map appears stable and pleasing to the eye (Figure 6.18). The point on the page that provides an initial natural focus for the map user is the **optical center**. Balancing the map elements around this point, which is slightly above the **geometric center** of the page, helps stabilize the final map layout. Research has shown that in left-to-right reading cultures, the eyes enter the visual space at the upper left, track to the optical center and exit toward the bottom right. Cartographers take advantage of this pattern to enhance stability by placing the mapped area in the vicinity of the optical center, then arranging the remaining map elements so that the highest ranking elements fall within that path; the less important elements are placed off the path in secondary spaces.

The divisions of the image space, as well as the visual weight of the individual map elements, also play roles in balancing a map layout. As the

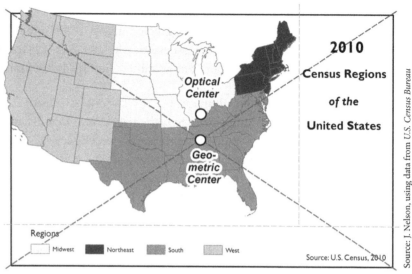

FIGURE 6.18
Implementing concepts of visual balance.

Source: J. Nelson, using data from *U.S. Census Bureau*

map elements are being arranged, for example, dividing the space into unequal parts as opposed to a more even and symmetrical design will add visual interest and imbue the space with life (Dent et al., 2009). The visual weights of the map elements, when considered in relation to one another, add yet another dimension that can affect balance (Arnheim, 1965). Larger objects, for instance, tend to be visually "heavier" and claim more attention, so they should be balanced against smaller objects. Objects to the right of center, as well as those toward the upper part of the layout, are likely to appear heavier, or draw more attention, than those on the left or those positioned toward the bottom of the layout. White space, which most treat as a negative quality, also affects final stability and should be considered using the same approach as applied to map elements.

VISUAL HIERARCHY

The elements of a map are arranged both on a single visual plane, as with the concept of balance, and from the perspective of an intellectual hierarchy of planes. For any given map, each map element will have a relative intellectual rank that corresponds to the importance of the element in communicating the information presented by the map. Elements with higher ranks are more important to the "story," so their visual importance relative to all the other map elements should reflect that. To reflect different levels of importance in this manner, designers use the concepts of **figure-ground** and **contrast**. Figure-ground is a perceptual tendency to categorize what we are seeing into two levels: figures, which are more important and tend to stand out visually, and grounds, which are less important and tend to form a background on which the figures rest. Figure-ground relationships between objects can be enhanced by using *contrast* in the design of map elements. Contrast is the property of an object that makes it distinguishable from other objects. In the visual world, it could be a contrast in weight or detail of an object, such as line thickness, or label detail, or in any of the basic visual variables used in map design: hue, value, saturation, size, shape, orientation, or texture. Varying these properties creates visual interest and improves our ability to visually organize objects into more important and less important objects. Thicker lines, for instance, are usually seen as more important than thin ones; areas with more detail attract more attention than those with fewer details (Dent et al., 2009). In the realm of color, brighter hues seem to attract more attention than darker hues, and in value, darker values trump lighter ones in visual importance.

Key Terms

Thematic mapping

Isoline map

Isarithm

Isotherm

Isobar

Isohyet

Isohypse

Isoplethic

Isometric

Isoline interval

Choropleth map

Natural breaks

Quantile

Equal interval

Manual breaks

Jenks Optimization Algorithm

Histogram

Sequential single hue scheme

Sequential multi-hued scheme

Standardize (data)

Dot density map

Graduated symbol

Proportional symbol

Visual balance

Optical center

Visual hierarchy

Map elements

Geometric center

Figure-ground

Questions

1. What is a thematic map, and how does it differ from a general reference map?

2. What does an isoline map show, and what are three specific types?

3. What's the difference between an isoplethic and an isometric map?

4. What is an isoline interval, and why is it important?

5. What is a choropleth map?

6. Why is data standardization important? Give an example.

7. What is a dot density map?

8. What's the difference between a proportional symbol and a graduated symbol map?

9. What are some of the more essential map elements, according to Foote and Crum?

10. When discussing visual balance, what's the difference between the optical center and the geometric center of a map?

11. What is "figure-ground"?

Bibliography

Andrienko, G., Andrienko, N., and A. Savinov. *Choropleth Maps: Classification Revisited.* Last accessed January 21, 2019. http://geoanalytics.net/and/papers/ica01.pdf.

Arnheim, R. 1965. *Art and Visual Perception.* Berkeley, CA: University of California Press.

Barnes, J. 1978. "Control Area and Control Points in Isopleth Mapping." *The American Cartographer* 5 (1): 65-69.

Bradley, M. "Charles Dupin and His Influence on France." Last accessed January 21, 2019. http://www.cambriapress.com/cambriapress.cfm?template=4&bid=467.

Brewer, C. and L. Pickle. 2002. "Evaluation of Methods for Classifying Epidemiological Data on Choropleth Maps in Series." *Annals of the Association of American Geographers. V* 92 (4), 662-681.

Campbell, J. 2001. *Map Use and Analysis.* 4th ed. Boston, MA: McGraw-Hill.

Chang, K. 2016. *Introduction to Geographic Information Systems.* 8th ed. New York, NY: McGraw-Hill Companies, Inc.

Delamarre, L. 1909. "Pierre-Charles-François-Dupin." In *The Catholic Encyclopedia.* New York, NY: Robert Appleton Company. Accessed September 21, 2019. http://www.newadvent.org/cathen/05205a.htm.

Dent, B.D., Torguson, J.S., and T.W. Hodler. 2009. *Cartography: Thematic Map Design.* 6th ed. New York, NY: McGraw-Hill.

Dramowicz, K., and E. Dramowicz. 2004. "Choropleth Mapping with Exploratory Data Analysis." *Directions Magazine.* Accessed September 21, 2019. http://www.directionsmag.com

Friendly, M., and D. Denis. "Milestones in the History of Thematic Cartography, Statistical Graphics, and Data Visualization." Accessed September 21, 2019. http://www.datavis.ca/milestones/.

Foote, K. and S. Crum. (2000). "Cartographic Communication." , Last accessed April 4, 2019. https://foote.geography.uconn.edu/gcraft/notes/cartocom/cartocom_f.html.

NCGIA. "Data Classification." Accessed September 21, 2019. http://www.ncgia.ucsb.edu/cctp/units/unit47/html/comp_class.html.

Robinson, A. 1982. *Early Thematic Mapping in the History of Cartography.* Chicago, IL: University of Chicago Press.

Slocum, T. A., McMaster, R. B., Kessler, F.C., and H.H. Howard. 2009. *Thematic Cartography and Geovisualization.* 3rd ed. Upper Saddle River, NJ: Pearson Prentice Hall.

Warf, B. 2010. *Encyclopedia of Geography.* Thousand Oaks, CA: SAGE Publications, Inc.

Wright, J. 1942. "Mapmakers are Human." *Geographical Review. V* 32 (4): 527-544.

Creating a Choropleth Map

In this exercise, you will design a choropleth map and create a layout that highlights population change in the Southeast Region of the United States from 2000 to 2010.

The U.S. Department of the Census reported an increase of over 9% in the total population of the United States, from 281.4 million people in 2000 to 308.7 million people in 2010. You have been asked to create a choropleth map highlighting changes in the southern census region.

OBJECTIVES

- Standardize and classify attribute data
- Apply color schemes
- Design a map

SOFTWARE

This exercise uses ESRI's ArcGIS Pro 2.3.2.

DATA

The data for this exercise are available from the Kendall Hunt Student Ancillary site. See the inside front cover for access information. You may also be directed to download the data from a different location by your instructor.

1. Download the data as directed by your instructor
2. Save the file to a location where you have read/write privileges

The files are compressed and must be decompressed prior to use.

Add the Data

1. Start ArcGIS Pro.
2. Select *Map* under the *New > Blank Templates* in the dialog box.
3. Leave the defaults for *Name* and *Location*. Click OK. ArcGIS Pro creates a default folder to store all components of a project, but, for this lab, we will use the folder provided in the class data.
4. Right-click on the *Topographic* layer in the *Contents pane* and select *Remove*. This base map automatically loads anytime you start a new project. We do not need the base map for this exercise.
5. In the *Catalog pane*, right-click the *Folders* icon and select *Add Folder Connection*.

6. Navigate to and select your *Chapter06* class folder.
7. Click OK
8. Expand your *Folders* and *Chapter06* folders and your *Exercise_06.gdb* by clicking on the arrow to the left of each icon to view the contents (Figure 6.1).

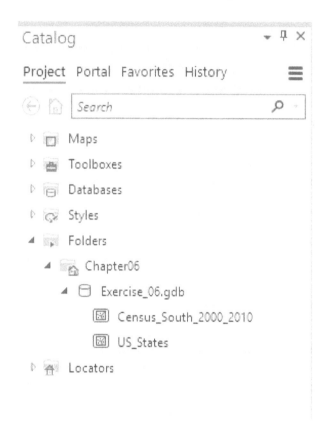

FIGURE 6.1

9. Click and drag *Census_South_2000_2010* to the *Contents pane* to add it to the *View*.

Setting up the Basemap

Thematic maps almost always require an equal-area map projection for the basemap because users will be comparing values between different areas on the map. The *Census_South_2000_2010* basemap is not projected to an *equal-area* projection. In this section, you will project the basemap to an equal-area projection and then calculate the area for each county in the attribute table.

Checking the Current Coordinate System of the Basemap

1. Right-click on *Census_South_2000_2010* in the *Contents pane*.
2. Select *Properties* and then *Source*.

3. Expand *Spatial Reference* by clicking on the arrow.
4. Scroll down and note the *Geographic coordinate system* (it should read as *GCS North American 1983*). Although this layer has a geographic coordinate system, it is not projected.
5. Click *Cancel* to close the *Layer Properties* dialog box.

Projecting the Basemap to an Equal-Area Projection

1. Click on the *Analysis* tab located on the *Ribbon*.
2. Press the *Tools* icon to open the *Geoprocessing* dialog box.
3. Type *Project* in the *Find Tools* prompt box and select *Project (Data Management Tools)*.
4. Add the *Census_South_2000_2010* to the *Input Dataset or Feature Class* by clicking on the arrow and then the layer.
5. Under *Output dataset or Feature Class* select the folder icon and navigate to your *Exercise_06.gdb*.
6. Name the layer *MyCensus_South_2000_2010_projected* and press *Save*.
7. Under *Output Coordinate System*, press the *World* icon.
8. Expand *Projected coordinate system*.
9. Expand *Continental* and *North America*.
10. Scroll down and select *North America Albers Equal Area Conic* and press *OK*.
11. Press *Run*.
12. Close the *Geoprocessing* window by pressing the X. The projected file is automatically added to your *Contents pane*.
13. Right-click and *Remove* the *Census_South_2000_2010* layer.
14. Right-click on the *Map* frame and select *Properties* and then *Coordinate Systems*.
15. Scroll to find and expand *Layers*.
16. Select *North America Albers Equal Area Conic* and click *OK*. This sets your *Map* frame to match the projection of your *MyCensus_South_2000_2010_projected* layer.
17. Press the *Map* tab to return to the *Ribbon* for the map.

Re-centering the Layer

Once projected, the layer needs to be re-centered to remove the skewed or tilted appearance.

1. Right-click on the *Map* frame and select *Properties* and then *Coordinate Systems*.
2. Expand *Layers*.
3. Right-click on *North America Albers Equal Area Conic* and select *Copy and Modify*.
4. Change the Central Meridian to -90.
5. Press *Save* and *OK*.
6. Press the *Full Extent* button located in the *Navigate* tools group to re-center your map view.

Calculate Area

When creating a choropleth map such as population density, it is necessary to calculate area and convert it to a unit that makes sense such as acres, square miles, or square kilometers.

1. Right-click on *MyCensus_South_2000_2010_projected* and select *Attribute Table*.
2. Scroll and find the field called *Area*.
3. Right-click on *Area* and select *Calculate Geometry*.
4. In the *Geoprocessing* dialog box, the *Target Field* should be *AREA*.
5. Under *Property*, press the drop-down arrow and then select *Area*.
6. Under *Area Unit* select *Square miles (United States)*.
7. Click *Run*.
8. Close the *Geoprocessing* dialog box by clicking on the X. The AREA field should be populated with the area values in square miles.

What is the area in square miles for Abbeville County in South Carolina? Hint: Right-click on the *NAME* field and *Sort Ascending*.

a. 658.23 square miles
b. 430.17 square miles
c. 975.12 square miles
d. 517.25 square miles

What is the area in square miles for Zavala County in Texas? Hint: Right-click on the *NAME* field and *Sort Descending*.

a. 1,658.21 square miles
b. 1,327.24 square miles
c. 1,975.12 square miles
d. 1,517.23 square miles

Design a Choropleth Overlay

There are several fields in the attribute table that are associated with population. Examine the table to become familiar with the name of the attribute field and its description.

Attribute Field	Field Description
POP2000	Total population, year 2000
POP2001	Total population, year 2001
POP_2010	Total population, year 2010
POP00_SQMI	Population per square mile, year 2000
POP_CHG	Change in total population
PPOP_CHG	Percent change in total population

Your map will highlight changes that occurred between the 2000 and 2010 censuses. A field for change in total population has been created (POP_CHG), but has yet to be populated with data.

1. Scroll and find the field called *POP_CHG* and select *Calculate Field*.
2. Under *Fields*, double-click *POP_2010*.
3. Press the minus (−) button (to the right of the *Insert Values* text).
4. Under *Fields*, double-click *POP2000*.
5. Your Python code should look exactly like this: *!POP_2010! - !POP2000!*
6. Click *Run*.
7. Close the *Geoprocessing* dialog box by clicking on the X. The *POP_CHG* field should be populated with the change values.

QUESTION 6.3

What was the population change for Wichita County in Texas from 2000 to 2010?

a. +370 people
b. −170 people
c. −164 people
d. −114 people

QUESTION 6.4

What was the population change for Alcorn County in Mississippi from 2000 to 2010?

a. −1,287 people
b. +4,588 people
c. +2,499 people
d. −6,321 people

Standardizing Attribute Data

Even at the county level, administrative regions can vary widely in size, which can influence the visual perception of count data, such as the change in population counts between two years. With choropleth maps, this often translates into big areas getting undue emphasis by being grouped into the higher, or darker-colored, classes, even when those big areas have smaller percentages of change over the two years. To offset this potential problem, cartographers do not map count data using this method; instead differences in the areal extents of regions are processed out statistically prior to visualization by changing the count data to derived data.

To standardize our change in population data, we will convert it to a percent change over the ten years.

1. To calculate the percent change in population between 2000 and 2010, right-click the field *PPOP_CHG* and choose *Calculate Field*.

2. Under *Fields*, double-click *POP_CHG*.
3. Click the division sign (/).
4. Double-click *POP2000*.
5. Click the multiplication sign (*), then click to the right of the multiplication sign in the expression window and type 100.
6. Your Python code should look exactly like this: *!POP_CHG! / !POP2000! * 100*
7. Press the *Run* button.
8. Close the *Geoprocessing* dialog box by clicking on the X. The *PPOP_CHG* field should be populated with the change values.
9. Answer the following questions, then close the *Attribute Table* by clicking on the X.

QUESTION 6.5

What was the percentage of population change for Young County in Texas from 2000 to 2010?

a. 5.12
b. 1.34
c. 3.38
d. 6.12

QUESTION 6.6

What was the percentage of population change for Yalobusha County in Mississippi from 2000 to 2010?

a. −2.86
b. −0.05
c. −1.78
d. −3.24

Classifying Attribute Data

Data visualized using the choropleth map technique are typically classified by grouping the data values into a smaller set of four to six classes. This generalizes and highlights the major patterns or trends in the data for the map user. It also limits the number of color values the user must discriminate between reliably. Choosing a classification method and an appropriate number of classes relies on the cartographer's knowledge of those methods and how they relate to the data's statistical distribution.

1. Right-click on *MyCensus_South_2000_2010_projected* and select *Symbology*.
2. Change the *Primary symbology* to *Graduated Colors*.
3. Change the *Field* to *PPOP_CHG*.

4. Experiment with the method and the number of classes until you have a combination you believe best tells the story of population change in the South Region.
5. Explore the *Histogram* and *Show Statistics* (for statistics, click the drop-down arrow next to the More option) to better understand and describe the data you are mapping.

What is the data's Count, Minimum, Maximum, Mean, and Standard deviation?

a. 1,423, −46.60, 92.04, 7.76, 14.24
b. 2,341, −13.98, 89.03, 6.54, 12,32
c. 1,213, −32.12, 90.00, 8.41, 15.12
d. 3,414, −90.32, 91.00, 9.34, 11.24

Traditionally, the histogram is a graphic display of the distribution of the attribute data where the data values are plotted along the x-axis and the frequency with which they occur is plotted along the y-axis (Figure 6.2). There are several common distribution patterns, and they can be described in terms of their shape, center, and spread among other features. The shape of the histogram can help you choose a reliable classification method. Skewed distributions, for example, often make use of Natural Breaks to classify the data set. Multipeaked distributions also make use of Natural Breaks. Equal Intervals and Quantiles, on the other hand, which do not take the shape of the distribution into account when grouping data values, tend to serve uniform and normal distributions more effectively.

In ArcGIS Pro, notice that the histogram has been changed from its traditional orientation. The ranges of the data values are plotted on the y-axis (from negative values showing a decrease in population to positive values showing an increase in population). The frequency with which the data values occur is on the x-axis.

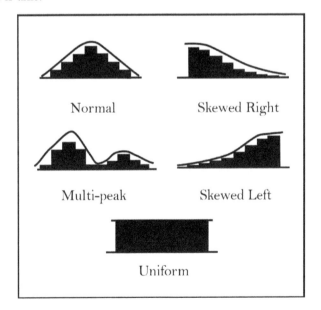

FIGURE 6.2

What is the shape of the histogram for the data?

    a.   More *Multipeak*
    b.   More *Uniform*
    c.   More *Normal*

Selecting a Color Scheme

The next step is to select a color scheme that will shade your polygons according to the data class to which they are assigned. In choropleth mapping, when ordered or numerical data are being mapped, the rule is to pick a scheme in which a light-to-dark ramp of shades predominates. Lighter shades should be assigned to lower data values, while darker shades should be reserved for higher data values.

1.   Choose an appropriate color by clicking on the drop-down arrow in the *Color Scheme* box.
2.   When you are satisfied with your map, close the *Symbology* dialog box by clicking on the X.

QUESTION 6.9

When the goal is to showcase variation in numerical data, like percentage of change in population, the best choice is a color scheme that

    a.   emphasizes a progression of light to dark values that match the progression of lower to higher changes in numerical data
    b.   emphasizes a progression of dark to light values that match the progression of lower to higher changes in the numerical data

Design a Map Layout

Right now, you have a data visualization in the *View*, but you will need a printed final product for your employer. This product should include your main map of the South Region as defined by the U.S. Census Bureau. You will also want a map title, map legend, map scale, and source statement for your finished design.

1.   Select the *Insert tab* and choose *New Layout*.
2.   Select *ANSI-Landscape > Letter* (8.5" × 11"). A blank layout page should appear.
3.   Under the *Map Frames* tool group, press the *Map Frame* button and select *Map > Default Extent*

4. Left-click, hold, and drag your cursor over the blank page to draw a box. This will insert your map into the layout.
5. Right-click on *Map Frame* and select *Properties*.
6. Rename your layout map to *MyPopChange*.
7. Roll your mouse cursor over each button icon to become familiar with their descriptions (highlighted in Figure 6.3).

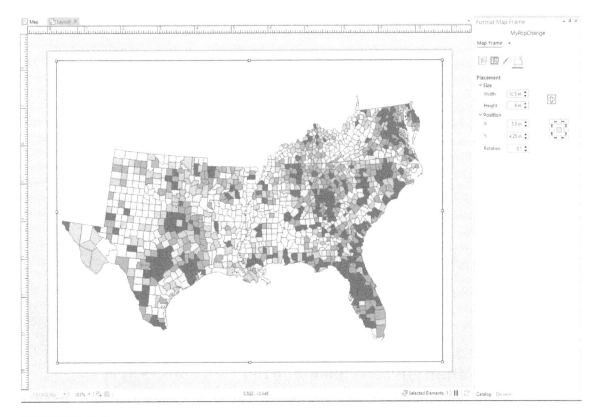

FIGURE 6.3

8. Press the *Display Options* button.
9. Under *Constraint*, select *Fixed Scale*.
10. Under *Scale*, type in 11,000,000 and press *Enter* on your keyboard. When you set your layout map to a *Fixed Scale*, it will not change even if you change scales in the *View*.
11. Now press the *Placement* button.
12. Under *Placement*, type 10.5 for the *Width* and 8 for the *Height*.
13. Center your map by holding down the left mouse button and moving the cursor. The size and position of your map should look like the one in Figure 6.3.
14. Right-click on your map, select *Activate*, and move your map slightly up so that it is placed in the visual center rather than the geometric center of the page.
15. Once you have moved your map, click on the left-pointing arrow to *Close activated map frame* (top left portion of your layout *View*).

Modifying the Neat Line

1. Make sure the *Insert* tab in the *Ribbon* is selected.
2. In the *Element pane*, press the *Display* icon and change the *Border > Symbol* color to *No Color*.
3. Select *Rectangle* from the *Graphics* tool group and draw a box around the entire map.
4. Resize and center as necessary.
5. When you are satisfied with its placement, check the *Locked box* in the *Format Polygon* dialog box to lock the neat line in place.

Adding a Title

1. In the *Text* tool group, click the arrow beside *Rectangle* and then *A Text*.
2. Left-click on the map area to insert the text box.
3. Click on the text box and type *Southeastern United States* (press the Enter key) *Population Change 2000–2010*.
4. Click on an area outside your *Layout* page to deselect the text box, then double-click the text box to bring up the *Element* dialog box
5. In the *Element* dialog box, select *Text Symbol > Properties*, and then expand *Appearance*.
6. Next to *Font name*, select *Arial* and **Bold** for *Font style*.
7. Press Apply.
8. Use some of the other *Element* options to change the size of font and center the text.
9. Your map, thus far, should look like the one in Figure 6.4.

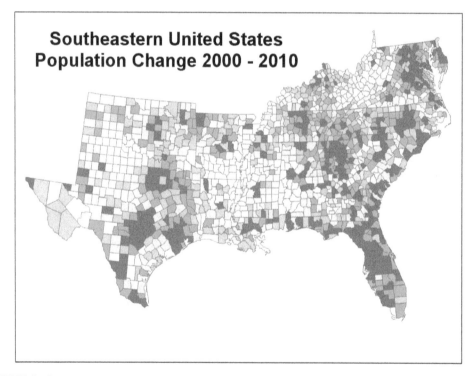

FIGURE 6.4

1. Click on *Legend* in the *Map Surrounds* tool group.
2. Draw a box on your map layout to insert the legend. You may have to expand the box to see the entire contents.
3. In the *Contents pane*, double-click on *Legend*. The *Element* dialog box will appear to your right.
4. In the *Element* dialog box, press *Show properties* (under the *Legend Items* heading).
5. Turn off *Layer name* and *Headings* by unchecking the box.
6. Click the back-arrow button and check the box next to *Show* and type *Percent Change* in the *Title* under the *Legend* heading.
7. Resize the legend to a size that you like and move it to the left corner of your map.
8. Close the *Element* dialog box by clicking on the X.

Adding the Scale Bar

1. Press the *Scale Bar* drop-down arrow in your *Map surrounds* tool group and select *Double Alternating Scale Bar 1*.
2. Draw a box in your map layout to insert the scale bar. Resize the scale bar so that the highest value is 300 miles.
3. Place the scale bar at the bottom middle of your map layout. Your map should look like the one in Figure 6.5.

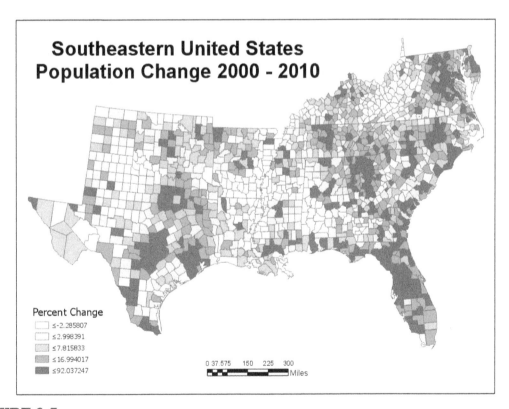

FIGURE 6.5

Adding the North Arrow

1. Press the *North Arrow* drop-down arrow in your *Map surrounds* tool group and select *ArcGIS North 17*.
2. Draw a box in your map layout to insert the north arrow.
3. Place the north arrow centered above the scale bar (Figure 6.6).

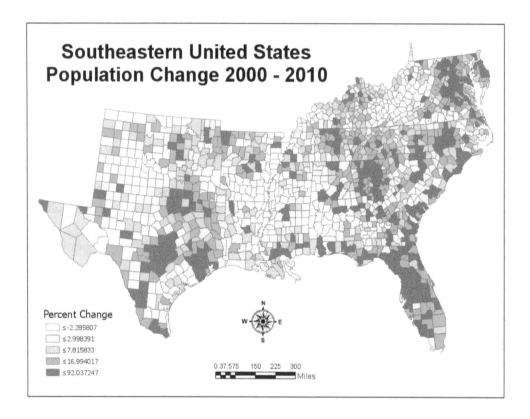

FIGURE 6.6

Adding the Data Source

1. In the *Text* tool group, select *Text* and *A Text*.
2. Left-click on the layout area to insert the text box.
3. Click on the text box and type *Source: U.S. Census Bureau, 2010*.
4. Click on an area outside your *Layout* page to deselect the text box, then double-click the text box to bring up the *Format Text* dialog box
5. In the *Element* dialog box, select *Text Symbol* and then *Appearance*.
6. Next to *Font name*, select *Arial* and *Italic* for *Font style*.
7. Make the *Size* 11.

8. Press Apply.
9. Place the source text on the bottom right of your map layout (Figure 6.7).
10. Close the *Element* dialog box by pressing the X.

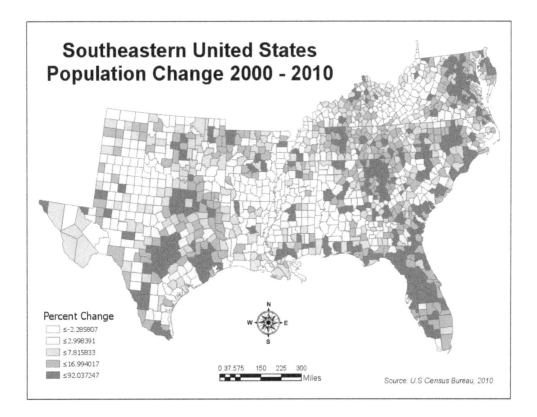

Southeastern United States Population Change 2000 - 2010

Percent Change
☐ ≤-2.285807
☐ ≤2.998391
☐ ≤7.815833
☐ ≤16.994017
☐ ≤92.037247

0 37.575 150 225 300
Miles

Source: U.S Census Bureau, 2010

FIGURE 6.7

Save the map
1. In the *Catalog pane*, expand *Layouts*.
2. Right-click on the *Layout* file in this folder and select *Export to File*.
3. Navigate to your *Chapter06* folder.
4. Name the map *MySEPopMap_yourlastname* and save it as a PDF.

CHAPTER 7
Spatial Data in the Digital Environment

Over the past few decades, computer technology has revolutionized mapmaking. Now, both reference and thematic maps have not only a printed presence but also a digital presence. Moving from a real-world, printed map to a digital representation is known as **data modeling**. Data modeling for spatial data got its official start with the development of the **Canada Geographic Information System** (CGIS). CGIS was the first industry-scale computer-based GIS, and most GIScientists recognize it as a primary milestone in the development of today's GIS packages. The concept of CGIS was born in 1963, when the Canadian government became concerned with decision-making practices regarding land use in its country. Maps with sufficient detail for making land use decisions were accessible, but the manual process of analyzing and interpreting them to arrive at those decisions were too time-consuming and labor-intensive for the government to support the tasks. Even if the money had been available, in reality there weren't enough people trained in these skillsets to perform the work for such a large expanse of land.

The idea of harnessing computer power to conduct these analyses originated with *Roger Tomlinson*, who had encountered similar issues while working on projects for an aerial survey company. As someone who saw this need as critical, he began experimenting with the notion of converting a printed map into a format that a computer could analyze. Computers can't "see" graphics and images like we can; their reality is a world of numbers. One of the first challenges Tomlinson faced, then, was how to create a map model the computer could "see" and interpret that would mimic what we as humans see and interpret when the same map is put in front of us.

Data Models

Data modeling consists of a series of steps: Worboys (1995) has one of the more easily understood descriptions (Figure 7.1). He breaks the process down using four hierarchical levels, which range from **Application Domain** (the original printed map) to the **Physical Computer Model** (actual computer code that implements the model). The two levels of most interest here are the second and third levels. The second level, **Conceptual Computer Model**, translates a map into a numerical model. Two basic models that have evolved over the years are the **raster data model** and the **vector data model**. The third level, **Logical Computer Model**, translates the conceptual model into a computer-based data structure.

Raster Data Model. Tomlinson's first stab at designing a conceptual computer model for CGIS was based on scanning the needed data. He had the area features traced from the original maps to create an uncluttered overlay and then used a drum scanner to scan the new line work into a digital format. During scanning, the scanner head moved back and forth across a revolving drum onto which the overlay was attached, detecting reflected light intensity levels every 1/250 of an inch. Each sampled light intensity level was stored as a *pixel*, or picture element, using a grid format. For each cell in the grid, the computer recorded a value of either 1 or 0; the presence of a line meant no light was reflected due to absence of ink (1), while the absence of a line meant light was reflected (0). These values, in the order in which they were written, produced a grid of cells representing the original line work. Each cell (and corresponding value) in the grid had an assigned row and column number that gave it a unique location in the file. The result was a prototype for the *raster data model* (Figure 7.2). A more generic description would be to describe the process as overlaying a grid onto the printed map, then numerically coding the primary geographic feature occupying each cell.

The first raster data model was a success in terms of converting geographic features to numbers, but beyond simply spitting out what Tomlinson already had in printed form, it was severely limited. There was no way, for example, to record any descriptive data about the scanned features, and Tomlinson knew he would need this data to calculate statistics and produce reports about the natural resources of Canada. He also envisioned a model that would (1) convert row and column numbers to latitude and longitude to tie features to real-world locations, (2) store descriptive data about each feature, (3) calculate areas, (4) overlay and/or merge features, (5) select feature subsets, and (6) create buffers around features.

Vector Data Model. Tackling the descriptive data issue first, Tomlinson decided to keep the locational information about the areas separate from the descriptive data about them. To link the de-

Application Domain

Conceptual Computer Model

Logical Computer Model

Physical Computer Model

Source: E. Nelson

FIGURE 7.1
Worboy's (1995) data modeling hierarchy.

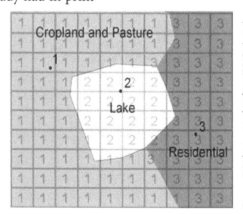

FIGURE 7.2
Raster Data Model.

Source: E. Nelson, using data from U.S. Geological Survey, Department of the Interior.

scriptive data to the feature, he needed to treat each feature as a separate entity rather than a series of grid cells. His solution was to use a geometric shape, the polygon, to represent the different map features (Figure 7.3). To convert the scanned features to geometrical figures based on digital coordinates, he placed the traced overlay of the area features, along with the original map, onto a *digitizing table* (an electronically sensitive device) and used the computer to record the latitude and longitude of the four corner points of the original map, along with a point inside each area feature. He then let the computer figure out the real-world coordinates of each of the scanned features. The point inside each of the resulting polygons was assigned a feature identification number *(FID)*, which was also embedded in the tables used to store the descriptive, or *attribute*, data associated with each feature. This model was the prototype for the *vector data model*, a model in which graphics are defined using geometric primitives instead of grid cells.

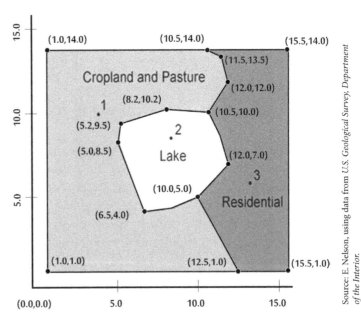

Source: E. Nelson, using data from U.S. Geological Survey, Department of the Interior.

FIGURE 7.3
Vector Data Model.

Data Structures

Both the raster and vector data models are concepts until they are implemented as *data structures* that can be used in a GIS. A variety of structures are available for implementing both raster and vector data models. These structures, which can affect both the efficient processing of data and the amount of data storage required, are members of Worboy's *Logical Computer Models*, the third level of his hierarchy.

Raster data structures. Raster data structures are implemented using *arrays*, which are groups of contiguous cells, each holding a value of the same data type. These values are accessed using indices, or row and column addresses, that represent location coordinates. Tomlinson's prototype architecture, known as a *bitmap image*, represents the simplest structure for raster data. The grid cell values of this format are numerical but are limited to ones (white) and zeroes (black) to indicate the presence or absence of a particular feature. In 1967, researchers at the *Harvard Lab for Computer Graphics and Spatial Analysis* modified this prototype to represent and analyze digital landscapes for environmental planning applications. While conducting a regional study, they found that the land use and elevation data available for analysis were stored in a grid cell format, leading them to expand on Tomlinson's structure (Chrisman, 2006). They developed a grid-based input system that could record both **discrete data values**, such as multiple land use codes, and **continuous data values** like elevation measurements. In these cases, the data values were expanded from the simpler 0/1 structure to include a variety of integers and floating-point data values to represent changes in discrete and continuous data, respectively.

For each cell in the grid to house these expanded data values required manipulating each pixel's **bit depth**. Bit depth refers to how much computer memory (or how many unique data values) a pixel in a raster file can store. It is based on the equation 2^n, so a bitmap with a bit depth of 1, like Tomlinson's raster prototype, has pixels with enough memory to store 2^1 or two, unique data values. Files with a bit depth of 2, then can store 2^2 or four unique data values. Some of our current raster files, like ESRI's Grid Format, can store 2^{32} or 4,294,967,296 unique data values per pixel.

Each cell in the array not only houses an attribute value for the area, its size is also correlated to the level of details the image can show (Figure 7.4). This characteristic is called **spatial resolution**. A grid cell might be 30 m × 30 m or 1 m × 1 m, for example. The cell with 30-m resolution is bigger and covers more ground than the cell with the 1-m resolution. The more ground a cell covers, the less detailed the features and patterns of the area will be, since each cell can represent only one data value. Smaller cells provide better detail or finer resolution, but have the disadvantage of requiring more data storage and longer processing times.

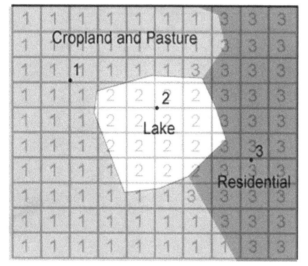

Smaller Cell, Finer Spatial Resolution   Larger Cell, Coarser Spatial Resolution

FIGURE 7.4
Comparing spatial resolutions and associated detail changes.

Vector data structures. In Tomlinson's vector data structure, the polygon was the geometric figure used to describe areal features mathematically. Like his raster prototype, this one was also modified by researchers at the *Harvard Lab for Computer Graphics and Spatial Analysis* in the 1960s. To produce the first graphic output for a mapping system, researchers designed a new mapping package known as SYMAP. This package, which produced thematic maps and output them to a line printer, used a vector data structure that supported line and point features as well as polygons. Attribute values, like those in the CGIS prototype, were kept in a separate file from the geography with the two files linked by a feature ID (Chrisman, 2006).

The points, lines, and polygons comprising this data structure are represented by (*x, y*) coordinates that are tied to a spatial reference system such as latitude and longitude (Figure 7.5). The point, represented by a single (*x, y*) coordinate, is the simplest geographic feature. It could be a city, or an archaeological site, perhaps. Lines, such as roads or railroads, are represented by storing strings of coordinates that must be connected by the computer when drawn. Areas, or polygons, are also represented by storing a string of coordinates, except in this case the first and last coordinate pairs are the same, resulting in a closed figure when drawn. Storing these features using coordinates allows us to (1) transfer the data to the computer, (2) use the data to redraw the map digitally, and (3) perform basic calculations, such as the distance between two features.

This next-generation vector data structure was aptly named "**cartographic spaghetti**," after a comment made by Nick Chrisman in which he described the data structure adopted by the CIA for its World Data Bank as "…unstructured as a plate of spaghetti" (Chrisman 2006, 105). ESRI's *shapefile* format is a modernized version of this vector data structure. In the shapefile, each set of features on a map (points, lines, polygons) are stored in their own data file using these coordinates. Stored in this manner, the computer can draw the features, but it has no way to differentiate them symbolically within any data file. For this to occur, we need to supply the computer with *attribute* data for each feature. Attribute data are recorded in a flat file, or spreadsheet form, for each geographic feature. This file is linked to the file of feature geometry using a Feature ID Number (FID). The FID is included in both the geometry and attribute files and is a unique code supplied to each geographic feature (Figure 7.6). Because it exists in both files, the computer can use it to associate the correct attribute data with the correct geometry. For example, by linking city coordinates (points) to a table that lists the population for each city, we can use different circle sizes for each city, depending on how many people reside there. This setup, where we use multiple tables that are linked by FIDs, is called a **georelational database**.

FIGURE 7.5
Non-topological vector data structure

Points Layer		Points Attributes		
FID	Coordinates	FID	Name	Population
1	(3.5, 13.5)	1	Colfax	2,469
2	...	2	...	

FIGURE 7.6
Example of a georelational database setup.

Cartographic spaghetti is considered a simplistic vector data structure by today's standards. Its initial purpose was to provide the functions necessary to reproduce a map using the computer; functions to analyze spatial relationships were missing entirely, making this more a mapping package and less a GIS. Even as a mapping package, it was soon clear that there were weaknesses in its design. Polygons, for example, were entities unto themselves; if two polygons happened to share a border, such as the state border between North and South Carolina, the shared border of each polygon would be stored twice.

At least two problems arise from this situation. Common borders between polygons, for instance, are going to be stored more than once, which is a waste of computer memory. Further, those shared borders might not match precisely, creating *slivers* and *gaps* upon printing that are distracting and diminish the quality of the map. In the earlier days of computer mapping and GIS, creating digital data to be used by these systems was a critical component in the process. To reproduce print maps as numerical structures, someone has to digitize each polygon's boundaries. A tedious and time-consuming task, it would not be uncommon that the shared border would differ at least slightly in point placement from one polygon to the next. When that happens and the map is printed, mismatches between the shared borders are likely to be visible. Slivers and gaps also make analysis difficult and creates error in the results.

The U.S. Census, around the same time, was also experiencing redundant digitizing operations as they worked to develop an automated system to increase the efficiency of census procedures. Their research on the development of geographic base files eventually produced the **GBF-DIME** file, which incorporated the system of **map topology** to eliminate redundant digitizing and to enhance analytical and map production procedures (U.S. Census, 2019). GBF-DIME stands for **Geographic Base File—Dual Independent Map Encoding**, and map topology refers to the mathematical concept that "…explicitly expresses the spatial relationships between features, such as two lines meeting perfectly at a point and a directed line having an explicit left and right side" (Chang, 2008, 7).

Topology is a critical concept for GIS; building it into base files as they are converted from print to digital formats allows digitizers to eliminate shared boundaries when building polygons and helps them reduce graphic clutter. With the DIME encoding scheme, intersections were treated as points, streets as lines, and blocks or areas as polygons. Intersections (*nodes*) and areas were each numbered. Street segments were then tagged with the areas to the left and right of each segment, as well as address ranges for both sides of the street, and for the two nodes (*From-nodes* and *To-nodes*) each segment connected (Figure 7.7). The street segment, also known as a *chain* or *arc*, is the basis for this system; the tagged areas explicitly encode spatial **adjacency** relationships and the From and To nodes explicitly encode **connectivity** and **contiguity** relationships. During the 1970s, GBF-DIME files were created for all cities in the United States. This is the structure upon which many of the modern vector systems are built, including the Census' **Topologically Integrated Geographic Encoding and Referencing (TIGER)** files, the USGS's **Digital Line Graphs** (DLGs), and ESRI's **coverages**.

The newest vector data structures are object-oriented implementations, such as ESRI's **geodatabase** (Figure 7.8). A geodatabase, at its most functional level, can be thought of as a container that houses data, both spatial and attribute together, as opposed the georelational database that stores the files separately. Non-spatial data are stored in **geodatabase tables** and spatial data in *feature classes*. Each **feature class** may be comprised of only one spatial data type (points, lines, or polygons), and whatever that type is, each feature in the class must have the same attribute fields and spatial reference system associated with it. Feature classes that are tied to each other via spatial relationships, such as a county feature class and a corresponding census tract class, can be stored together as a *feature data set* to make modeling those relationships in the GIS easier using **geodatabase topology** rules. Census tracts, for example, make up a county, so they share some boundaries with the county feature class. If the boundary of a tract changed, that change might also need to be made at the county level as well. By storing both in a feature data set, where a common spatial reference system is required, these updates are easier to implement (ESRI, 2013). **Relationship classes** can be used to link feature classes and geodatabase tables; an example here might be the need to create a permanent association between a feature class of parcels and a non-spatial table of parcel owners.

Source: E. Nelson

FIGURE 7.7
Topological data structure.

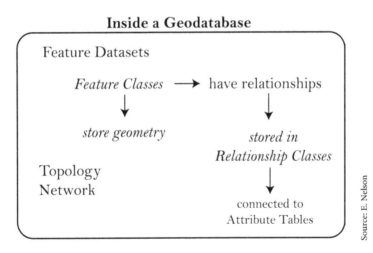

Source: E. Nelson

FIGURE 7.8
Basic view of the geodatabase

Key Terms

Data modeling

Canada Geographic Information System

Application Domain

Physical Computer Model

Conceptual Computer Model

Raster data model

Vector data model

Logical Computer Model

Physical Computer Model

Discrete data value

Continuous data value

Bit depth

Spatial resolution

Cartographic spaghetti

Georelational database

GBF-DIME

Map topology

Base File—Dual Independent Map Encoding

Adjacency

Connectivity

Contiguity

Topologically Integrated Geographic Encoding
  and Referencing

Digital Line Graph

Coverage

Geodatabase

Geodatabase table

Feature class

Geodatabase topology

Relationship classes

Questions

1. What is data modeling?

2. What's the importance of the Canada Geographic Information System?

3. What were some of the limitations Tomlinson saw in early raster modeling?

4. What are the two types of data models, and how are they different?

5. What is an FID, and why is it important?

6. Why was the Harvard Lab for Computer Graphics and Spatial Analysis important?

7. What is "cartographic spaghetti," and how did this term come about?

8. What is map topology, and why is it important?

9. What is GBF-DIME, and why is it important?

10. What is TIGER, and why is it important?

11. What is the latest type of vector data structure, and how does it differ from past structures?

Bibliography

Chang, K. 2008. *Introduction to Geographic Information Systems.* 5th ed. New York, NY: McGraw-Hill Companies, Inc.:.

Chrisman, N. 2006. *Charting the Unknown: How Computer Mapping at Harvard Became GIS.* Redlands, CA: ESRI Press.

Davis, B. 2001. *GIS: A Visual Approach.* 2nd ed. Albany, NY: Onword Press.

Demers, M.N. 2000. *Geographic Information Systems.* 2nd ed. New York, NY: John Wiley & Sons, Inc.

Environment Canada. 1973. "The Canada Geographic Information System." *Cartographica, v.* 10(3): 62-86.

Foresman, T.W., ed. 1998. *The History of Geographic Information Systems: Perspectives from the Pioneers.* Upper Saddle River, NJ: Prentice Hall.

National Academy of Sciences. 2006. *Beyond Mapping: Meeting National Needs Through Enhanced Geographic Information Science.* Washington, DC: National Academies Press.

NCGIA. "The GIS History Project." Accessed September 21, 2019. http://www.ncgia.buffalo.edu/ncgia/gishist/bar_harbor.html.

Shekhar, S., and H. Xiong. "Encyclopedia of GIS 2008." Accessed September 21, 2019 https://link.springer.com/referencework/10.1007/978-0-387-35973-1.

Slocum, T. A., McMaster, R. B., Kessler, F.C., and H.H. Howard. 2009. *Thematic Cartography and Geovisualization.* 3rd ed. Upper Saddle River, NJ: Pearson Prentice Hall.

U.S. Census. Dual Independent Map Encoding. Retrieved from https://www.census.gov/history/www/innovations/technology/dual_independent_map_encoding.html, October 20, 2019.

Wise, S. 2002. *GIS Basics.* New York, NY: Taylor & Francis, Inc.

Worboys, M.F. 1995. GIS: *A Computing Perspective.* London, England: Taylor & Francis.

Spatial Data, Digital Environment

This exercise explores the vector and raster data models used in GIS. You will work with both raster and vector data to understand the different ways in which spatial data can be used and stored in a computer to represent real-world features.

OBJECTIVES

- Examine the characteristics of vector data
- Examine the characteristics of raster data
- Learn how to access and read metadata

SOFTWARE

This exercise uses ESRI's ArcGIS Pro 2.3.2.

DATA

The data for this exercise are available from the Kendall Hunt Student Ancillary site. See the inside front cover for access information. You may also be directed to download the data from a different location by your instructor.

1. Download the data as directed by your instructor
2. Save the file to a location where you have read/write privileges

The files are compressed and must be decompressed prior to use.

Scenario Summary

The exercise is contextualized by the following scenario:

Fracking is coming to an area near you. More properly termed hydraulic fracturing, fracking is a method of extracting natural gas from an organic-rich, fine-grained sedimentary rock known as shale. This method involves injecting chemicals, sand, and millions of gallons of water under high pressure directly into the ground to release natural gas in the shale deposits.

Detractors claim that the negative effects of fracking outweigh any possible benefits. Some of the effects they list include the following:

- The mixture of chemicals, sediment, and natural gas injected may make its way to the surface and enter rivers
- By-products and natural gas can leach into groundwater

- Fracking can weaken existing fractures in the rock, known as faults, leading to an increase in earthquakes

The North Carolina State Legislature has passed a law allowing fracking. The town of Oak Ridge, located in the northwest quadrant of Guilford County in the central part of North Carolina, wants to be proactive and has asked you to examine the data they have collected that might be used for future mitigation and emergency management strategies. This exercise examines the data structures and metadata associated with geospatial data sets that could be used in a fracking analysis.

Metadata

GIS data sets consist not only of spatial data and attribute data but also metadata. Metadata is typically included as a text file and describes relevant details about the spatial data to which it is attached. These details can be crucial to evaluating the data and deciding whether to use it in the context of a specific GIS project. In GIS, metadata can be accessed using the *Catalog pane*. Like Microsoft's Windows Explorer, the *Catalog pane* organizes your spatial data using a tree view and provides detailed information about data sets.

1. Start ArcGIS Pro.
2. Select *Map* under the *New > Blank Templates* in the dialog box.
3. Leave the defaults for *Name* and *Location*. Click OK. ArcGIS Pro creates a default folder to store all components of a project, but, for this lab, we will use the folder provided in the class data.
4. Right-click on the *Topographic* layer in the *Contents pane* and select *Remove*. This base map automatically loads anytime you start a new project. We do not need the base map for this exercise.
5. In the *Catalog pane*, right-click the *Folders* icon and select *Add Folder Connection*.
6. Navigate to and select the *Chapter07* class folder.
7. Click OK.
8. Expand your *Folders* and *Chapter07* folders and the *NorthCarolina.gdb* and *CensusData* (this is a *Feature Dataset*) by clicking on the arrow to the left of each icon to view the contents (Figure 7.1).

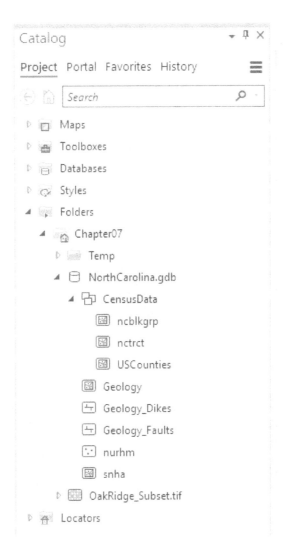

FIGURE 7.1

QUESTION 7.1

Which of the following files is NOT listed in the *Contents pane* once you have expanded the items in your *Chapter07* folder?

a. nctrct
b. Geology
c. nurhm
d. NC_MjrRds

1. Click on your *Project* tab (upper left corner of your session).
2. Select *Options* and then *Metadata*.
3. Click on the arrow to expand the *Metadata style* list and select *North American Profile of ISO19115 2003*. This sets the style template of ArcGIS Pro to match the style of the metadata text associated with the layers.
4. Click OK.
5. Click the *Back Arrow* (upper left corner of your session).
6. In the *Catalog pane*, right-click on *nurhm* and select *View Metadata*. This will open the details of the metadata in the *Catalog view* window. Note: The *Catalog view* is a different component than the *Catalog pane,* and, although they have similar capabilities, they are designed to do different tasks.
7. In the *Catalog view* window, click *nurhm.*
8. Scroll through the metadata description until you find the *Fields* heading, and click on the arrow if the *Fields* heading is not already expanded.
9. Find and examine the fields named *FAC_TYPE* and *TOT_STAFF.* The metadata provide the details of each field, including the *Data type.*

QUESTION 7.2

What is the data type for the FAC_TYPE field?

   a. Double
   b. BLOB
   c. Date
   d. String

QUESTION 7.3

What is the data type for the TOT_STAFF field?

   a. Double
   b. BLOB
   c. Date
   d. String

10. Click on the *Geography* tab in the *Catalog view*. This map shows the locations of the facilities as points.
11. Click on the *Table* tab in the *Catalog view* to see all the fields for the *nurhm* layer. Use the scroll bar at the bottom of the *Catalog view* to examine all the fields.

What is the data type for the STATELICID field? (Hint: Go back to the *Metadata* tab to view the data type for this field).

a. Double
b. BLOB
c. Date
d. String

Does the *nurhm* have the same projection as the *Geology* feature class? (Hint: Find the projection for each feature class under the Spatial Reference heading in the metadata).

a. Yes
b. No

12. Close the *Catalog view* (not the *Catalog pane*) window by clicking the X.

Vector Data

A data model is a conceptual representation of reality. When that model is implemented in a computer, the data must be organized or structured so that they can be stored and retrieved. The vector data model builds complex representation from primitive objects, namely points, lines, and polygons.

1. Right-click on the *Geology_Dikes* feature class and select *Properties*.
2. Click on the *Source* option from the list.

The *Geometry type* for *Geology_Dikes* is which of the following?

a. Point
b. Line
c. Polygon
d. TIN

3. Click *Cancel* to close the *Feature Class Properties* dialog box for *Geology_Dikes*.

4. Right-click on the *snha* feature class and select *Properties*.
5. Click on the *Source* option from the list.

The *Geometry type* for *snha* is which of the following?

   a. Point
   b. Line
   c. Polygon
   d. TIN

6. Click *Cancel* to close the *Feature Class Properties* dialog box for *snha*.
7. Right-click on the *Geology_Faults* feature class and select *Properties*.
8. Click on the *Source* option from the list.

The *Geometry type* for *Geology_Faults* is which of the following?

   a. Point
   b. Line
   c. Polygon
   d. TIN

9. Click *Cancel* to close the *Feature Class Properties* dialog box for *Geology_Faults*.
10. Right-click on the *nurhm* feature class and select *Properties*.
11. Click on the *Source* option from the list.
12. Close the *Properties* dialog box.

The *nurhm* feature class has which *Geometry* type?

   a. Point
   b. Line
   c. Polygon
   d. TIN

13. Click *Cancel* to close the *Feature Class Properties* dialog box for *nurhm*.

Geodatabases

The geodatabase organizes and stores spatial data of various types in one common folder. It is the native data structure for ArcGIS Pro. A geodatabase can contain points, lines, or polygons. Within the geodatabase, you can also create and store feature data sets. A feature data set stores a collection of feature classes that share a common coordinate system and extent. Feature classes can be part of a feature class data set or they can be stored as a standalone feature class (Figure 7.2). This exercise contains one geodatabase with one feature data set. The feature data set contains three feature classes. The geodatabase also stores five standalone feature classes. You can view the thumbnail next to the name of each feature class to determine whether they were created using points, line, or polygons. The raster data set is stored directly in the *Chapter07* folder and is not included in the geodatabase. We will work with the raster data set later in this exercise.

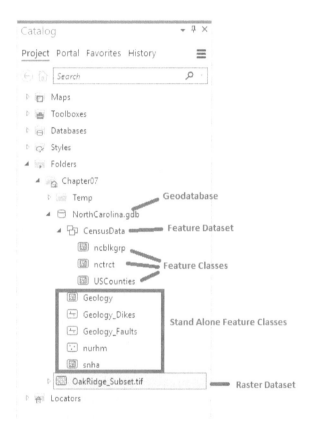

FIGURE 7.2

1. Expand all items in the *Catalog pane.*

Which of the following feature classes is NOT part of the feature data set?

a. Geology
b. ncblkgrp
c. nctrct
d. USCounties

Most of the data examined up to this point focuses on demographics (census geography and attributes) and at-risk populations, such as nursing home residents. There is a physical geography side to the fracking issue as well, however. Fracking is intimately tied to the Earth's geology, so you will also need to organize the physical geography standalone feature classes into a feature data set to make the analysis easier.

1. Right-click on *NorthCarolina.gdb* and select *New* and *Feature Dataset*.
2. Under *Feature Dataset Name*, type *NC_Physical*.
3. Under *Coordinate System*, select the *World* icon.
4. Expand *Projected coordinate system*.
5. Expand *State Plane*.
6. Expand *NAD 1983 (US Feet)*.
7. Scroll down and select *NAD 1983 StatePlane North Carolina FIPS 3200 (US Feet)*.
8. Press *OK* and then *Run*.
9. Close the *Geoprocessing* dialog box.
10. Right-click *NC_Physical* and select *Import* and then *Feature Class(es)*.
11. Under *Input Features*, click on the folder icon, navigate to and double-click on your *NorthCarolina.gdb*.
12. Press and hold the *CTRL* key on your keyboard and select *Geology*, *Geology_Dikes*, and *Geology_Faults*.
13. Press *OK* and then *Run* to add the standalone features classes to the feature data set.
14. Once finished, close the *Geoprocessing* dialog box.
15. In the *Catalog pane*, expand the *NC_Physical* feature data set to verify that each of the feature classes were imported. Each of the imported feature classes are renamed to include an underscore 1 so that you can distinguish them from the original feature classes.
16. In the *Catalog pane*, right-click each of the original standalone feature classes and delete them.

Feature classes in a feature data set must share a common coordinate system and extent.

a. True
b. False

Raster Data

The raster data model represents the environment by dividing it into discrete, coded cells that make up a grid format. Each cell in the grid is coded with a value that represents a specific quality or quantity of that location. These values can be codes, such as the primary land use occurring in the cell, or continuous numerical values like the elevation or temperature measured for each cell. The size of the individual cells, as well as their bit-depth (the number of bits used to encode the information in the computer), play roles in how much detail can be recorded.

In many instances, aerial photographs, in the form of raster data, are included in projects to use as background reference material when creating presentations of your analyses to the public.

1. Uncheck the check boxes for all the layer in the *Contents pane* to make them invisible.
2. Click, hold, and drag the *OakRidge_Subset.tif* into the *Contents pane.*
3. Right-click on *OakRidge_Subset.tif* and select *Zoom To Layer.*
4. Zoom in and explore the aerial photograph. Be sure to zoom in close enough to see individual pixels (cells).
5. In the *Contents pane*, right-click on *OakRidge_Subset.tif* and select *Properties.*
6. In the *Layer Properties* dialog box, click on *Source* from the list and expand the headings to answer the following questions.

QUESTION 7.12

What is the data type for this aerial photograph?

a. Raster
b. BLOB
c. String
d. Double

QUESTION 7.13

What is the cell size (*X* and *Y*)?

a. 0.5 m
b. 0.5 ft.
c. 0.5 yards
d. 0.5 km

The aerial photograph does not have a projected coordinate system.

    a. True
    b. False

What is the pixel depth of the aerial photograph?

    a. 4 bit
    b. 8 bit
    c. 12 bit
    d. 32 bit

A vehicle in the aerial photograph is represented by more than one pixel (cell).

    a. True
    b. False

    7. Exit ArcGIS Pro. You do not need to save the changes.

CHAPTER 8
Basic Spatial Analysis

The vector and raster data structures discussed in Chapter 7, along with any associated attribute data, form the basic inputs of a GIS. When the data embedded in these structures are used to examine the geographic features they represent, then the GIS is being used to conduct **spatial analysis**. *Spatial analysis* is the process of studying geographic features based on their locations. This can be as simple as selecting the features on the basis of some shared characteristic, or more complex, like studying how multiple geographic features relate to each other spatially. Many of these techniques did not originate with GIS, but stemmed from the use of maps before the advent of computer technology. One of the earlier examples, for instance, occurred during the American Revolution. At the Battle of Yorktown in 1781, French cartographer Louis Alexandre Berthier produced a set of maps that depicted the positions of the British troops over time. He did this by hinging the maps together to produce *overlays* that could be flipped through to "see" temporal changes (Foresman, 1998).

Overlays are used to store geographic features as multiple layers of information. This technique can be used, as Berthier did, to visualize changes in the movement of features, or it can be used to combine, visually or analytically, two or more layers that store different geographic data occurring in the same location. When used in the latter context, the process is known as **overlay analysis**. Widely touted as a classic example of pre-GIS overlay is the map Dr. John Snow made in 1854. Snow's map is popular because it is an example of how a problem was solved using geographic relationships. In an effort to find a possible cause for a cholera outbreak in London, he mapped the deaths caused by cholera in relation to well locations; the graphic result allowed him to hypothesize that there was a link between the two. When he convinced officials to remove the pump handle from the well closest to the most deaths, the outbreak was contained, proving the link.

The Canada Geographic Information System (CGIS) marks one, if not the earliest, attempt to automate the overlay process. Their use of computer technology marks the beginning of a revolution in geographic analysis. Today's GIS offers an abundance of analytical techniques, ranging from simple queries of attributes to more complicated combinations that include both attribute and spatial queries, as well as techniques that create new data.

Data Queries

Data queries are an essential aspect of GIS; they provide a mechanism for users to request information about spatial features. Different from **geoprocessing**, which generates new data by combining data already stored in the GIS, queries are used simply to retrieve already stored data about feature locations. They do not change the underlying data already present or create new data. Data queries can be approached from two distinct perspectives: *attribute queries,* which return information about feature attributes, and *spatial queries,* which return information about feature locations.

Attribute Queries

Attribute queries select records of spatial features in a database using attribute values as the criteria for selection. An example might be to request that the GIS select and return just the counties of the United States in which the estimated housing value is greater than or equal to $75,000. Such queries are typically expressed using Structured Query Language (SQL), or some variation of SQL. SQL was designed specifically to manipulate data in relational databases. It uses attribute fields in the GIS database in conjunction with user-defined values for that field and set algebra ($<$, $>$, $=$, $\leq$, $\geq$) and/or **Boolean algebra** (AND, OR, NOT) to structure the request. In the example posed above, if the field in the database is [EST_HOMEVAL], then the expression needed to satisfy the request would be: [EST_HOMEVAL] $\geq$75,000.

Those new to GIS, while most likely comfortable with set algebra, may not be as familiar with Boolean algebra. Boolean algebra is used to design more complex or composite attribute queries. The most common Boolean operators in GIS include AND, OR, XOR, and NOT. The Boolean operator AND is used when two conditions must both be true to select a feature, while OR selects features when either of the two conditions is true. XOR selects features when one condition is true, but the other is false, and NOT is used when a condition must be negated for the feature to be selected. Figure 8.1 provides a visual of how these functions work. If the request to the GIS was to select just the counties of the United States that belong to the state of Colorado in which the estimated home value is equal to or greater than $75,000, for example,

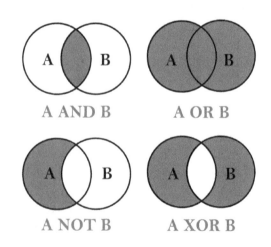

A AND B   A OR B

A NOT B   A XOR B

FIGURE 8.1
Common Boolean functions.

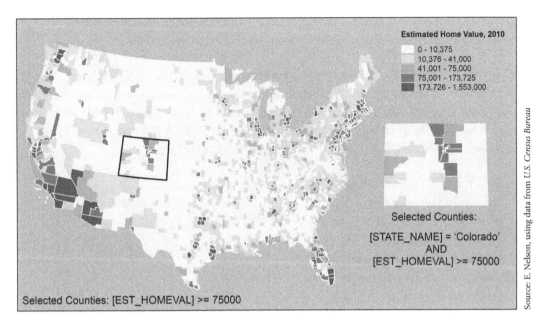

FIGURE 8.2
Composite query requiring the AND operator.

then it becomes a composite query that requires the Boolean operator AND: [STATE_NAME] = 'Colorado' AND [EST_HOMEVAL] ≥ 75,000 (Figure 8.2, selected counties are outlined in white). If, instead, the request was to return just the counties of the United States that belong to the state of Colorado in which the estimated household value is over $75,000 or the level of educational attainment is more than four years of college, the query increases in complexity. It now requires not only the AND operator, but also the OR: [STATE_NAME] = 'Colorado'

AND ([EST_HOMEVAL] ≥ 75,000 OR [EDUCATION] ≥ 4). Notice the addition of parentheses around the OR clause; queries are treated as mathematical statements, so they are evaluated from left to right using the mathematical principles of PEMDAS, which outlines the order in which one should evaluate each component (parentheses, exponents, multiplication, division, addition, subtraction). The results of this more complex statement can be seen in Figure 8.3. If the parentheses had been left out of this expression, then the GIS would have first

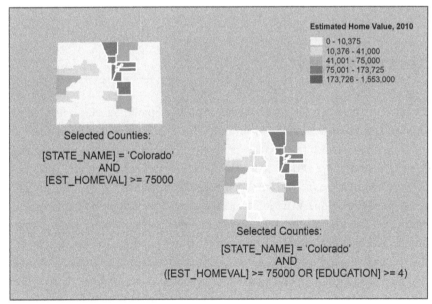

FIGURE 8.3
Complex query requiring both the AND and OR operator.

selected all of the counties in Colorado with the requisite estimated home value, then the subset of any county in the United States meeting the educational requirement would have been added.

The NOT operator is most likely the easiest to comprehend, while the XOR the most difficult. If, for instance, the GIS was requested to return all counties in the United States except those that have estimated home values less than $50,000, the expression required would be NOT ([EST_HOMEVAL] < 50,000). If the expression loaded was [EST_HOMEVAL] < 50,000 XOR [EDUCATION] > 4, then only those counties in which one condition is true while the other condition is false are selected.

In many cases, the feature attribute table will come with several attributes, but there is always the chance that the data you want to analyze or map are not among those. Since we want a flexible system, the GIS needs a way to incorporate "outside" attribute tables. These tables are *non-spatial*; they are not tied to the spatial database. The challenge, then, is to find a way to connect the table to the GIS databases. This is usually accomplished by (1) defining a common field between the non-spatial table and the feature attribute table, then (2) using that field to *join* the two tables. The result of a join is a virtual link to the non-spatial table via the feature attribute table. Once tables are joined (Figure 8.4), you can then query and analyze that data as well.

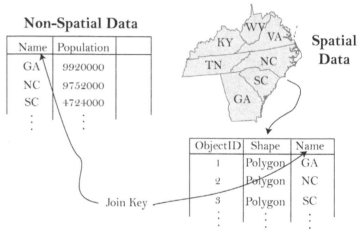

FIGURE 8.4
Using a common field to join non-spatial attribute data to a geographic database.

Spatial Queries

It is also possible to query the database spatially. Spatial queries select features using the geometric characteristics of the database; features from one GIS layer are selected using features from a second layer. The spatial relationships between the two layers are the basis for selection. You might, for example, select all the parks in a parks layer that are within 30 miles of a school in a schools layer. This option is classified as *selecting features that are within a specified distance of another feature* and is an example of using the spatial relationship of **proximity** to answer a query. In a GIS, such queries are built using a dialog box that requires a *target* layer that is connected to a *source* layer by using a *spatial relationship* of interest. The target layer holds the spatial features to be selected; the source layer contains the features to which the target layer features are being compared. A **spatial query** using the **Intersect** option, for instance, would be looking for overlapping areas of interest between two layers; it might be specified as *selecting Counties that intersect Interstates* (Figure 8.5).

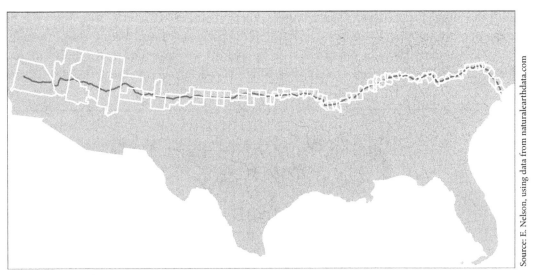

FIGURE 8.5
Spatial query in which counties are selected on the basis of their intersection with a selected interstate.

The Intersect relationship is an example of using the spatial property of **intersection** to answer a query. *Proximity* and *Intersection* are two of the four basic spatial relationships commonly used to query features in a GIS; the other two are **Containment** and **Adjacency**. A containment query can be specified using multiple relationship descriptions; a common example might be to select the *Elementary schools that are completely within New Hanover County*. An example of using the adjacency relationship might be to select the *Counties that touch the boundary of New Hanover County*.

Geoprocessing Functions

Geoprocessing refers to those functions of a GIS that produce new data from the original data sets. Many methods fall under the geoprocessing umbrella, and they range from simple buffer operations to more complex statistical analyses. The most common of these include those that *extract* subsets of features from the original data, *aggregate* original features into larger features, *buffer* original features, and create new data by *overlaying* multiple data layers. More often than not, the question that prompted the analysis requires some subset of functions to be implemented sequentially to provide an answer.

Extracting Spatial Features

The **Clip** tool is used when the features in one data layer extend beyond the boundaries of the area a project is set up to analyze. A data layer that serves as the outer boundary of the project is used to extract the required information from the layer covering the larger extent. From an anecdotal perspective, this can be thought of as using a cookie cutter to cut out a section of a data layer. This process overlays the outer boundary layer and the target feature layer, then computes their geometric difference to extract the data lying within the extent of the clipping boundary. The result of the process is a new feature class in which the area outside the outer boundary has been discarded, leaving only the data bounded by that polygon. A common example would be using the boundary of a county to clip point data covering the entire state (Figure 8.6).

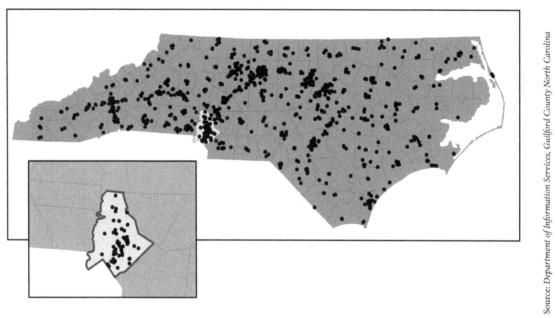

Source: Department of Information Services, Guilford County, North Carolina

FIGURE 8.6
Clipping point features to restrict the selection to those within one county.

Aggregating Spatial Features

Dissolve. The **Dissolve** tool in a GIS creates new map features by collapsing adjacent areas or line features in a data layer. Also a form of cartographic generalization, these features must share a common attribute value for the dissolve to be implemented. Features that are adjacent and have the same attribute values are generalized into a common larger polygon. If, for example, you needed a data layer showing the census regions of the United States, but only had a comprehensive U.S. states data layer, you could use an attribute that identifies each state's region to dissolve state boundaries on that basis. When complete, a new data layer organizing the states into larger census regions' polygons would be created. The capability to dissolve similar, adjacent polygons can greatly simplify a database by removing unnecessary boundaries and duplicate attributes.

Merge. While the *Dissolve* tool collapses adjacent features in a data set, the **Merge** function works by combining multiple data layers into a single output layer. The input layers can be points, lines, or polygons, as long as all the data layers involved are the same data type. When the two data layers are adjacent, this is similar to a process called tiling, which is the primary purpose of the tool. If, for example, two teams were assigned adjacent areas of a park and tasked with collecting GPS points outlining the trails of their section, a merge could be used later to combine the two files into one comprehensive layer of data.

Buffering Spatial Features

The concept of **buffering** refers to creating a zone around specified spatial features. This zone, which can be of constant or variable width, is then used to select a second set of features that surround the buffered features. Points, lines, and polygons can be buffered in a GIS. When point data are buffered, for example, a circle whose radius is the specified buffer distance will be created. These are saved to a new polygon file, where the polygons create an *inside region* and an *outside region*. The inside region, or area that is within the specified buffer distance, represents the **buffer zone**, and the outside region represents the area that is more than the specified buffer distance away from the feature.

Buffering applications often have the purpose of protecting some area, such as creating drug-free buffer zones that can be drawn around schools. Hospitals can also be buffered, if, for example, there is a need to determine how many in a region are within one mile of a major transportation artery. A feature can also have more than one buffer zone associated with it; a point source of pollution, for instance, could be buffered with multiple distances as part of an assessment of how it influences wetlands (Figure 8.7).

Source: U.S. Geological Survey, Department of the Interior

FIGURE 8.7
Multiple buffer rings around point sources of pollution.

Overlaying Spatial Features

From the earliest implementation of GIS with the *Canada Geographic Information System*, users wanted to compare two maps of the same region analytically. An example of this might be the need to overlay a city's boundary file with a county's land-use file. Prior to the development of GIS, cartographers created composite maps by overlaying two or more separate maps on a light table to visualize the results. To automate the process and create new spatial features resulting from the overlay, a combination of algorithms and Boolean algebra were used to join or fuse separate data layers as a function of the space they occupied. When working with vector data, these overlays allow polygon features to be combined with a second data layer of point, line, or polygon features. Different combinations of layers produce different results. For *Polygon-on-Polygon* overlays, the two most common ways of combining the input layers is by *intersecting* or *unioning* the data sets.

Intersect. The function of the *Intersect* command in a GIS is to select those areas that two data layers have in common spatially and create a new data layer on the basis of those features. This overlay uses the Boolean AND operator to determine the geometric intersections of all the polygons from both layers (refer to Figure 8.8). The polygons in the new data layer are then reconfigured geometrically by recalculating the coordinates, areas, and centroids of each to reflect the new polygons created, and each is tagged with all the attributes from the original layers. In our example above, intersecting the city boundary with the county's land use would result in a new file containing the city boundary and just the land-use polygons within that

FIGURE 8.8
Intersection of county land use polygons with a city limits polygon.

boundary. Where the extents of the two input layers differ, those polygons within one extent but not the other are eliminated.

Union. The **Union** command, on the other hand, takes the two input layers and combines all the polygons from both using the Boolean OR operator (refer to Figure 8.9). In this instance, the extents of both layers

FIGURE 8.9
Union of county land use polygons with a city limits polygon.

GEOGRAPHIC INFORMATION SCIENCE

are combined. The polygons that are within either of these extents are kept in the new data layer. They are reconfigured geometrically in the new layer, with the attribute data combined as necessary. Looking at the city-boundary and land-use data from this perspective, all the polygons from both layers would be kept, with the spatial and attribute data recalculated to match the new configurations.

Point-in-polygon. Points and polygons, as well as lines and polygons, can also be overlaid. The **Point-in-Polygon** method makes use of a **spatial join** to append the attributes from a polygon layer to a point layer, where each point is a feature with attributes from the polygon surrounding it. When a target layer of point features, such as schools, is overlaid onto a join layer of polygon features, like census tracts, the result is a new point features layer in which each school has all the attributes of the surrounding census tract appended to its attribute table. This might be useful if you wanted to know something about the population living near the school, such as median family income, or median housing values.

The algorithm used to determine which polygon surrounds a point falls into the category of computational geometry. A common solution to the problem of calculating which polygon a point is in, is to count how many times a line, parallel to one of the axes of the coordinate systems and extending from the point in question toward the increasing end of the coordinate system, intersects the polygon boundary in question. If it crosses the boundary an even number of times, the point is outside the polygon; if the number of intersections is an odd number, the point is inside the polygon (Figure 8.10).

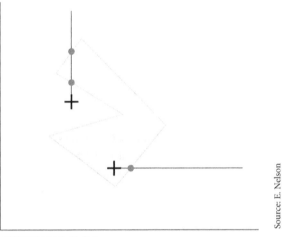

FIGURE 8.10
Solving the point-in-polygon request.

Map algebra. Overlay operations using vector data can be complicated, and the results of their implementation are quite different from the results of the same operations on raster data. Generally, overlays processing raster data are much more efficient because the grid data structure can use arithmetic expressions and Boolean operators to combine the layers on a cell-by-cell basis. These types of operations are expressed using **map algebra**, a structure developed by Dana Tomlin (1990), who created a raster software package and an accompanying textbook that popularized these concepts.

Map algebra expressions are composed of data layers and operations; expressions can be created for individual grids (NewGrid = SquareRoot (InputGrid)) or multiple grids (NewGrid = InputGrid A + InputGrid B). Expressions are also grouped by their function: **local**, **focal**, **zonal**, or **global**. The simplest function is *local*; these expressions process cell values on a cell-by-cell location. If you had daily precipitation totals for North Carolina during Hurricane Floyd, for example, and the data were recorded in raster form with a layer for each day, finding the total precipitation amounts that each cell recorded for the entire weather event would simply be a matter of adding the cells' values of all of the raster layers. *Focal* functions are expressions that use neighboring cell values from the input grid to calculate individual grid values for the new grid. The neighboring cell values form a *moving window*; for each cell in the middle of that window, an operation can be performed that uses the surrounding cell values to calculate the value at the middle cell. If you have an elevation grid, for instance, you could use surrounding cell values to average each cell as you move across the surface, essentially smoothing out variation in elevation differences (Figure 8.11). *Zonal* functions use zones of cell values in calculating new grid values, and *global* functions take into account all cells in the grid in calculating each new grid value.

665	624	583	541	583
624	524	483	441	483
583	483	383	341	383
624	524	321	241	200
441	341	300	200	200

Value to be averaged

Moving window

	550	489	469	
	505	416	364	
	444	348	285	

New averaged value

Source: E. Nelson

FIGURE 8.11
Example of a focal function, in which a moving window is used to average cell values.

One useful way to explore the effects of raster overlays is to examine overlay results when using grid values of 0 (absence of feature) and 1 (presence of feature) only. As an example, let's work with two raster layers, one showing the presence of sparsely populated areas and the other showing the presence of geologically stable areas. Using these layers to help site a hazardous waste facility, the idea would be to find a location in a sparsely populated, geologically stable area. Thus, when the two layers are combined, the cells of interest should meet both criteria. If we multiply the two data layers, the data values for the new data layer would be either 0 or 1, where 1 would identify all the cells that met both criteria (Figure 8.12).

If, on the other hand, these constraints were relaxed so that only 1 of the 2 criteria had to be met, multiplying the two raster layers wouldn't provide enough detail since the 0 category also includes cells that meet neither of the criteria. In this case, adding the two raster layers would be the more appropriate choice. When adding, the cells in the new raster layer would take 1 of 3 values: 0, where neither of the criteria are met; 2, where both of the criteria are met; and 1, where 1 of the 2 criteria were met. Of course, you could consider cells with a value of 2 as well as 1 as being valid in this scenario. Another way of approaching these results would be to consider the values to consist of graded choices, where 2 would identify the most desirable areas, 1 would identify less desirable areas, and 0 would identify the least desirable areas.

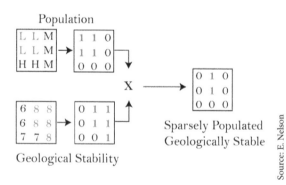

FIGURE 8.12
Example of a raster overlay in which the rasters are multiplied to mimic the AND Boolean function when binary values are used.

GEOGRAPHIC INFORMATION SCIENCE

Key Terms

Spatial analysis
Overlay analysis
Data queries
Geoprocessing
Attribute queries
Spatial query
Boolean algebra
Non-spatial (attributes)
Proximity
Intersect
Intersection
Containment
Adjacency

Clip
Dissolve
Merge
Buffering
Buffer zone
Union
Point-in-polygon
Spatial join
Map algebra
Local (function)
Focal (function)
Zonal (function)
Global (function)

Questions

1. Who was Dr. John Snow, and why was he important in the context of GIS?

2. What are two types of data queries, and how do they differ?

3. What is SQL?

4. What is a spatial join, and why is it important?

5. What are the four basic spatial relationships commonly used to query features in a GIS?

6. What is geoprocessing, and what are some examples of some of the more common types?

7. What tool is used to extract spatial features, and what is the input and resulting output?

8. How does the use of the Merge tool differ from the use of the Dissolve tool?

9. What is a buffer zone, and what does it delineate?

10. What are two common ways of combining the spatial features from two different polygon layers using vector data, and how are the results different?

11. What is map algebra, and why is it important?

12. How do the four groups, or categories, of map algebra functions differ?

Bibliography

Bolstad, P. 2013. "Buffering and Overlay in ArcGIS." Accessed September 22, 2019. https://giscourses.cfans.umn.edu/sites/giscourses.cfans.umn.edu/files/l9_buffering_pvbjune2017.pdf.

Chang, K. 2008. *Introduction to Geographic Information Systems*. 5th ed. New York, NY: McGraw-Hill Companies, Inc.

Chrisman, N. 2006. *Charting the Unknown: How Computer Mapping at Harvard Became GIS*. Redlands, CA: ESRI Press.

Clarke, K. 2003. *Getting Started with GIS*. 4th ed. Upper Saddle River, NJ: Prentice Hall.

Davis, B. 2001. *GIS: A Visual Approach*. 2nd ed. Albany, NY: Onword Press.

Demers, M.N. 200. *Geographic Information Systems*. 2nd ed. New York, NY: John Wiley & Sons, Inc.

Environment Canada. 1973. "The Canada Geographic Information System." *Cartographica*, v. 10(3): 62-86.

Escobar, F. 2013. "GIS Overlay Operations." Accessed September 22, 2019. https://geogra.uah.es/patxi/gisweb/VOModule/VO_Operations.htm

Foresman, T.W., ed. 1998. *The History of Geographic Information Systems: Perspectives from the Pioneers*. Upper Saddle River, NJ: Prentice Hall.

National Academy of Sciences. 2006. *Beyond Mapping: Meeting National Needs Through Enhanced Geographic Information Science*. Washington, DC: National Academies Press.

Schmandt, M. 2013. *GIS Commons: An Introductory Textbook on Geographic Information Systems*. Last accessed January 26, 2019. http://www.giscommons.org.

Slocum, T. A., McMaster, R. B., Kessler, F.C., and H.H. Howard. 2009. *Thematic Cartography and Geovisualization*. 3rd ed. Upper Saddle River, NJ: Pearson Prentice Hall.

Theobald, D.M. 2007. *GIS Concepts and ArcGIS Methods*. 3rd ed. Fort Collins, CO: Conservation Planning Technologies.

Tomlin, C. D., 1990. *Geographic information systems and cartographic modeling*. Prentice Hall: Englewood Cliffs, N. J.

Wise, S. 2002. *GIS Basics*. New York, NY: Taylor & Francis, Inc.

Worboys, M.F. 1995. *GIS: A Computing Perspective*. London, England: Taylor & Francis.

Solving Spatial Problems

In this exercise, you will analyze the spatial data created in the last exercise (Chapter 7) to assess the potential impacts of fracking in North Carolina, Guilford County, and the Town of Oak Ridge.

OBJECTIVES

- Create a new layer using a subset of another layer
- Dissolve features to create a generalized layer
- Create a buffer
- Overlay two polygon layers
- Perform a point-in-polygon analysis

SOFTWARE

This exercise uses ESRI's ArcGIS Pro 2.3.2.

DATA

The data for this exercise are available from the Kendall Hunt Student Ancillary site. See the inside front cover for access information. You may also be directed to download the data from a different location by your instructor.

1. Download the data as directed by your instructor
2. Save the file to a location where you have read/write privileges

The files are compressed and must be decompressed prior to use.

Analysis Overview

The Town of Oak Ridge has specific questions about water contamination potential and earthquake risk potential. These questions will be used to frame your analysis.

For water contamination potential, the questions they have are:

- Are any potential fracking sites within 5/10/20 miles of Oak Ridge?
- Which water supply watersheds overlap Triassic Basins in North Carolina?

For earthquake risk potential, their questions are:

- How many faults and dikes are in North Carolina, Guilford County, and Oak Ridge?
- How many at-risk sites are within a mile of these faults and dikes?

1. Start ArcGIS Pro.
2. Select *Map* under the *New > Blank Templates* in the dialog box.
3. Leave the defaults for *Name* and *Location*. Click OK. ArcGIS Pro creates a default folder to store all components of a project, but, for this lab, we will use the folder provided in the class data.
4. Right-click on the *Topographic* layer in the *Contents pane* and select *Remove*. This base map automatically loads anytime you start a new project. We do not need the base map for this exercise.
5. In the *Catalog pane*, right-click the *Folders* icon and select *Add Folder Connection*.
6. Navigate to and select your *Chapter08* class folder.
7. Click OK.
8. Expand your *Folders* and *Chapter08* folders and your *Exercise_08.gdb* by clicking on the arrow to the left of each icon to view the contents.
9. Click on *Project* (upper left corner of your session) and select *Save as*.
10. Navigate to your *Chapter08* folder and save the project as *Ex08_yourlastname*.

Where Are the Potential Fracking Sites in North Carolina?

The *NC_Physical* feature data set contains a layer, *Geology*, which lists information on all the rock types in the state. One of the columns in the attribute table (BELT) will allow you to create a new layer of the geologic features that are likely to be drilled—these are the Triassic Basins. Your first task is to identify and isolate the Triassic Basins so that you can work with them.

1. In the *Catalog pane*, expand the feature data sets (*Guilford_Co*, *NC_Physical*, and *NC_Water*) by clicking on the arrows next to each of their names.
2. Left click, hold, and drag the *Geology* layer into the *Contents pane*.
3. Right-click on the *Geology* in the *Contents pane* and select *Attribute Table*.

Each of the polygons in the table belongs to a specific geological belt. The name *Triassic Basins* is the name given to the region or belt where fracking is likely to occur in North Carolina.

4. Right-click on the field named *BELT* and select *Sort Descending* to promote the records containing *Triassic Basins* to the top of the attribute table.
5. Click on your *Map* tab in the *Ribbon*.
6. Under the *Map* tab, locate the *Select by Attributes* tool in the *Selection* tool group and click it.
7. In the *Geoprocessing* dialog box, make sure the *Selection Type* is set to *New selection*.
8. Press *Add Clause*.
9. Click on the *drop-down* arrow next to the *Where* text and select the field name *BELT*.
10. Expand the second drop-down arrow and select *is equal to*.
11. Expand the third drop-down arrow and select *Triassic Basins*. Your clause should read as: *BELT is equal to Triassic Basins*.
12. Press *Add* and then *Run*.
13. Close the *Geoprocessing* dialog box by clicking on the X.
14. At the bottom left of the table, locate and press the *Show selected records* button (Figure 8.1).

FIGURE 8.1

QUESTION 8.1

How many Triassic Basins records were selected?

a. 0
b. 40
c. 61
d. 1,843

15. Close the attribute table window by clicking on the X (the X is located to the right of the table name: Geology) but leave the records selected.
16. Zoom in on the *Map* to view the *Triassic Basins*. Note that many of the polygons are contiguous.
17. Zoom to the full extent.

Dissolving the Polygons

Extracting the Triassic Basins to a new layer was a good first step. Next, you need to clean up this new layer.

1. Make sure your Triassic Basins are still selected. You can view the map to see if they are still highlighted.
2. Right click on the *Geology* layer in the *Contents pane.*
3. Select *Data* and then *Export Features.*
4. Under *Output Feature Class*, click on the *Folder* icon and navigate to *NC_Physical* feature data set which is located in the *Exercise_08.gdb.* Be sure to double-click on the *NC_Physical* feature data set.

EXERCISE 8 Basic Spatial Analysis

209

5. Name the exported feature class *Triassic_Basins*.
6. Click *Save* and then *Run*. *Triassic_Basins* will be automatically added to your *Contents pane*.
7. Close the *Geoprocessing* dialog box by clicking on the X.
8. Click on the *Analysis* tab in the *Ribbon*.
9. Under the *Tools* group of tools, select the drop-down arrow (highlighted in Figure 8.2) to expand the selections.

FIGURE 8.2

10. Find and press the *Dissolve* button. It is located under the *Manage Data* heading.
11. Under *Input Features*, click the drop-down arrow and select *Triassic_Basins*.
12. Under *Output Feature Class*, press the folder icon and navigate to the *NC_Physical* feature data set that is located in the *Exercise_08.gdb*. Be sure to double-click on the *NC_Physical* feature data set.
13. Name the output feature class *Triassic_Basins_Dissolve*.
14. Click *Save*.
15. Under the *Dissolve Field(s)*, select *BELT*.
16. Press *Run*.
17. Close the *Geoprocessing* dialog box by clicking on the X.
18. Uncheck the box for *Trassic_Basins* to make it invisible.
19. In the *Map* tab, press *Clear*. It is in the *Selection* tool group.
20. Change the color of your *Triassic_Basins_Dissolve* to red by right-clicking on the rectangle symbol below its name.
21. Save your project.

How many features are listed in the attribute table for *Triassic_Basins_Dissolve*?

    a. 1
    b. 4
    c. 10
    d. 11

Based on the locations of the Triassic Basins in North Carolina, potential fracking sites appear to be in:

a. Western North Carolina
b. Eastern North Carolina
c. Central North Carolina
d. Only on the coast of North Carolina

Buffering

In order to answer the following question, you need to be able to visualize distances from the Triassic Basins. The way to do this is to use the *Buffer* tool.

Are any of the Triassic Basins (potential fracking sites) within 5, 10, or 20 miles of Oak Ridge?

1. Close the *Triassic_Basins_Dissolve* attribute table.
2. Click on the *Analysis* tab in the *Ribbon*.
3. Under the *Tools* group of tools, select the drop-down arrow (highlighted in Figure 8.2 shown previously) to expand the selections.
4. Find and press the *Buffer* button. It is located under the *Determine Proximity* heading.
5. Under *Input Features*, click the drop-down arrow and select *Triassic_Basins_Dissolve*.
6. Under *Output Feature Class*, press the folder icon and navigate to the *NC_Physical* feature data set that is located in the *Exercise_08.gdb*. Be sure to double-click on the *NC_Physical* feature data set.
7. Name the output feature class *Triassic_20mi_Buffer*.
8. Press *Save*.
9. Under the *Distance [value or field]*, type 20 and set the units to *Miles* (the drop-down box to the right of the *Distance [value or field]* box).
10. Under *Dissolve Type*, choose *Dissolve all output features into a single feature*. Leave the defaults for the other options.
11. Press *Run*.
12. Close the *Geoprocessing* dialog box by clicking on the X.
13. Click, hold and drag your *Oak_Ridge_Limits* into the *Contents pane*. Reorder the layers as shown in Figure 8.3.

FIGURE 8.3

QUESTION 8.4

Oak Ridge is within 20 miles of a potential fracking site.

    a. True
    b. False

14. Repeat the buffering operation to create a 5- and 10-mile buffer around *Triassic_Basins_Dissolve*. Use the steps above for the 20-mile buffer as a guide.

QUESTION 8.5

Oak Ridge is within 10 miles of a potential fracking site.

    a. True
    b. False

QUESTION 8.6

Oak Ridge is within 5 miles of a potential fracking site.

    a. True
    b. False

15. From the *Project* tab, click *Save As*, and save your project as *Ex08_yourlastname*.
16. Close the *Geoprocessing* dialog box by clicking on the X.

Which Watersheds Overlap Triassic Basins?

This second analysis examines the potential impacts of fracking on water supplies.

Creating a Polygon Overlay

Where do the underlying geologic features known as the *Triassic Basins* intersect with water supplies? A type of analysis that can answer this question is the *Intersect*, which will create a new layer of polygons that show the intersection of the two.

1. Right-click and select *Remove* for all layers except for *Triassic_Basins_Dissolve*.
2. In the *NC_Water* feature data set, click, hold, and drag *Water_Supply_Watersheds* into your *Contents pane*.
3. In the *NC_Physical* feature data set, click, hold, and drag *NC_Counties* into your *Contents pane*.
4. Click on the *Analysis* tab in the *Ribbon*.
5. Under the *Tools* group of tools, select the drop-down arrow to expand the selections.
6. Find and press the *Intersect* button. It is located under the *Overlay Data* heading.
7. Under *Input Features*, click the drop-down arrow and select *Triassic_Basins_Dissolve*.
8. Repeat the process to add *Water_Supply_Watersheds*.
9. Under *Output Feature Class*, press the folder icon and navigate to *Exercise_08.gdb*.
10. Name the output feature class *Triassic_Water_Intersect*. Leave the defaults for all the other options.
11. Press *Save* and then *Run*.
12. Close the *Geoprocessing* dialog box by clicking on the X.
13. Right-click on *NC_Counties* and select *Label*.
14. Turn *Trassic_Basins_Dissolve* and *Water_Supply_Watersheds* off by clicking on the check boxes.

QUESTION 8.7

What is the name of the river basin that lies in both Rockingham and Stokes Counties that could be potentially polluted?

a. Neuse
b. Roanoke
c. Yadkin
d. Cape Fear

Are There Faults and Dikes in the Study Region?

The second series of questions the town of Oak Ridge wants to explore involves earthquake potential. The east coast of the United States is thought to be much more geologically stable than the west coast, but increasing the level of fluids in the underlying rock strata could act as a lubricant and allow areas that have previously been considered more stable to see an increase in earthquake activity. The first issue they would like you to address is whether any faults or dikes are in the region. Most people have heard of faults, and know that a fault is a fracture in the earth, with one of the most active faults in the U.S. being the San Andreas. A dike is a sheet of newer rock that has formed in a fracture running through pre-existing rock.

1. Under the *Insert* tab in the *Ribbon*, select *New Map*.
2. Right-click on the *Topgraphic* layer and select *Remove*.
3. Right-click *Map(1)* in the *Contents pane*, then select *Properties*.
4. Select *General* from the list.
5. In *Name* option, name your new map *Earthquake Impacts*, then press *OK*.
6. In the *NC_Physical* feature data set, click, hold, and drag *Geology_Dikes, Geology_Faults, Trassic_Basins_Dissolve, and NC_Counties* into your *Contents pane*.
7. Reorder the layers so that *Geology_Dikes* is on top followed by *Geology_Faults*, *Trassic_Basins_Dissolve*, and then *NC_Counties*.
8. Right-click on *NC_Counties* in the *Contents pane* and select *Label*.

QUESTION 8.8

Are there geologic faults in Guilford County, North Carolina?

a. Yes
b. No

QUESTION 8.9

Are there geologic dikes in Guilford County, North Carolina?

a. Yes
b. No

QUESTION 8.10

Are there geologic dikes in Oak Ridge, North Carolina (hint: You must add the layer to the *Contents pane*)?

a. Yes
b. No

Point-in-Polygon Analysis (Select by Location)

Because of the potential for increased earthquake activity, the town of Oak Ridge would like to know if there are any vulnerable, at-risk populations who might be impacted.

1. In the *Exercise_08.gdb*, click, hold, and drag *NC_Nursing_Homes* into the *Contents pane*.
2. Click on the *Analysis* tab in the *Ribbon*.
3. Under the *Tools* group of tools, select the drop-down arrow to expand the selections.
4. Find and press the *Buffer* button. It is located under the *Determine Proximity* heading.
5. Under *Input Features*, click the drop-down arrow and select *Geology_Dikes*.
6. Under *Output Feature Class*, press the folder icon and navigate to *Exercise_08.gdb*.
7. Name the output feature class *Dikes_1mi_Buffer*.
8. Press *Save*.
9. Under the *Distance [value or field]*, type 1 and set the units to *Miles*.
10. Under *Dissolve Type*, choose *Dissolve all output features into a single feature*. Leave the defaults for the other options.
11. Press *Run*.
12. Close the *Geoprocessing* dialog box by clicking on the X.
13. In the *Map* tab, press the *Select by Location* button in the *Selection* tool group.
14. In the *Input Features*, click on the drop-down arrow and select *NC_Nursing_Homes*.
15. Under *Relationship*, select *Intersect*.
16. Under *Selecting Features*, choose *Dikes_1mi_Buffer*.
17. Press *Run*.

QUESTION 8.11

How many nursing homes in North Carolina are within 1 mile of a dike?

a. 7
b. 72
c. 59
d. 1,027

1. In the *Map* tab, press *Clear*. It is in the *Selection* tool group.
2. Add *GC_Schools* to the *Contents pane*.
3. Repeat the point-in-polygon analysis for *CG_Schools* using the *Dikes_1mi_Buffer*.

Which of the following schools among the six selected are within 1 mile of a dike?

a. Kernodle Middle School
b. General Greene Elementary
c. Page High School
d. Southwest Elementary

4. Save the project and exit ArcGIS Pro.

CHAPTER 9
Aerial Photography

The foundation of modern mapping, as we saw in *Chapter 5*, occurred with the development of surveying techniques. As other countries began to implement France's new techniques for their own national surveys, the demands of this new standard in mapping quickly became evident. The sheer number of bodies, for example, required to carry out the surveys was a problem; this was solved by using armies to complete the work. Involving the military, however, changed the perception of the need for these surveys. Before national surveys were associated with military applications, many countries, especially those lacking the financial and technological means to conduct them, did not see a need for such detailed mapping within their borders (Dickinson, 1979).

World War I (1914-1918) was the tipping point that truly changed most minds, though. The reality of a global war made accurate mappings of foreign lands critical. This is where the need for better equipment and improved technology also became an issue. One problem in mapping foreign lands was accessibility; being able to produce or obtain a map of such an area tied to surveying technology was exceedingly rare. Most countries, at the time, resorted to compilation, or piecing a map of an area together by using one or more, usually inferior, sources (Dickinson, 1979). World War I, however, spurred developments in technology on several fronts, including expanding on the idea of combining photography with manned flight. Both the development of photography and the ability for man to fly occurred before the 20th century, but the full impact of *aerial photography*, or taking photos of Earth from a position above its surface, was not fully realized until well into that era.

Photography, for example, is rooted in studies of the nature of light, which can be traced as far back as ancient Greece. It is the principles derived from these studies, along with advances in chemistry and optics, that helped Joseph Nicéphore Niépce produce the first known photograph in the 1800's. Taken in 1826, Niépce's photo is believed to show the courtyard outside of his house in France (Thrower, 1996).

From this inauspicious start, it was merely a matter of time before someone would conceive of photographing his or her location from above the ground. *Gaspard-Félix Tournachon* (also known as *Nadar*) was that man. In 1858, he used a camera from an anchored balloon to take a picture of the terrain of Biévre, France. This image, captured on glass, no longer exists. It is, however, the first record we have of an attempt at aerial photography. Nadar's work captured the imagination of the public, and the demand for aerial photographs was officially born (Aronoff, 2005). Two short years later, Boston photographer *James Wallace Black* teamed up with balloon navigator *Samuel Archer King* to take the first aerial photograph in the United States. King took Black up in his hot-air balloon 1,200 ft. over the city of Boston and Black took an image. This image, titled *Boston, as the Eagle and the Wild Goose See It*, is the oldest known aerial photograph that still exists (Lillesand et al., 2007).

In 1862, the Union Army adopted this form of aerial photography to assess Confederate defenses during the Civil War (1861-1865). While useful in theory, the Army soon found it less than practical, as the balloons made easy shooting targets. What they needed was a sturdy platform that could take photographs as it moved. The answer to this, unfortunately, was some decades away. The U.S. Army Balloon Corp disbanded in 1863, and it was not until *Orville and Wilbur Wright* unveiled their airplane in 1903 that technology provided a more suitable platform. Their first attempt at flight, on December 14, only lasted 3 seconds, but before the week was out, they were covering hundreds of feet at altitudes of up to 10 ft. (Gray, 2002). By 1908, the first public flights had been witnessed both in the United States and Europe, and in 1909, while in Italy conducting flight training for the military, the first aerial photograph was taken from a plane (Aronoff, 2005).

During World War I, planes became a key component of military strategy, and the continued development of air photo technology and interpretation became crucial. The first cameras developed specifically for aerial photography were in place by 1915, and skilled photo interpreters, the "eyes of the armed forces" (Aronoff, 2005, 13), became a new career in high demand by the war's end. The mainstreaming of aerial photography and its associated photointerpretation methods revolutionized the civilian fields of surveying and map production. Those working in forestry, geology, agriculture, and cartography, among other fields, began to adopt **photogrammetry** as a way to reduce the costs and time required to produce and update large-scale maps. Photogrammetry concerns itself with obtaining accurate measurements from aerial photographs and using those measurements to produce even higher-quality maps than traditional surveying of both easy-to-access as well as difficult-to-access areas.

The Aerial Photograph: Key Characteristics

Using aerial photographs as the basis for producing large-scale maps, such as topographic quadrangles, fundamentally changed the mapping sciences. Understanding some of the basic characteristics of these images is a good place to start when exploring how they have influenced mapping. A raw aerial photograph may never be treated as equivalent to a map, as there is uncontrolled distortion embedded in its geometrical foundation. The field of photogrammetry, in fact, evolved from the need for surveyors to correct these distortions and extract real-world dimensions. A classic way to envision these types of problems is to examine the shape of a feature on an unprocessed aerial photo and compare it to its real-world shape on both **orthophotographs**, aerial photographs in which distortions have been corrected, and topographic maps. In Figure 9.1, for example, the land cleared for a power line in the unprocessed photograph (the straight lighter-colored line running through the middle of the photo) bends and dips in places due to changes in elevation as it crosses the landscape. The changes in elevation recorded by the camera causes the scale of the photograph to vary, making it unsuitable for use as a map or as the basis for creating a map. To use the photograph as the foundation for creating a map, these types of distortions must first be removed, which results in an *orthophotograph*. The orthophotograph is the basis for creating the topographic map. The following discusses the key characteristics of aerial photographs that influence these types of distortions.

Source: U.S. Geological Survey, Department of the Interior

FIGURE 9.1
Unprocessed aerial photograph, orthophotograph and topographic map of the Altavista, Virginia area. The land cleared for the power line appears to bend in the unprocessed photograph due to distortion caused by relief displacement.

Types of Aerial Photographs

Aerial photographs can be grouped into two broad categories: *oblique* and *vertical*. Oblique photographs are probably the type most familiar to the public. Taken when the axis of the camera is tilted at an angle to the ground during imaging, the result is a *perspective* view of an area, which mimics what we might see ourselves if we were viewing the same area at a similar height (Figure 9.2a). Unfortunately, the tilt of the camera further exaggerates the geometric distortion inherent in the image. Vertical photographs, on the other hand, are far less complicated to correct geometrically, which makes them ideal for using them as the foundation for a map. These photographs are imaged with the camera pointed vertically to the ground. The result in this case is a *plan view*, in which the area is seen as if the viewer is directly overhead (Figure 9.2b).

a.

b.

FIGURE 9.2
Aerial photograph types: (a) Oblique view of Starmount area in Greensboro, NC, 1985; (b) Vertical view of Cardinal neighborhood in Guilford County, NC, 1989.

Aerial Photograph Format

The standard vertical air photo is a black and white print, approximately 9 square inches. Centered along the sides of the photograph are **fiducial marks**, which are images of markers built into the aerial camera. These images are used as fixed references; by connecting opposite pairs of fiducial marks on an image with perpendicular lines, the point at which the camera's optic axis intersects with the film plane can be determined. This **principal point** (PP) is the location on the photograph with the least geometric distortion and is important in assessing patterns of distortion across the image (Figure 9.3). In vertical photography, the principal point coincides with the **nadir**, the point on Earth below the camera when the image was recorded (Monmonier and Schnell, 1984).

FIGURE 9.3
Fiducial marks and the principal point on an aerial photograph.

Most aerial photographs are imaged during a series of parallel, overlapping flight lines the aircraft follows when taking the images (Figure 9.4). The resulting photographs are configured into long strips, with the final prints oriented 90° to the flight line. Adjacent strips differ by 180° in orientation, as the plane turns at the end of each run. As flight lines can be flown in any direction, the orientation of the images relative to cardinal directions can vary. This is unlike most map products, which tend to place north toward the top of the map. The overlap of flight lines is required to ensure complete coverage and to facilitate the use of photogrammetric methods for creating maps from the imagery. Complete coverage of an area is addressed by having flight lines imaged with approximately 30% side lap. Along any given flight line, overlap between adjacent photographs is typically 60%. Although this increases the cost of obtaining full coverage of an area, imaging the same portion of the Earth's surface in adjacent photos by this amount creates **stereopairs** (Figure 9.5).

Source: E. Nelson

FIGURE 9.4
Photographic overlap along flight lines and sidelap between adjacent flight lines.

Source: Department of Geography Environment and Sustainability, UNC Greensboro. Reprinted by permission

FIGURE 9.5
Stereopair of Norfolk, Virginia, 1983.

CHAPTER 9 Aerial Photography

Stereopairs show the same portion of the Earth's surface, but from slightly different camera positions. When viewed together, using the appropriate photogrammetric equipment, the images are perceived as a 3D model, or **stereomodel**, of the area. The principle behind this concept rests on our own eye–brain system. Each of our eyes views its surroundings from a slightly different position; the brain takes the information gathered from each eye and merges it, allowing us to generate depth perception and view our world in 3D.

GEOMETRIC DISTORTION

The geometric distortion found in unprocessed aerial photos takes several forms. Some of the most important include height (scale) distortion, **tilt displacement**, and relief (topographic) displacement. **Height distortion** occurs because the height, or elevation, of the terrain varies as the plane flies along a flight line. Objects at higher elevations are closer to the camera and will appear larger in the photograph than similar objects at lower elevations, which means that scale varies over the photograph (Figure 9.6).

When the optical axis of the camera is not precisely vertical during image acquisition, the resulting photograph will also show effects of *tilt displacement*. Almost all vertical photographs will have at least a small degree of tilt

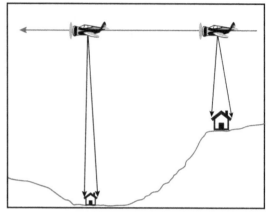

FIGURE 9.6
Height Distortion: An object at a higher elevation will appear larger than an identical object at a lower elevation.

due to a variety of factors, including wind and aircraft maneuvers like banking and climbing. What is interesting about tilt displacement is that there is an order to the severity of the distortion. Tilt displacement affects the shapes of objects in the image, with object distortions increasing radially inward or outward with respect to the *isocenter*. The isocenter, on a true vertical photograph, would be the same as the principal point and nadir. Since all vertical photographs have some degree of tilt distortion, though, a better definition would be the line on the photograph that bisects a line connecting the principal point and nadir (Jensen, 2000). Because this type

of distortion has a regular pattern, computer algorithms can be used to remove it from an image.

With *relief* or *topographic displacement*, the tops of objects in an image are displaced relative to their bases. There is also a radial pattern to this type of distortion, with objects located above the terrain leaning away from the nadir of the photograph (Figure 9.7). Distortion, again, increases toward the edges of the photograph. This type of displacement is caused by a combination of the perspective geometry of the camera lens and the varying elevation of the terrain in the image. While it may be processed out of the image to create a product that can be used as a base for mapping, **relief displacement** can also be useful to the photointerpreter, as it is harnessed for both stereoviewing and for calculating heights of objects in the image.

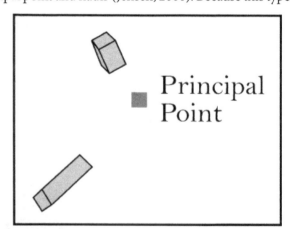

FIGURE 9.7
Relief (topographic) displacement: Tops of objects are displaced relative to their bases as you move away from the nadir due to changes in topography.

Basic Photogrammetric Techniques

Photogrammetric techniques range from methods for determining distances, areas, and heights of objects on an image to using the image to generate **digital elevation models (DEMs)**, orthophotos, and other related products. Following are a few examples of some of the simpler techniques involved in this science, along with an overview of a few products that can be derived from aerial photography.

As with maps, scale is a central feature of the aerial photograph. By defining the size relationship between a real-world feature and its corresponding image on the aerial photo, photogrammetrists can use it to both measure features and plot distances. The scale of a photo is formally defined as the ratio of the camera lens focal length (f) to the flight altitude (H) of the plane, written mathematically as $\frac{f}{H}$. Although this ratio looks nothing like the standard $\frac{\text{map distance}}{\text{ground distance}}$ ratio we are used to working with when handling maps, some simple geometry proves it is a surrogate form (Jensen, 2000). As Figure 9.8 shows, line XY on the ground is imaged as line xy on the photograph. The ratio $\frac{xy}{XY}$, then, is equivalent to $\frac{\text{photo distance}}{\text{ground distance}}$. From similar triangles ZXY and zxy, then $\frac{f}{H}$ is also equivalent to $\frac{\text{photo distance}}{\text{ground distance}}$. Remember, however, this scale is not consistent across the image. Much like a projected map's principal scale is only true at the point or line of tangency, the photo's scale is only true at the principal point and may vary somewhat across the image due to changes in object heights and terrain elevations.

The focal length and flight altitude are usually stamped at the top of the image. To compute the ratio, both parameters must first be transformed into the same units of measurement. For example, on a photograph with a 6-in. focal length and flight altitude of 5,000 ft., the steps are to convert both measure-

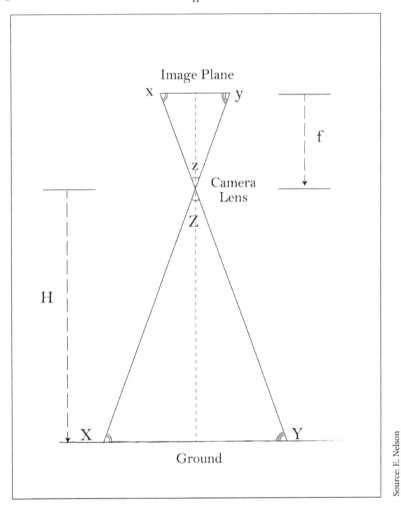

FIGURE 9.8
Photo scale, defined as the ratio of the camera lens focal length (f) to the flight altitude (H) of the plane.

Source: E. Nelson

ments to inches, calculate the ratio, then convert the ratio to representative fraction form by dividing out the numerator to arrive at 1 for the upper part of the ratio:

[handwritten: 1.85 /1070]

$$\text{6 in. focal length / 5,000 ft. flight altitude}$$

[handwritten: 1070 × $\frac{12}{1}$ = 12840]

Convert feet to inches: $5{,}000 \text{ ft.} \times \frac{12 \text{ in.}}{1 \text{ ft.}} = 60{,}000 \text{ in.}$ *(feet in the numerator and denominator cancel each other)*

Plug the numbers into the equation and simplify *(Inches in the numerator and denominator cancel each other)*

[handwritten: $\frac{1.85}{12840} = \frac{\frac{1.85}{1.05}}{\frac{12840}{1.05}} = \frac{1}{6940.5}$]

$$\frac{6 \text{ in.}}{60{,}000 \text{ in.}} = \frac{\frac{6}{6}}{\frac{60{,}000}{6}} = \frac{1}{10{,}000} \text{ or 1:10,000}$$

If the image is not annotated with focal length and flying altitude, another way to estimate its scale would be to measure the distance on the image between two features, then to compare that distance to one between the same two features on a map that has a defined scale. Two formulae are useful here (Avery and Berlin, 1992). For maps, this formula would be *Ground Distance = Map Distance ×* **Map Scale Factor** where the *Map Scale Factor* is defined as the inverse of the map scale. The corresponding formula for an air photo would be *Ground Distance = Photo Distance × Photo Scale Factor*. Since both formulae represent ground distance, the equation can be rewritten as follows:

Map Distance × Map Scale Factor = Photo Distance × Photo Scale Factor

Suppose, then that the distance between **A** and **B** on an image with an undefined scale is 0.2 in. On a map of the same area, with a scale of 1:10,560, the same distance between those features measures 0.1 in. If we input the 'knowns' of our problem into the formula above, we have one unknown we can solve for: **Photo Scale Factor**.

$$0.1 \text{ in.} \times 10{,}560 \text{ in.} = 0.2 \text{ in.} \times \text{Photo Scale Factor}$$

$$\frac{1{,}056}{0.2} = \frac{0.2}{0.2} \times \text{ Photo Scale Factor}$$

$$5{,}280 = \text{Photo Scale Factor}$$

Since *Photo Scale Factor* is the inverse of *Photo Scale*, inverting the answer will yield the photo's estimated scale.

$$1{:}5{,}280 = \text{Photo Scale}$$

DETERMINING OBJECT HEIGHTS

Aerial photographs are 2D representations of a 3D world. In photographing that environment, all the 3D attributes of features, such as object heights, are forced onto a plane with no vertical dimension. Unlike a **planimetric** map, however, in which the features are all plotted as if they were located at the same elevation, those same feature locations on an air photo are influenced by many factors, including the local scale at that point, the feature elevation and its distance from the nadir. These relationships result in a distinct topographic displacement pattern, where any feature above or below the mean ground level of the photo is displaced from its true horizontal location, and the tops and bases of many features can be easily discerned. This displacement can be harnessed to estimate the heights of objects in the image by using the following formula (Avery and Berlin, 1992):

$$\text{Object Height} = d/r\,(H)$$

where: d = length of the object from top to bottom

r = distance from top of object to principal point of the image

H = flying height of aircraft during image acquisition

If, as Figure 9.9 shows, the length (d) of the object being measured was 0.10 in., the top of the object was 0.40 in. from the principal point (r), and the flying height (H) was 2,000 ft., then the object height would be estimated as:

0.10 in. / 0.40 in. (2,000 ft.) = 500 ft.

UNDERSTANDING STEREOSCOPY

Another area in which the height or relief displacement of objects on a vertical photograph can be used to an advantage is when working with pairs of adjacent aerial photographs. Because such images are planned with a 60% overlap, the images can be aligned in such a way that each eye can essentially view the same scene, with a slight distance shift occurring in feature positions from one image to the next. This shift, or **parallax displacement**, is converted by the eye–brain system into a 3D model of the area. Experts often view such images with their unaided eyes and perceive depth; most others, however, will find that using a **stereoscope** in conjunction with the aligned images to be the most efficient means of creating the necessary depth perception.

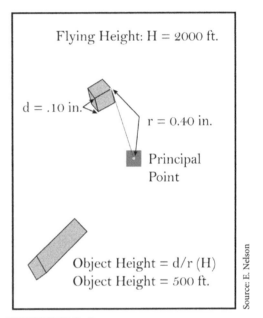

FIGURE 9.9
Estimating the heights of objects using topographic displacement.

Source: E. Nelson

The stereoscope is a photogrammetric instrument that enhances one's ability to fuse visually two images of an area with slightly different perspectives into a *stereomodel* or 3D environment. It works by presenting one image to the left eye and the other image to the right eye. The parallax displacement between the two images is used by the eye–brain system to perceive the images in 3D form. The geometry of the resulting stereomodel then allows scientists to make precise 3D measurements. Over time, many techniques and instruments have been developed to enhance this basic process. One instrument, particularly important to topographic mapping, is the *stereoplotter*.

Stereoplotters allow the operator to not only view the environment in 3D but also trace paths of constant elevation, creating the contours we see on our topographic maps series. This type of instrument is designed to control both the horizontal and vertical movements of a measuring mark. By setting the height of the measuring mark to rest on the terrain surface, the operator can trace contour lines for that particular elevation and store them digitally. The topographic maps produced today follow this procedure, not only for creating the contours but also for identifying and measuring all other features. Operators even add attributes to each feature as they work, creating both a topographic map and additional vector GIS data that can be used in GIS analyses (Aronoff, 2005).

CORRECTING GEOMETRIC DISTORTION

Whereas photogrammetric analyses are crucial for creating stereomodels and calculating relief displacements, there are also other ways those in GIScience might use aerial photographs. One example would be to pair or overlay a photograph with vector GIS data. Because of the distortions inherent in the raw imagery, however, alignment issues with these data sets will cause problems. The key in this instance is to process relief displacement and other geometric distortions out of the photograph prior to using it. An *orthophotoscope* is the instrument used to remove relief displacement and produce an *orthophoto* from the original aerial photograph. With the distortions removed, every point in the orthophoto appears as if it was viewed from directly above, producing a photo that is equivalent to a planimetric map.

Today's orthophoto technology is capable of producing a variety of other products as well, including digital arrays of terrain elevations called *Digital Elevations Models* (DEMs), *orthophotomaps*, and **orthophotoquads**. DEMs are useful for creating digital relief maps, 3D representations of an environment, and analyzing terrain. Orthophotomaps are orthophotos in quadrangle form that have been enhanced by overlaying map grids, placenames, symbols, and contours. Black and white orthophotoquads are similar to our 1:24,000 topographic series, but typically they have less information than the standard quadrangle. They tend to be used in specific applications, such as site selections or tax assessments (Monmonier and Schnell, 1984).

Landscape Interpretation

In addition to the information derived from aerial photographs using photogrammetric techniques, photointerpreters also use a variety of visual indicators to identify objects and infer information about a region. The traditional framework from which they work makes use of eight visual elements: shape, size, tone, texture, shadow, site, association, and pattern (Aronoff, 2005). What follows are examples to introduce you to these elements and how they are used in landscape interpretation. Today's applications of these elements in specific fields, such as archaeology, forestry, agriculture, and urban landscapes, will require additional knowledge of those fields.

SHAPE

As we saw in our discussion of basic visual variables used in mapping, shape is a property of objects to which we are sensitive visually. Unique shapes, such as athletic fields, or the building footprint of a structure like the Pentagon, are easily identified using this element alone if you know the characteristics for which you are looking (Figure 9.10).

Absent the unique distinctiveness, you can typically designate an object as at least of cultural or natural origins. Objects with regular, geometric shapes and straight lines (roads, for example) are usually the result of human construction, making them a cultural object. Naturally occurring features like rivers, on the other hand, are more likely to be irregular in shape and non-geometric. With a little more expertise or additional information, you can even distinguish between objects that have similar shapes but lack unique

Source: U.S. Geological Survey, Department of the Interior

FIGURE 9.10
Identifying features using the visual element of shape: Pentagon (left), William-Brice football stadium, Columbia S.C. (right).

distinctive features. One example here would be identifying an object as a road versus a railroad (Figure 9.11). While these features tend to look similar on many photographs, a closer look will reveal that railroads are often more linear, have gentler curves than roads, and lack perpendicular intersections (Rabenshorst and McDermott, 1989).

Source: U.S. Geological Survey, Department of the Interior

FIGURE 9.11
Identifying features using the visual element of shape: roads, railroads, and rivers, Lynchburg, V.A.

ASSOCIATION

Another instance in which shape may be useful even when it is not unique is when it is considered in the context of surrounding land use. Take as an example a public school in the United States. The building shape itself will look similar to many other types of buildings, but playing fields, parking lots, and residential areas will surround it. Each of these, when considered in conjunction with the building, helps to identify it as a school, as opposed to a mall or a single-family residence (Figure 9.12). *Association* is the interpretive element that describes this process of using the functional connections of surrounding features to help identify an object.

Source: U.S. Geological Survey, Department of the Interior

FIGURE 9.12
Identifying features using the visual element of association: schools versus malls, Greensboro, N.C.

SIZE

Size, the measure of an object's dimensions, is another fundamental visual variable of which we make use in landscape interpretation. Object sizes can be used in both an absolute sense and a relative sense to help identify a feature. Absolute sizes are calculated photogrammetrically and are often used to classify a feature as belonging to a particular group. Houses, for example, could be categorized by absolute size. Doing this then allows the photointerpreter to use house sizes to infer housing values (Avery and Berlin, 1985). Absolute sizes of known features also help us to appreciate the sizes of adjacent, sometimes unknown, features. This use of relative size refers to the process of comparing an object's size to those nearby. Jensen (2000) provides an interesting example of this, where the average lengths of trailers on tractor-trailer rigs (45-50 ft.) can be used to gauge how large adjacent warehouse buildings are on an image.

SHADOW

Aerial photographs also provide access to *shadow* information if an object has height. Shadows are important because they sometimes expose details that are difficult to see from directly overhead. The shadows of steeples, for example, are often used in identifying buildings as churches.

TONE AND TEXTURE

Tone or value refers to how bright an object is or to its dominant color. Tone in a traditional aerial photograph is created through a chemical reaction during the development of the camera's film. This film is light-sensitive; the camera records the amount of light energy reflected from the portion of Earth being imaged, and when the film is developed, variations in light intensity shows up as differences in tone.

This interpretive element is somewhat trickier than the previous, because an object's tone is dependent upon (1) how much light it reflects and how much of that light is captured by the camera as it records the image, and (2) its texture. If an object reflects a lot of light, then it will appear lighter on the resulting image. Smoother surfaces, such as roads and bare fields, generally tend to have higher reflectance values and show up on an image as lighter tonal values. Rougher textures, on the other hand, scatter light so that less is reflected back to the camera, resulting in darker tones on the image. Areas of forest are a good example here (Figure 9.13). Leaves and branches intermix and create shadows so that when imaged, the area appears coarser and darker (Aronoff, 2005). *Texture* is considered an interpretative element in and of itself; it is used frequently to distinguish types of agriculture, where some crops appear coarser than others. Corn, for example, generally has a coarser texture than wheat (Rabenshorst and McDermott, 1989).

PATTERN

When objects are arranged in a repetitive way, the result is a design called *pattern*. Trees that are planted in rows create a pattern we associate with orchards. Tombstones in a cemetery also create a distinctive pattern that can be recognized on aerial photographs. Another interesting example of pattern in the United States is the presence of long lots along the Mississippi River (Figure 9.14). While much of the United States was surveyed using the Public Land Survey System, this was not the case along the Mississippi River, which had already been surveyed by the French during the time they held the land. The French survey created long, narrow parcels of land that gave each owner access to the Mississippi, as it was the primary means of travel during that time. This pattern also ensured each owner had similar areas of land quality, which tended to vary as distance from the river increased (Rabenshorst and McDermott, 1989).

SITE

While both the French long lot and the Public Land Survey System produced rectangular patterns, the character of the French long lots—their orientations and the ratios of the sides of the rectangles—make them distinct on imagery. The French long lot in the United States is also an example of a *site*, which is an interpretive element that has a unique physical or socioeconomic characteristic. In this case, the French survey created a land-tenure system unique to the Mississippi River.

While these eight elements have been discussed largely in isolation, in practice they most often are considered simultaneously during interpretation. Whether alone or in combination, however, they can be used to complete tasks that produce derived information from the raw photograph. These tasks include classifying the imagery, counting objects visible on an image, measuring objects, and delineating regions with homogenous tones and textures (Aronoff, 2005).

FIGURE 9.13
Identifying features using the visual elements of tone and texture: Forests, roads, and fields, Reidsville, N.C.

FIGURE 9.14
Identifying features using the visual elements of pattern and site: French long lots along the Mississippi River, St. James Parish, Louisiana.

Key Terms

Photogrammetry

Orthophotograph

Oblique (aerial photo)

Vertical (aerial photo)

Fiducial marks

Principal point

Nadir

Stereopair

Stereomodel

Height distortion

Tilt displacement

Relief displacement

Map scale factor

Photo scale factor

Planimetric

Stereoscope

Parallax displacement

Orthophotoquad

Digital elevation model (DEM)

Questions

1. What is aerial photography? What circumstances spurred its development?

2. With what platform was the first aerial photograph captured?

3. The oldest known aerial photograph still existing is of what area of the world?

4. What is photogrammetry? What would be an example of a photogrammetric process?

5. Why is it not a good idea to use a raw aerial photograph as a map?

6. How do fiducial marks, principal points, and nadirs relate to the standard vertical aerial photograph?

7. Describe the three most important types of geometric distortion in an aerial photograph.

8. What is parallax displacement?

9. What are the eight basic visual elements of landscape interpretation?

10. Explain how the Mississippi long lot is an example of both pattern and site in terms of landscape interpretation.

Bibliography

Aronoff, S. 2005. *Remote Sensing for GIS Managers*. Redlands, California: ESRI Press.

Avery T. E. and Berlin, G. L., 1985. *Fundamental of Remote Sensing and Airphoto Interpretation*. 5th ed. Macmillan: New York.

Avery, T.E. and G.L. Berlin, 1992. *Fundamentals of Remote Sensing and Air Photo Interpretation*. 5th ed. New York, NY: Macmillan Publishing Company.

Campbell, J.C. 1984. *Introductory Cartography*. Englewood Cliffs, NJ: Prentice-Hall, Inc.

Campbell, J.B. 1996. *Introduction to Remote Sensing*. New York, NY: Guilford Press.

Dickinson, G.C. 1979 *Maps and Air Photographs*. 2nd ed. London, England: Edward Arnold, Ltd.

Gray, C. 2002. "The First Five Flights: The Slope and Winds of Big Kill Devil Hill—The First Flight Reconsidered." Last accessed March 11, 2019. http://www.thewrightbrothers.org/fivefirstflights.html.

Jensen, J.R. 2000. *Remote Sensing of the Environment: An Earth Resource Perspective*. Upper Saddle River, NJ: Prentice-Hall, Inc.

Lillesand, T., Keifer, R.W., and J. Chipman. 2007. *Remote Sensing and Image Interpretation*. 6th ed. New York, NY: John Wiley & Sons.

Monmonier, M. and G.A. Schnell. 1984. *Map Appreciation*. Englewood Cliffs, NJ: Prentice-Hall, Inc.

Rabenshorst, T.D. and P.D. McDermott, 1989. *Applied Cartography: Introduction to Remote Sensing*. Columbus, OH: Merrill Publishing Company.

Thrower, N.J.N. 1996. *Maps and Civilization: Cartography in Culture and Society*. Chicago, IL: University of Chicago Press.

Concepts in Photogrammetry and Landscape Interpretation

In Exercise 9, you will gain experience in the basic photogrammetric and landscape interpretation concepts used in aerial photography.

OBJECTIVES

- Use an image's fiducial marks to determine its principal point
- Estimate the scale of a photo
  - Using flying height and camera lens focal length
  - Using known features
  - Using the distance between two features and a map
- Estimate the height of an object using flying height and distance from the photo's principal point
- Use visual elements to identify and infer information about landscape features

SOFTWARE

The questions for Exercise 9 require Adobe's Acrobat Reader DC.

DATA

The data for the exercise are available from the Kendall Hunt Student Ancillary site. See the inside front cover for access information. You may also be directed to download the data from a different location by your instructor.

1. Download the data as instructed by your instructor
2. Save the file to a location where you have read/write privileges

Fiducial Marks and the Principal Point

Fiducial marks are images of markers built into the aerial camera. When a photo is taken, these marks are reproduced on the sides or in the corners of the photograph. Connecting opposite pairs of fiducial marks with perpendicular lines will determine the photo's principal point. The principal point is the geometric center of the photograph.

1. Navigate to the *Chapter09* class folder.
2. Double-click the folder to see its contents.
3. Right-click *Aerial_Photo_1.pdf* and *Open with Adobe Acrobat Reader DC*.

Aerial_Photo_1.pdf is a photo of the Norfolk, Virginia area (Figure 9.1). It is a coastal city known for its transportation and military presence. The largest Navy base in the world is located here as is the corporate headquarters of Norfolk Southern Railway.

FIGURE 9.1

4. Click on the *Tools* tab.
5. In the *Find your tools here* search box, type *line* to search for the *Line* tool.
6. Click the down arrow next to *Drawing Tools* and then select *Expand Drawing Tools*. The *Drawing Tools* are now added to the menu bar above the aerial photo.
7. From the *Menu Bar*, expand the *Drawing Tools* by clicking on the down arrow. Select *Line* (Figure 9.2).

FIGURE 9.2

To find the principal point on the aerial photo, you will now draw two intersecting lines using the fiducial marks.

8. To draw the first line, position the cursor over the upper left fiducial mark, click and hold the left mouse button, and drag a line to the lower right fiducial mark.
9. Again, from the *Menu Bar*, expand the *Drawing Tools* by clicking on the down arrow. Select *Line* and draw the second line to connect the upper right fiducial mark to the lower left fiducial mark.

QUESTION 9.1

What cultural landscape feature is located at this photo's principal point?

a. Airport
b. Storage tanks
c. Warehouses
d. Ships

Estimating Photo Scale

You can derive the scale of an aerial photograph in several ways: as the ratio of camera lens focal length (*f*) to flying height (*H*), by comparing the distance between two objects on both the photo and a map with a scale, and by using an object on the photo with known length.

QUESTION 9.2

You have been given a folder of imagery with no annotation; however, the folder does contain a sheet of paper with the following information:

COMBAT—Commercial Block Analytical Triangulation
Project: University of North Carolina Greensboro; Strip 3, 3 Photos
Photo scale:a
Flight altitude (AMT): 8,325 ft. *H*
Camera focal length: 6 in. *f*

1

Based on the Flight Altitude and the Camera Focal Length, compute the scale for this photo, stating it as a representative fraction for your final answer. What is the scale of the photograph, stated as a representative fraction?

$8,325 \times 12 = 99900$

a. 6:8,325
b. 1:1,388
c. 6:99,900
d. 1:16,650

$$\frac{99900}{6} = 16650$$

Aerial_Photo_1.pdf, of Norfolk, Virginia, as previously shown in Figure 9.1 is a 30-year-old image you found in the back of a filing cabinet. You do not know who took the image, what kind of camera they used, or the altitude of the plane.

You need to estimate the scale of the image. You believe that you can work with an aircraft carrier in the upper left quadrant of the photo to acquire the scale of the image. Aircraft carriers are easy to identify because they have angled flight decks for landing planes (Figure 9.3).

The number on the bow (facing toward land) identifies the carrier. A little detective work via the internet turns up a list of all U.S. Navy aircraft carriers by number. CV-62 is the *Independence*, which is listed as 1,070 ft. in length.

FIGURE 9.3

Use *Aerial_Photo_1.pdf* to measure the image length of the ship.

1. Go to the *Tools* menu and type *measure* in the *Search (Find your tools here)*. Click *Open*. The *Measuring Tool* should appear in the toolbar above the photo.
2. Zoom in on the aircraft carrier to 400% by clicking the *View* tab > *Zoom*, then *Zoom To...*, then use the slider bars to center the aircraft carrier on the screen.
3. Click on the *Measuring Tool* and use it to estimate the ship's length in inches on the photo.

Based on your measurement from the photo and the ship's real-world length, compute the scale for this photo, stating it as a representative fraction for your final answer.

$$\frac{1.85 \text{ in}}{1070 \text{ ft}} \qquad \frac{1.85}{12840}$$

$$.85\sqrt{1070}$$

$$\downarrow$$
$$12840 \text{ in.}$$

What is the scale of this image, stated as a representative fraction?

a. 1:25,000
b. 1:6,903
c. 1:9,900
d. 1:22,882

Aerial_Photo_2_Map.pdf contains a photograph and a map of the University of North Carolina Greensboro campus in Greensboro, North Carolina. Figure 9.4a is a section of a digital aerial photograph. The scale of the photograph was not included in the metadata, but you have access to a 1:14,500 scale reference map of the area (Figure 9.4b) that you can use to estimate the photo's scale.

1. Right-click *Aerial_Photo_2_Map.pdf* and choose *Open with Adobe Acrobat Reader DC*.

Measure the distances between points A and B on the photo and the map.

2. Go to the *Tools* menu and type *measure* in the *Search (Find your tools here)*. Click *Open*. Your *Measuring Tool* should appear in the toolbar above the photo.
3. Click on the *Measuring Tool*.
4. On the photo, click the point at A, then move to point B and double-click to finish the measurement.
5. Repeat the process to measure the distance between point A and point B on the map.

1.49 in

.42 in

FIGURE 9.4a

FIGURE 9.4b

In inches, how far is the distance between point A and point B on both the photo and the map? Pick the answer that is closest to your measurements.

   a. Photo: 2.9 in.; Map: 1.9 in.
   b. Photo: 1.5 in.; Map: 0.6 in.
   c. Photo: 1.1 in.; Map: 0.9 in.
   d. Photo: 2.9 in.; Map: 0.9 in.

Using the results obtained in Question 9.4, calculate the scale of the photo. What is the scale of the photo, stated as a representative fraction?

   a. 1:1,200
   b. 1:5,800
   c. 1:6,400
   d. 1:12,000

$$.6 \times 14500 = 1.5 \times P$$
$$\frac{8700}{1.5} = \frac{1.5}{1.5} \times P$$
$$5800 = P$$

$\times 1 = 14500$

Using the map's scale factor, determine the **real-world** length of road segment on the map that lies between these two points.

Which of the following best estimates the length in feet?

    a. 725
    b. 900
    c. 1,231
    d. 8,845

.6 × 14500 = 8

Estimating an Object's Height

Features above or below the mean ground level of a photo are displaced from their true horizontal location, and often both the tops and bases of some objects can be seen. If this is the case, then the displacement can be used to estimate the height of an object if you also know the flying height of the plane and can locate the principal point of the photo:

Object height = d/r (H)

where

        d = length of the object from top to bottom
        r = distance from top of the object to the principal point of the image
        H = flying height of the aircraft during image acquisition

Aerial_Photo_3_AppState.pdf is a photograph of the Appalachian State University campus in Boone, North Carolina (Figure 9.5). The photo shows a building just north of the football field (A).

FIGURE 9.5

1. Open *Aerial_Photo_3_AppState.pdf* in Adobe Acrobat Reader DC.
2. Use the *Line* tool to find the principal point of the photograph and use the *Measure* tool to find *d* and *r*.

(handwritten: ↓ .20   ↓ 2.47)

Which of the following best approximates the height of the building labeled A (*d*) and its distance from the principal point (*r*)?

a. *d* = 0.2 in.; *r* = 2.3 in. *(circled)*
b. *d* = 0.5 in.; *r* = 4.3 in.
c. *d* = 0.7 in.; *r* = 0.3 in.
d. *d* = 0.7 in.; *r* = 2.3 in.

If the flying height of the plane that took this photograph was 1,500 ft., approximately how tall is the building labeled A?

a. 30 ft.
b. 103 ft.
c. 120 ft. *(circled)*
d. 174 ft.

(handwritten:
$$d/r \ (H)$$
$$\frac{.2}{2.3}(1500)$$
$$130?$$
)

Identifying Landscape Features

In addition to the information derived from aerial photographs using photogrammetric techniques, photo interpreters also use a variety of visual indicators to identify objects and infer information about a region. The traditional framework from which they work makes use of eight visual elements: shape, size, tone, texture, shadow, site, association, and pattern.

Use Figures 9.6a to 9.6d and your knowledge of the eight visual variables to answer the following questions.

FIGURES 9.6a to 9.6d

9 + V 2 .

QUESTION 9.9

What is the feature in Figure 9.6a?

   a. Mall
   b. School
   c. Church
   d. Hospital

EXERCISE 9 Aerial Photography

241

What is the feature in Figure 9.6b?

a. Amusement park
b. Golf course
c. School
d. Farm

What is the feature in Figure 9.6c?

a. Parking Deck
b. Shopping Center
c. Tennis Courts
d. Football Stadium

What is the feature in Figure 9.6d?

a. Grain Silo
b. Lighthouse
c. Cell Tower
d. Water Tower

CHAPTER 10
Remote Sensing

Traditional aerial photography is but one method available today for acquiring imagery of the Earth. By the end of World War II, the demands of the military for more and better cameras, films, and platforms for capturing images of our landscapes had created another technological boom in the United States. With an influx of German scientists leading the way, the U.S. Space Program gained momentum, and the rocket became the new platform for this growing geospatial technology (Thrower, 1996). Rocket technology, along with the development of artificial satellites and non-photographic scanning systems, prompted the director of the U.S. Office of Naval Research, *Evelyn Pruitt*, to coin a new term for this expanding field: **remote sensing**. She considered this new technology, based on electronics (scanners) and radiation physics (the entire **electromagnetic spectrum**), to be a separate field from traditional aerial photography, the foundations of which are in chemistry (film) and optics (cameras). Today, however, the term *remote sensing* covers both and is typically defined as the process of acquiring information about the Earth using any technology that is not in direct contact with the Earth's surface (Monmonier and Schnell, 1984).

Electromagnetic Radiation

All remote sensing technology, whether based on traditional aerial photographic techniques or the non-photographic technology of satellites and electronic scanner systems, is designed to sense light energy that is either reflected or emitted from ground-based objects. The principal type of light energy detected is **electromagnetic radiation**, released from the sun. This radiation is composed of vibrating electric and magnetic fields that travel through space in waves. A stream of photons, or discrete bundles of light energy, comprises each wave and moves at the speed of light. Different types of radiation, such as visible light or radio waves, consist of photons with different energy levels, wavelengths, and wavelength frequencies.

ELECTROMAGNETIC SPECTRUM

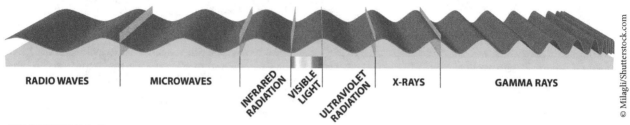

RADIO WAVES | MICROWAVES | INFRARED RADIATION | VISIBLE LIGHT | ULTRAVIOLET RADIATION | X-RAYS | GAMMA RAYS

© Milagli/Shutterstock.com

FIGURE 10.1
The electromagnetic spectrum: wavelength and frequency.

Of these radiation characteristics, two are key for understanding how scientists obtain information from remote sensing data: **wavelength** and **frequency**. A wavelength is defined as the distance from one wave peak to the next; a wave's frequency is the number of these peaks that pass a fixed point in a given timeframe. As Figure 10.1 shows, shorter wavelengths have higher frequencies and greater amounts of energy than longer wavelengths. This relationship can be modeled mathematically as:

$$c = f\lambda$$

where c is the speed of light (3×10^3 m/s), f is the frequency of the wavelength (cycles per second, Hz), and λ is the wavelength (m).

So that the product of f and λ is always equal to the speed of light, the frequency of the wave must always be inversely related to its wavelength.

Scientists categorize the continuum of electromagnetic radiation by frequency to apply these concepts and examine how they influence information extraction. Once categorized in this manner, the result is referred to as the *electromagnetic spectrum (EMS)*.

Atmospheric Interactions

Before the energy of the electromagnetic spectrum can be detected by remote sensing systems, it must first make it through the Earth's atmosphere and then back to the sensor. This is no easy feat, as the Earth's atmosphere contains a variety of particles and gases that can absorb, scatter, or refract many of these wavelengths before they ever reach the surface of the Earth. One of the interesting things about this interference is that it is *wavelength selective*, as Figure 10.2 shows. Some wavelengths pass through the atmosphere untouched, while others are restricted in some manner (Avery and Berlin, 1992; Campbell, 1996).

Restricted wavelengths are not as useful for remote sensing applications, as the amount of energy reaching the ground is reduced, leaving less to be detected when it is reflected off ground-based objects. These areas

FIGURE 10.2
Atmospheric interactions: absorption bands and atmospheric windows.

of the EMS are called **absorption bands**, because the wavelengths are absorbed by such atmospheric gases as carbon dioxide, water vapor, and ozone. Ozone, for example, absorbs portions of the ultraviolet wavelengths, while carbon dioxide absorbs portions of the mid-infrared and far-infrared wavelengths and water vapor absorbs portions of near-infrared and thermal infrared wavelengths.

These same atmospheric gases also play a role in *scattering* the shorter wavelengths of the EMS, including the visible blue wavelengths. As these wavelengths enter our atmosphere, they are absorbed, then redirected or *scattered*, away from their initial direction of travel by particles that are much smaller than the wavelengths. Known as **Rayleigh scattering**, these wavelengths are diffused throughout the sky, which is why the sky appears blue. Rayleigh scattering is heavily wavelength dependent; it is inversely proportional to the fourth power of the wavelength, so shorter wavelengths are much more affected than longer ones. This type of scattering also reduces image contrast.

Those wavelengths that are not restricted, on the other hand, form **atmospheric windows**. These regions are important for remote sensing because they are the most suitable regions of the spectrum around which to develop remote sensing systems. They include the visible wavelengths and near-infrared wavelengths, as well as the thermal infrared, microwave, and to some extent the shorter ultraviolet wavelengths (Avery and Berlin, 1992).

CHAPTER 10 Remote Sensing

245

The Visible Spectrum

In remote sensing, scientists further divide the electromagnetic spectrum into regions of wavelengths that have similar properties. The oldest known region, whose properties were studied by several ancient Greek scholars, is the *visible light* region or **visible spectrum**. Visible light is the region of the electromagnetic spectrum that humans can see. It ranges from 0.4 to 0.7 micrometers (μm) or 400 to 700 nanometers (nm). These wavelengths are grouped because they are the only ones out of the entire electromagnetic spectrum that the human eye–brain system is equipped to process (Figure 10.3). Notice the units of measure—a wavelength that is 700 nm long is only 7/10,000,000 of a meter in length (a nanometer is one billionth of a meter; a micron is one millionth of a meter). Our eye–brain system, since it processes visible light and assigns meaning to the various wavelengths, is, perhaps, the earliest of our remote sensing devices.

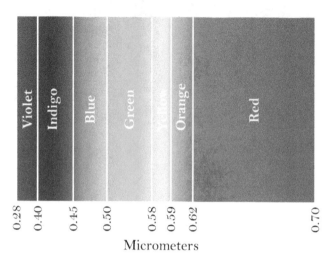

FIGURE 10.3
Visible spectrum.

To give you an idea of how our eye–brain system functions in such a manner, consider the following simplified description of the process. Imagine yourself walking through a wooded area on a sunny summer day. The sunlight shining down on you includes all the wavelengths of the visible spectrum in equal proportions. When this light shines on an object in your view, like the leaves on a tree, the chemical makeup of that object will *absorb* some of those wavelengths and *transmit* or *reflect* others. In the case of summer leaves, the shorter 0.4 to 0.5 μm wavelengths are absorbed by the leaves' chlorophyll, while those in the 0.5 to 0.6 μm range are reflected and processed by your eye–brain system as you look at the trees (Monmonier and Schnell, 1984).

What is particularly unique about our personal remote sensing system is the meaning the brain assigns to each of the wavelengths. As our system processes reflected light, it associates a hue, or dominant color, to each wavelength. In the case of the summer leaves, that hue would be green. If an object reflected primarily the 0.4 to 0.5 μm range, then we would perceive it as being blue; if it reflected primarily in the 0.6 to 0.7 μm range, we would see it as red. Each of these narrower wavelength frequencies is known as a **spectral band**.

Using Visible Spectral Bands in Remote Sensing

Because all objects absorb or transmit some wavelengths of the electromagnetic spectrum, while reflecting others, each has a unique pattern of reflected radiation, known as a **spectral signature**. These patterns form the basis for remote sensing, and they can be graphed using a **spectral signature graph** (Figure 10.4).

This graph creates the signature, or response curve, of an object by plotting the wavelengths of light along the x-axis of the graph and the percentage of that light that is reflected from each band on the y-axis.

The percentage *(p)* of reflected light is determined in a two-step process. First, the total amount of energy or *incident energy (I)* striking an object is calculated by measuring and summing the amounts of energy *reflected (R)*, *absorbed (A)*, and *transmitted (T)* per wavelength for that object: $I = R + A + T$

FIGURE 10.4
Spectral signature graph for grass and trees.

Then, the amount of reflected energy is divided by the incident energy, and the resulting fraction is multiplied by 100 (Shellito, 2012): $p = (R/I) * 100$

In the visible spectrum, for example, water, soil, and vegetation all form distinct spectral signatures that allow us to distinguish them on photographs or digital images.

Each of these bands has principal applications that help guide our use of them in remote sensing applications. The visible blue band, for example, is the best of the three primary visible bands (red, green, blue) for penetrating water, so examining the landscape through this particular lens may allow us to assess water quality or map coastal zones. The visible green band is also used in water quality studies, as well as for studying urban infrastructures. Remote sensors use the visible red band in vegetation studies and for determining soil and geologic boundaries. All three bands are useful for identifying cultural features (Aronoff, 2005).

DISPLAYING VISIBLE SPECTRAL BAND DATA

The hues that we associate with the wavelengths of the visible spectrum are not actual properties of light, but rather our eye–brain system's response to light. We are able to process light in the visible spectrum because our eyes are equipped with three types of color receptors or *cone cells* that are each sensitive to the red, green, and blue spectral bands of the visible spectrum. Through a sophisticated processing network, input from each of these cones is combined to create the full range of hues we associate with this spectrum. Red, green, and blue, then, when modeling color from the perspective of light, are called **additive primary colors**. They are primary because by varying these combinations of wavelengths, all the other hues associated with the visible spectrum can be created. They are additive because they are based on the **additive color model**, in which we begin with black, and then add light combinations to create different hues (Figure 10.5). Televisions and computer monitors are also built upon this model, with red, green, and blue phosphors built into each pixel of the screen as a triad. When individual electron beams produced by the hardware's color guns strike the phosphors, red, green, and blue lights are created and combined to display colors.

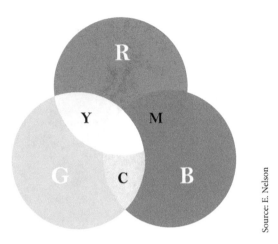

FIGURE 10.5
Additive color model (R=red, G=green, B=blue,
C=cyan, M=magenta, Y=yellow).

Remote sensing and GIS software can take this process a step further by compiling digital images from multiple spectral bands. Some sensors, for example, are designed to sense multiple spectral bands at the same time. In the case of the visible spectrum, this typically means collecting reflected light for the red, green, and blue spectral bands individually. These separate bands can then be displayed individually in grayscale or combined to create a **true color composite** image. For example, to examine an individual band, we assign that band of reflectance values to each of the three color guns in a computer display. Since each of the color guns creating the image reflects the same amount of light for each pixel in the image, a grayscale picture of the region is created. This image represents how the area looks when viewed only through the specific lens of that wavelength (Figure 10.6).

In creating the true color composite, on the other hand, we assign the red spectral band to the red color gun, the green spectral band to the green color gun, and the blue spectral band to the blue color gun. The software then displays the data from each band using the hues that we would normally associate with the features, and when it combines the different amounts of light reflectance from each hue on the screen, a rendering of the area that looks like a normal color photograph appears. If a black and white, or *panchromatic composite*, is preferred, reflected light for the area would be collected via a **panchromatic band**, which is a wider band sensitive to the entire range of the visible spectrum. In this case, the one band of panchromatic data would be loaded into each of the color guns; since each gun is reading the same set of reflectance values, the image produced is black and white. The difference between this image and one of a single band is that the panchromatic covers the entire visible spectrum, mimicking what our eyes would see if we only saw in black and white.

The Near-Infrared Spectrum

Working within the visible spectrum produces images that mimic our vision when color composites are the product, but the electromagnetic spectrum contains many additional wavelengths that we as humans cannot process visually. Just on either side of the visible spectrum, for instance, are shorter ultraviolet wavelengths (3-0.4 μm) and longer near-infrared wavelengths (0.7-1.3 μm). While our eye–brain system does not process

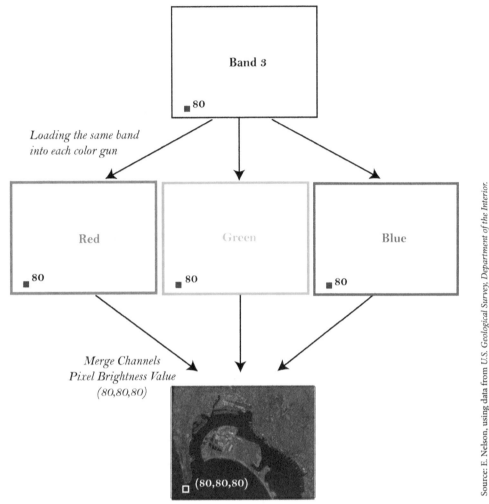

Source: E. Nelson, using data from *U.S. Geological Survey, Department of the Interior.*

FIGURE 10.6
Displaying an individual spectral band in grayscale. Pixel values are the same for each color gun, resulting in a series of gray shades, such as (80, 80, 80) for the highlighted pixel, representing reflectance values.

either of these, we do have cameras and digital sensors that provide access to them and allow us to "see" them. The development of sensors to accommodate this extended wavelength range has its roots in World War II and the need, during that time, to be able to detect camouflaged military equipment from the air.

As this equipment was either painted green or covered with cut, green vegetation, its spectral signature in the visible spectrum was very similar to other vegetation, causing it to blend in on panchromatic and true color composite images. There is a difference between live vegetation and camouflaged equipment, though. Live vegetation contains chlorophyll, which reflects not only green wavelengths in the visible spectrum but also longer near-infrared wavelengths just outside the visible spectrum. The same is not true of green paint or dead vegetation, neither of which contains chlorophyll. To take advantage of this, Kodak developed a panchromatic film with an expanded range sensitive to near-infrared wavelengths of light. When used to acquire images of an area, camouflaged equipment appears very dark and distinct from surrounding live vegetation, which reflects so much infrared light it appears almost white (Jensen, 2000; Scott, 1997).

Sensors designed to collect near-infrared energy create a *color infrared (CIR)* product or **false color composite**. For this type of image, reflected light is collected for the near-infrared, red, and green spectral bands individually. To create the standard *false color composite*, the software assigns the near-infrared band to the red color gun, the red spectral band to the green color gun, and the green spectral band to the blue color gun. The result is an image with false colors or colors we do not expect to see. Healthy vegetation, for example, since it reflects a higher percentage of infrared light than red or green light, now appears red on the image, whereas dying or dead vegetation appears as a less intense red, or more green or blue-green.

USING NEAR-INFRARED BANDS IN REMOTE SENSING

In addition to distinguishing healthy vegetation from dying or dead vegetation, the infrared region of the spectrum is also useful for identifying different types of vegetation that would appear too similar to tell apart on a traditional color image. The classic example that illustrates this idea uses deciduous and coniferous forests (Figure 10.7). On a traditional panchromatic or true color image, the two types of trees would appear similar in color and tone, as they both reflect approximately the same amount of visible light. Examine them using the infrared portion of the spectrum

Source: U.S. Geological Survey, Department of the Interior

FIGURE 10.7
Comparing panchromatic (top) and black and white infrared (bottom) imagery for distinguishing deciduous trees from conifers.

however, and deciduous trees will appear much lighter due to the composition of the leaves; conifers, on the other hand, will appear much darker (Avery and Berlin, 1992).

Beyond vegetation, scientists use the near-infrared band to highlight land/water contrasts and differences in soil moisture. Land or water contrasts and soil moisture content differentiation are common applications because water absorbs most near-infrared wavelengths, creating very dark representations of these features in comparison to dry land, which appears lighter because more infrared wavelengths are reflected (Avery and Berlin, 1992).

Digital Remote Sensing

While traditional photographic systems sense the ultraviolet, visible, and near-infrared spectral bands, atmospheric windows beyond these bands are only accessible through non-photographic technologies. During and following World War II, scientists were busy developing *electronic detection systems* capable of detecting radiant energy for any number of spectral bands. Using electronic detecting elements, **multispectral scanners** were designed to sense more spectral bands, in narrower bandwidths, over a much greater range of the electromagnetic spectrum. Extending the range from 0.3 to ~14 μm, scientists can now access not only the ultraviolet, visible, and near-infrared bands but also the mid-infrared and thermal infrared spectral regions (Lillesand et al., 2007). When an area is imaged in this way, with multiple separate images for each band, it is called **multispectral imagery**.

Multispectral scanners use electronic detecting elements to record reflected light from the ground; this light is then converted to an electrical charge, which is proportional to the amount of energy the detector element received. Elements that record higher amounts of energy will display on screen as areas lighter in tone or value than those that record lower amounts of energy. Each band sensed provides an energy reading for the same area, but the reflectance values recorded differ, as they are specific to the individual band (Figure 10.8). The bands of energy collected can be displayed and interpreted individually or combined into composites by loading them into the red, green, and blue color guns to view the merged bands on-screen.

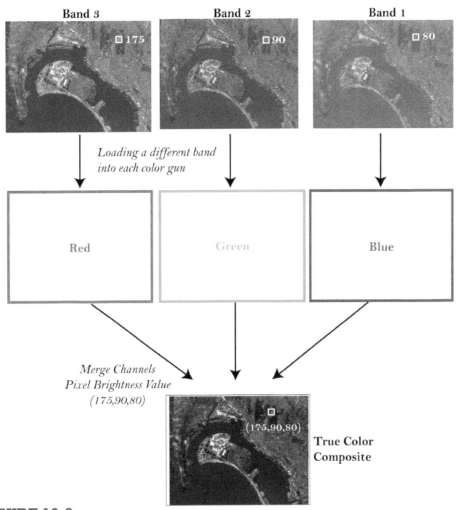

Source: E. Nelson, using data from U.S. Geological Survey, Department of the Interior.

FIGURE 10.8
Displaying three different spectral bands to create a true color composite. Pixel values differ for each band, resulting in different colors, such as (175, 90, 80) for the highlighted pixel, representing reflectance values.

A good example of how this technology expanded our ability to detect reflected energy in other parts of the electromagnetic spectrum is to examine how we harness it to explore *thermal infrared energy*. In this spectral region, the amount of energy emitted by objects correlates with their surface temperature, so warmer objects will appear lighter than cooler objects. Originally conceived for military applications, this spectral band is detectable both day and night. It is also useful for energy loss studies in housing and building designs (Dickinson, 1970).

CHARACTERISTICS OF DIGITAL IMAGERY

With the advent of electronic systems, the products of remote sensing expanded and new concepts came into use. Where the principal product of traditional remote sensing is the aerial photograph, electronic systems produce images, which have the capability of being displayed digitally. The term *photograph*, then, refers to any image or picture-like representation detected and recorded via film. The term *image* is a broader term, meaning any picture-like representation in digital form, including traditional photographs that have been scanned and saved in digital format (Aronoff, 2005). Within the electronic scanning systems, images are stored as a grid of equally sized square cells called **pixels**, short for picture elements. Each cell holds a number that represents a brightness value detected for that pixel, where the value is an average of the reflected radiation for all features with that cell. The detail that can be resolved with these systems is dependent, in large part, on the size of the pixel. Any object smaller than the pixel size will not be resolvable. Electronic systems vary in their resolutions, with four different types of resolution playing key roles in determining the final quality of any image for a given application. Understanding these resolutions will help you select data that are best suited for solving your particular problem.

The type of resolution related to an image's pixel size, for example, is its **spatial resolution**. The spatial resolution of a sensor refers to the smallest-sized feature you can expect to identify on its corresponding images. The smaller an image's pixels, the more detail you can expect to see and the higher (or finer) the sensor's spatial resolution (Figure 10.9). Larger pixel widths, such as 1 km, are useful for broad land cover studies and for identifying major water bodies, agricultural regions, and forested lands. A pixel width of 30 m, on the other hand, has much more detail and can be used to examine crop patterns and urban areas as well as to discriminate between vegetation types and identify major roads and airports (Aronoff, 2005).

Source: NASA

FIGURE 10.9
Comparing spatial resolutions of Landsat (28m, left), Atlas (10 m, center) and Quickbird (2 m, right) imagery.

Sensors and their images also have a **spectral resolution**, which describes the number and width of the spectral bands recorded for each image detected (Table 10.1). These bands may also be referred to as *channels*, and they can be narrow or broad depending on the sensor's specifications and the applications for which it was designed to detect imagery. For example, a panchromatic band is sensitive to the entire visible spectrum, making it a broader band or channel than one just sensitive to the red visible band. Because of this, more incoming light is sensed per pixel, allowing the sensor to detect changes in brightness over smaller areas. This band, then, is typically associated with higher or finer spatial resolutions, which require more storage because the image is divided using a finer grid of smaller pixels. A sensor composed of three narrower spectral bands, one sensitive to the red visible band, one to the blue visible band, and one to the green visible band, would require three separate storage locations for each pixel in the image. This also increases storage requirements, but in this case the extra storage is reserved for higher spectral resolutions. Higher spectral resolution is typically offset by decreasing an image's spatial resolution. The result is more spectrally flexible—you can view any one narrower band or combine any of the image bands to create different color composites, but the resulting image typically will not have the same level of detail as one generated from a broader band.

LANDSAT 5 MSS			LANDSAT 7 TM		
Bands	Spectrum	Wavelength	Band	Spectrum	Wavelength
1	Green	0.5 – 0.6	1	Blue	0.45 – 0.52
2	Red	0.6 – 0.7	2	Green	0.53 – 0.60
3	Near IR	0.7 – 0.8	3	Red	0.63 – 0.69
4	Near IR	0.8 – 1.1	4	Near IR	0.76 – 0.90
			5	Short Wave IR	1.55 – 1.75
			6	Thermal IR	10.40 – 12.40
			7	Short Wave IR	2.08 – 2.35
			8	Panchromatic	0.52 – 0.9

Source: NASA

TABLE 10.1
Spectral resolutions for LANDSAT MSS and TM sensors.

The number of brightness levels recorded for each pixel is a measure of **radiometric resolution** (Figure 10.10). This type of resolution is also tied to the storage capabilities of the sensor. Electronic devices, at their simplest, work as on/off switches, where each pixel would detect energy reflectance (and code it as a 1) or detect no energy reflectance (and code it as a 0). These values are called *bits* in the computer world; their foundations is base 2 (as opposed to base 10, with which we typically work), and they form the basis for storing information in a computer. The result in this case is a black and white image; differences in the percentages of reflectance do not matter because there is no way to record that detail within a binary scheme.

If, however, we design the system so that each pixel receives two bits of memory, then each pixel could store 1 of 4 different values. This increases the radiometric resolution and allows the sensor to record finer variations in reflectance values. A typical form today would be to allocate either 8 or 16 bits to each pixel to capture a range of brightness values useful for analytical processes. Eight bits, for example, will allow each pixel to record up to 256 different brightness levels, which mimics the range of gray tones our eyes can perceive. Like spectral and spatial resolution, radiometric resolution also affects the file size or storage requirements

2-bit (4 values)   **4-bit** (16 values)   **8-bit** (up to 256 values)

Subtle features become visible

Source: NASA

FIGURE 10.10
Comparing radiometric resolutions: 2-bit (left), 4-bit (center), 8-bit (right).

of an image. Take an image covering 60 km × 60 km. If the spatial resolution is 20 m, then the image must be divided into 3,000 pixels per side (3,000 × 20 = 60,000 m or 60 km). That is 9 million pixels to cover the area (3,000 × 3,000) completely. If we record each band using 8 bits (1 byte) of computer memory, we will need roughly 9 MB of storage to store this file on our computer.

The last type of resolution to consider is **temporal resolution**. Temporal resolution describes how frequently an image is acquired of a specific area. Sensors with higher temporal resolutions revisit areas more frequently. High temporal resolutions are useful for crop monitoring studies and studies examining change detection of an area.

Satellite Systems

In the United States, spaceborne platforms for remote sensing began with the launching of *American Explorer I*, the United States' response to the Soviet's launching of *Sputnik-I* in 1957. By 1960, the United States had generated the first space photographs, produced by using cameras and film aboard a spy satellite in the Corona program. Scientists designed the system to return the film via capsule and parachute, and then destroyed the satellite following the mission. These systems quickly moved to all digital components and stable, recurring platforms that provided better image resolutions, longer missions, and even the ability to reposition the satellites (Aronoff, 2005).

Satellite imagery offers several advantages over standard aerial photography, but it does not replace it. For example, satellite or spaceborne platforms provide continuous, global data acquisition, which increases temporal resolution, and provides access to more standardized products. Both make temporal comparisons used in change detection studies easier to conduct. The scale of the imagery, however, is small and provides minimal capability for the stereoscopic viewing required in large-scale topographic applications (Thrower, 1996). It also provides the same projective view as standard aerial photography, resulting in similar distortion properties, although these become slightly more complicated as they can vary depending on the type of orbit the satellite follows.

SATELLITE ORBITS

Some satellites, for example, are placed in **geostationary orbits**. These orbits are designed so that the satellite rotates at the same speed and in the same direction as Earth, keeping it over the same point on the equator at all times; this allows it to monitor the same area continuously (Figure 10.11). Geostationary orbits are most typical of weather satellites, whose primary purpose is to monitor patterns of cloud cover at high altitudes. The resulting imagery is global in scale, with the same geometric distortions common in small-scale maps. Other satellites are placed in *sun-synchronous, near-polar orbits*, in which the satellite rotates westward as the Earth rotates eastward, allowing it to cross different locations at approximately the same time each day (Figure 10.12). The result is less frequent imaging of the area and additional distortion due to rotation, but the images that are produced all have consistent sun angles for easier interpretation over time. The images are also more detailed because these orbits are typically lower in altitude than the geostationary ones. Satellite systems, then, serve as complementary approaches to traditional aerial photography, expanding the overall scope of remote sensing (Monmonier and Schnell, 1984).

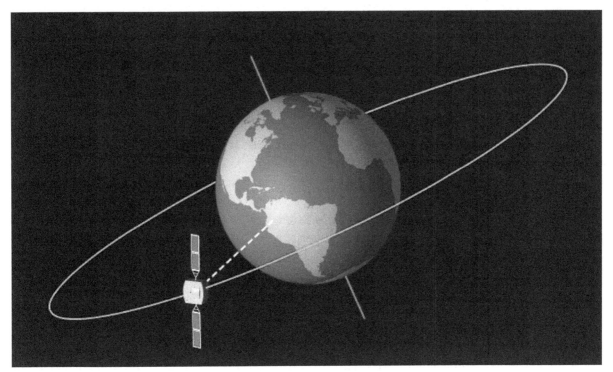

Source: NASA

FIGURE 10.11
Geostationary orbit.

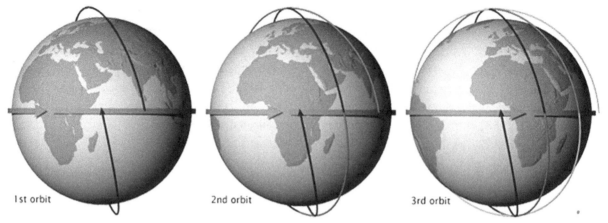

1st orbit   2nd orbit   3rd orbit

FIGURE 10.12
Sun-synchronous, near-polar orbit.

SATELLITE PLATFORMS

Different satellite systems are designed to address different remote sensing applications; sensor resolutions, coverage, frequency, cost, and speed of image delivery are all variables that are addressed within this context. Low-resolution systems, for example, monitor global conditions and are useful for assessing crop conditions and classifying regional land cover and land uses. The first of these satellites to be dedicated to a civilian application, meteorology, was **TIROS-1** (Television and Infrared Observation Satellite) which was launched in 1960. Its resolution was coarse, but it highlighted the potential of satellites to influence weather mapping. The technology behind this satellite series also formed the foundation for the United States' first earth resources satellite series, **ERTS** (Earth Resources Technology Satellites). This series, launched in 1972, marked the first continuous surveillance of Earth using satellites. Renamed **Landsat** in 1975, it has the backing of both the United States Geological Survey (USGS) and the National Aeronautics and Space Administration (NASA). Their support has allowed Earth resources remote sensing to develop at a rapid rate (Thrower, 1996).

Landsat, a medium resolution series, offered the first systematic repetitive coverage of Earth with enough detail to be useful for a variety of applications. The earlier satellites in this series used a multispectral scanner sensor (MSS) that operated in four spectral regions similar to color infrared film photography: the visible red, green, and blue bands, plus a near-infrared band. With a **sun-synchronous, near-polar orbit** at 900 km and a maximum spatial resolution of 80 m on earlier satellites, the final product from these systems were higher-quality images with significantly reduced distortion. Images could be acquired every 18 days for the same area. Industries such as agriculture, forestry, geology, archaeology, and urban and regional land use helped guide the development of later sensor designs, including choice of bandwidth and placement within the electromagnetic spectrum.

Today, the Landsat program is managed by a combination of NASA, NOAA, and the USGS, who operate the program under the *open skies policy*, allowing them to provide the data free to the public worldwide. Images from Landsats 1-3 (launched in 1972, 1975, and 1978) were digital products, and of high-enough quality that they prompted the development of **digital image processing**, a set of computer procedures and algorithms to enhance visual image interpretation. The launching of Landsat 4 in 1982 failed, but Landsat 5, launched in 1984, added a new sensor to the mix, the *Thematic Mapper* (Figure 10.13). This sensor offered a 30 m

FIGURE 10.13
Landsat program timelines.

spatial resolution and increased the spectral resolution from 4 bands (MSS) to 7, covering the visible, near-infrared and thermal infrared spectral regions, with the thermal band having a spatial resolution of 120 m. The temporal resolution improved from 18 days to 16 days. Like Landsat 4, Landsat 6 (1993) failed. Landsat 7, however, launched in 1999, again offered an improved sensor, the *Enhanced Thematic Mapper* (ETM+). This sensor offered 7 spectral bands at a 30 m spatial resolution, along with a 15 m panchromatic band, a 60 m thermal infrared band, and improved radiometric resolution. This system malfunctioned in 2003, leaving only Landsat 5 still functioning. Landsat 8 was launched in February 2013, adding a second working platform in the Landsat series of satellites. The Landsat 8 satellite provides enhancements from previous Landsat instruments. Two additional spectral bands were added: a deep blue visible channel (band 1) and a shortwave infrared channel (band 9). Band 1 is designed to help sense coastal zone and water resources investigation while band 9 is designed to detect cirrus clouds (Table 10.2). Landsat 9 is expected to launch sometime in 2020.

LANDSAT 8 Operational Land Imager (OLI) and Thermal Infrared Sensor (TIRS)		
Bands	Wavelength (micrometers)	Resolution (meters)
Band 1 – Coastal aerosol	0.43 – 0.45	30
Band 2 – Blue	0.45 – 0.51	30
Band 3 – Green	0.53 – 0.59	30
Band 4 – Red	0.64 – 0.67	30
Band 5 – Near Infrared (NIR)	0.85 – 0.88	30
Band 6 – Short Wave IR 1	1.57 – 1.65	30
Band 7 – Short Wave IR 2	2.11 – 2.29	30
Band 8 – Panchromatic	0.50 – 0.68	15
Band 9 – Cirrus	1.36 – 1.38	30
Band 10 – Thermal Infrared 1	10.60 – 11.19	100
Band 11 – Thermal Infrared 2	11.50 – 12.51	100

Source: NASA

TABLE 10.2
Landsat 8 Operational Land Imager (OLI) and Thermal Infrared Sensors (TIRS).

From 1972 to 1986, the United States was the only country with a satellite-based remote sensing system that was virtually global in scope. In 1986, France joined us with the launching of their system, **SPOT** (Système Pour l'Observation de la Terre), which offered a 10 m spatial resolution in its panchromatic band and a 20 m spatial resolution in the visible and near-infrared bands. Also unique to their satellite at the time was advanced optic capability, including not only nadir viewing but also off-nadir, or side viewing, which enabled scientists to produce stereopairs from the imagery more easily. SPOT has also seen an evolution in technology, including adding a 20 m mid-infrared band on SPOT 4 in 1998 and a 5 m panchromatic band on SPOT 5 in 2002.

Even with France's contributions in the 1980s, and other countries and entities like India and the European Union launching systems in the 1990s, Landsat was still the most detailed publicly available imagery until 1999. In that year, EOSAT (now Space Imaging) launched the first commercial high-resolution satellite system, **IKONOS**. Offering a spatial resolution of 1 m for its panchromatic band, IKONOS imagery gave civilian applications what before had only been available to the military: supreme spatial resolution with an increased temporal resolution of 11 days and redundant image acquisition. IKONOS was quickly followed by other ventures, like Quickbird by DigitalGlobe, Inc. DigitalGlobe tailors their systems to the needs of their clients, with prices varying according to the requested spatial, spectral, and radiometric resolutions, as well as the level of geometric correction required. Most offer a panchromatic band, as well as up to four multispectral bands, and unlike government and military systems, most produce oblique imagery using sensors that point to the side. Such capabilities make them quite valuable for monitoring urban infrastructure, providing emergency response to natural disasters, as well as evidence for breaking news stories (Aronoff, 2005).

Digital Image Processing

Using these digital images, particularly with other geographic data, requires that we be able to manipulate them digitally. While most of these procedures fall outside the scope of this text, it is important to introduce you to at least a few concepts. Here, we explore image restoration and rectification processes, image enhancement procedures, and the basic concept of image classification.

IMAGE RESTORATION AND RECTIFICATION

Many of the algorithms you will find under this heading are for processes that can also be performed by the sellers of the imagery prior to purchasing it. Correcting degraded data, removing systematic geometric distortions, and changing image geometry are examples of the types of tasks that must be done on raw imagery before it can be used in a GIS. The amount of reflected energy that sensors measure, for example, is influenced by shadows, haze, and other atmospheric conditions. If one of these issues is a systematic influence occurring across an image, algorithms that process the raw imagery can compensate for this.

Raw imagery must also be tied to ground locations to be used in a GIS. **Georectification** is the process of assigning a geographic coordinate to every pixel in an image. This is a two-step process that begins with a mathematical transformation to calculate the geographic coordinates that will tie the imagery to a map projection used by other GIS data. The most straightforward way of doing this is to identify a set of coordinates in the field or on a reference source, also called **ground control points**, and then locate those same points on the image. The transformation algorithm, using the data associated with the original pixels, then creates a new grid of pixels using the desired map projection and calculates new cell values. The simplest algorithm for this part of the process, and the only one that does not change the original pixel values, is the *nearest neighbor* algorithm (Aronoff, 2005). This algorithm calculates the pixel centers for the new grid, then finds the corresponding location on the original image, and assigns the value of the pixel nearest to that location to the new grid cell (Figure 10.14).

FIGURE 10.14
Georectification: nearest neighbor transformation.

IMAGE ENHANCEMENT

Image enhancement algorithms are used to improve our ability to interpret an image visually. They include processes to manipulate contrast, brightness, values, and image sharpness. The point of these algorithms is not to add information, but merely to exaggerate it. For instance, many satellite images originally look quite dark and have little contrast because the percentage of energy reflected to the sensor is in a rather narrow range compared to sensor's capabilities. It makes sense, then to process the original brightness values so that they take up the full range of brightness values the sensor can detect (Figure 10.15). **Contrast Stretch** algorithms do this by multiplying each pixel value by a function that stretches the original range of values so that they match the full range, increasing the image's contrast and making it easier to interpret visually.

IMAGE CLASSIFICATION

Image classification is popular because it allows scientists to classify pixels by brightness value into useful groups. There are two basic approaches for this: *supervised* and *unsupervised*. The key is that information classes are not known prior to these processes; they have to be generated from the original pixel values. In the supervised approach, the analyst defines the classes the algorithm will extract by selecting training areas on the original imagery. These are areas on the image the analyst can identify by experience, fieldwork, or use of other higher-resolution imagery. The computer then generates a spectral signature for these areas, plots the correspondences between bands on a scatterplot, and then uses that information to classify all of the pixels in the image.

The simplest means of **supervised classification** is by using an algorithm known as the *Minimum Distance to Means*. It compares the spectral value of each pixel to the arithmetic mean for each training class in each spectral band and then assigns the pixel to the class that minimizes the difference between average pixel value for the class in each band and the pixel's values in each band. The algorithm is simple and fast, but it has a tendency to misclassify pixels because different training areas have different ranges of spectral reflectance, which can affect the arithmetic mean calculated for the class (Aronoff, 2005). The final accuracy of the classification is then assessed using independent data for verification purposes.

Original Image

Modified Image

Source: E. Nelson, using data from *U.S. Geological Survey, Department of the Interior*

FIGURE 10.15
Contrast stretch: Original image (top), modified image (bottom).

Unsupervised classification algorithms classify pixels by finding statistical groupings in the image's data values. The resulting groups are generally well defined spectrally, but the analyst must assign meaning or labels to groups, which can be difficult if the group does not correspond well to the information classes with which the analyst is working. The most common approach under this scenario is to use an algorithm called *ISODATA* (Aronoff, 2005). With ISODATA, the analyst specifies the number of clusters for the computer to find. The computer than randomly seeds a cluster mean for each cluster in the multispectral space. Each pixel in the image is then assigned to one class using the Minimum Distance to Means Algorithm. When complete, the computer recalculates the cluster means using the assigned data and then reclassifies the image using these new means. This iterative process continues for either a specified number of rounds or until the computer can make no further adjustments.

Key Terms

Remote sensing
Electromagnetic spectrum
Electromagnetic radiation
Wavelength
Frequency
Absorption band
Rayleigh scattering
Atmospheric window
Visible spectrum
Spectral band
Spectral signature
Spectral signature graph
Additive primary colors
Additive color model
True color composite
Panchromatic band
False color composite
Multispectral scanner
Multispectral image

Pixel
Spatial resolution
Spectral resolution
Radiometric resolution
Temporal resolution
Geostationary orbit
TIROS-1
ERTS
Landsat
Sun-synchronous, near-polar orbit
Digital image processing
SPOT
IKONOS
Georectification
Ground control points
Contrast stretch
Supervised classification
Unsupervised classification

Questions

1. Who coined the term "remote sensing," and why did she initially consider it a field separate from traditional aerial photography?

2. What are the two key characteristics of electromagnetic radiation that scientists need to understand and use in order to obtain information from remote sensing data?

3. What is an absorption band in the context of the electromagnetic spectrum? Why is it important?

4. How does an atmospheric window differ from an absorption band in remote sensing?

5. What is the visible spectrum and why is it important?

6. What is a spectral signature? How can it be visualized?

7. A panchromatic image and a true color composite of the same area are created from remote sensing data. Both images use data from the same wavelength ranges. Why is the panchromatic image black and white and the true color composite a color image?

8. What is a false color composite and how is the image created?

9. What four types of resolution play a role in the final quality of a digital image?

10. Explain why a digital image with a higher spectral resolution usually has a lower spatial resolution.

11. Which satellite system offered the first systematic repetitive coverage of Earth with enough detail to be useful for a variety of applications?

Bibliography

Aronoff, S. 2005. *Remote Sensing for GIS Managers*. Redlands, CA: ESRI Press.

Avery, T.E. and G.L. Berlin, 1992. *Fundamentals of Remote Sensing and Air Photo Interpretation*. 5th ed. New York, NY: MacMillan Publishing Company.

Campbell, J.C. 1984. *Introductory Cartography*. Englewood Cliffs, NJ: Prentice-Hall, Inc.

Campbell, J.B. 1996. *Introduction to Remote Sensing*. New York, NY: Guilford Press.

Dickinson, G.C. 1970 *Maps and Air Photographs*. 2nd ed. London, England: Edward Arnold, Ltd.

Jensen, J.R. 2000. *Remote Sensing of the Environment: An Earth Resource Perspective*. Upper Saddle River, NJ: Prentice-Hall, Inc.

Lillesand, T., Keifer, R.W., and J. Chipman. 2007. *Remote Sensing and Image Interpretation*. 6th ed. New York, NY: John Wiley & Sons.

Monmonier, M. and G.A. Schnell, 1984. *Map Appreciation*. Englewood Cliffs, NJ: Prentice-Hall, Inc.

Rabenshorst, T.D. and P.D. McDermott. 1989. *Applied Cartography: Introduction to Remote Sensing*. Columbus, OH: Merrill Publishing Company.

Shellito, B. 2012. *Introduction to Geospatial Technologies*. New York, NY: W.H. Freeman and Co.

Thrower, N.J.N. 1996. *Maps and Civilization: Cartography in Culture and Society*. Chicago, IL: University of Chicago Press.

Exploring Satellite Imagery

In Exercise 10, you will learn to load and manipulate spectral bands associated with multispectral satellite imagery.

- Load satellite bands into remote sensing software to display imagery
- Manipulate imagery scale and identify locations by coordinates
- Create and interpret different color composites
- Create spectral profiles and compare brightness values of different features

SOFTWARE

This exercise uses a freeware multispectral image data and analysis system called *MultiSpec*. If the software is not available in your geospatial lab, you may download it for free at https://engineering. purdue.edu/~biehl/MultiSpec/

DATA

The data for the exercise are available from the Kendall Hunt Student Ancillary site. See the inside front cover for access information. You may also be directed to download the data from a different location by your instructor.

1. Download the data as instructed by your instructor
2. Save the file to a location where you have read/write privileges

The files are compressed and must be decompressed prior to use.

Displaying Imagery

This assignment uses imagery from the Landsat 7 satellite. Launched as a joint project between NASA, NOAA, and the USGS, Landsat 7 is equipped with the Enhanced Thematic Mapper Plus (ETM+) multispectral sensor. ETM+ collects eight bands of data ranging from the visible to the thermal infrared.

Each of these bands may be visualized by loading them individually or in any combination into the color guns of your monitor using remote sensing/GIS software. Different combinations lend themselves to different interpretations of the landscape, as we will see below.

1. Start *MultiSpec*.
2. From the *File* menu inside the application select *Open Image*.

3. Navigate to your *Chapter10* class folder.
4. Select *GSO_ETMplus_7bands.tif* and click *Open*.
5. A dialog box requesting information for display parameters will appear (Figure 10.1). The default bands or channels being displayed are bands 4, 3, and 2.

FIGURE 10.1

6. Click *OK*.
7. If prompted, click *OK* again.

QUESTION 10.1

When bands 4, 3, and 2 of the ETM+ sensor are assigned to red, green, and blue respectively, what type of image results?

a. True color composite
b. False color composite
c. Panchromatic
d. Thermal infrared

QUESTION 10.2

Areas that appear bright red on this image are reflecting energy primarily from which part of the electromagnetic spectrum?

a. Infrared
b. Blue visible
c. Red visible
d. Green visible

Identifying Imagery Locations and Scale

Imagery in *MultiSpec* can be viewed at multiple scales that can enhance your ability to detect and identify features in the landscape. Features can be located by rolling the mouse cursor over the image and locating them by latitude and longitude or by the lines and columns that make up a raster image.

1. Zoom in and out on the image by using the *Mountain* icons on the toolbar (Figure 10.2).
2. The *Coordinates View* bar displays the location and scale information when the image is active and when you zoom in and out.

FIGURE 10.2

3. The scale of the image will show in the bar (Figure 10.3); keep zooming in until the scale reads between 1:10,000 and 1:16,000. You should be able to see individual pixels at this scale.

FIGURE 10.3

The default display units are Latitude/Longitude in *Decimal Degrees*. As you scroll your cursor over the image, numbers in the *Coordinates View* window change.

4. Find an interesting-looking pixel. Move your cursor over it and click it. The *Coordinates View* bar has captured numbers related to the pixel you have selected. Note: Once you have double-clicked the pixel, *MultiSpec* should keep the image centered on it as you zoom in and out.

Select the single red pixel in the top left corner of the image. What are the latitude and longitude coordinates for this pixel?

a. 37.004289—37.004029; 80.107048—80.106731
b. 37,004,289—37,004,029; 80,107,048—80,106,731
c. 37.004289—37.004029; −80.107048—−80.106731
d. 37.4289—37.4029; 80.888048—80.888731

5. *MultiSpec* also gives you the ability to navigate to a specific pixel. In the drop-down window on the left side of the *Coordinates View* bar (Figure 10.4), click the "down arrow" button and change the coordinates from Lat-Long (Decimal) to Lines-Columns. Note: Each time you click the drop-down window and when you use some of the other tools, you deactivate the map. When this happens, a single click on the map will reactive it, then your next single click will select pixels.

FIGURE 10.4

Individual pixels can be found by navigating through the grid. Grid locations are laid out and numbered from left to right (Columns) and from top to bottom (Lines).

Study the numbers to the right of the *Coordinates View* bar as you move your cursor vertically and horizontally through the image. Notice that the numbers decrease as you move up and left and increase as you move down and right.

Manipulating and Interpreting Color Composites

Imagery created from bands 4, 3, and 2 of ETM+ tend to have several distinct characteristics:

- Water does not reflect much energy from any of these bands.
- Urban features reflect a lot of energy from bands 3 (red wavelengths displayed using the monitor's green color gun) and 2 (green wavelengths displayed using the monitor's blue color gun).
- Healthy vegetation reflects a tremendous amount of energy from band 4.
- Different types of vegetation reflect varying amounts of energy. Deciduous trees, for example, would have higher reflectance values in band 4 than conifer trees.

QUESTION 10.4

Scroll over the image and double-click the pixel at each location specified below. Match the pixel to the type of land-use feature.

a. Line 3,673, Column 2,345   _C_ Water
b. Line 3,692, Column 3,740   _A_ Airport
c. Line 1,744, Column 7,339   _B_ Urban/City
d. Line 3,680, Column 3,914   _D_ Golf Course

The bands comprising the image can easily be changed to provide a different visualization of the landscape, which can help enhance interpretation of features.

1. To change band combinations, go to the *Processor* menu and select *Display Image*.
2. In the dialog box that appears change the band assignments of the red, green, and blue channels to bands 3, 2, and 1, respectively (Figure 10.5).
3. Click *OK*.

FIGURE 10.5

What type of image results when Band 3 (red wavelengths) is assigned to the red color gun, Band 2 (green wavelengths) to the green color gun, and Band 1 (blue wavelengths) to the blue color gun?

a. True color composite
b. False color composite
c. Panchromatic
d. Thermal infrared

Creating and Examining Spectral Profiles

Each pixel in a band holds a brightness value (BV) between 0 and 255 that represents the amount of light in that band reflected from the Earth's surface at that point. The values for a pixel can be collected from multiple bands and graphed, placing bandwidth or channel number along the x-axis and BV along the y-axis. This is called a spectral profile.

1. Go back to the *Processor* menu—*Display Image* and change the bands back to 4, 3, 2 for red, green, and blue, respectively.
2. Click *OK*.
3. Zoom out to see the entire image, then click once in the area marked *A) Airport* in Figure 10.6 and zoom in to that region.

FIGURE 10.6

4. As you zoom, center your viewer on the area that is bluish white. You should notice a linear feature (Piedmont Triad International Airport) at a scale of about 1:80,000 or larger, and Greensboro should be to the east (right).
5. Zoom in close enough to see the pixels that make up the airport runway.
6. Click the bluish gray pixel located at Line 3,681 Column 2,342.
7. From the menu bar, click on *Window*, then *New Selection Graph*.
8. Resize the chart as needed to view the graph and the information along each axis. Hint: Hover your cursor over the icons in the top right corner and click on the Restore Down icon, then resize the chart by clicking and dragging the edges as needed.

Which of the graphs below best represents the spectral signature of the pixel on the runway at the airport?

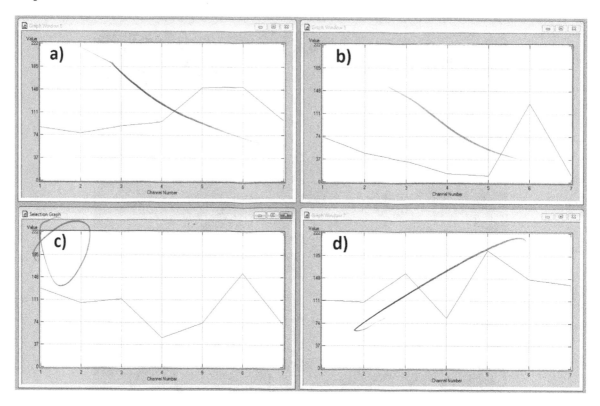

Which channel number has the highest spectral reflectance value for the pixel on the runway at the airport?

    a.   Channel 2
    b.   Channel 4
    c.   Channel 6
    d.   Channel 7

9.   Minimize the selection graph window, and then zoom out (approximately 1:600,000) from the runway in Area A (Figure 10.6).
10. South of the runway, center your display on the lake (Area B: a very dark blue/black object).
11. Click once to activate the map.
12. Click on one of the lake's pixels to select it, then zoom in on the object.

13. Once you have zoomed in far enough to see individual pixels, select the black pixel located at Line 6,247, Column 1,837.
14. From the menu bar, click on Window, then *New Selection Graph*.
15. Resize the chart as needed to view the graph and the information along each axis.

QUESTION 10.8

Which of the graphs below best represents the spectral signature of the pixel on the lake?

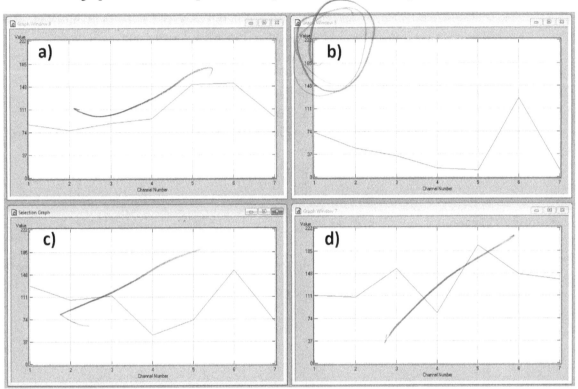

QUESTION 10.9

Which channel number has the highest spectral reflectance value for the pixel on the lake?

a. Channel 2
b. Channel 4
c. Channel 6
d. Channel 7

The lake reflects less Channel 4 energy than the airport.

a. True
b. False

16. Close the selection graph windows, and then zoom out again until you see the area marked B in Figure 10.6.
17. Activate the map by clicking once, then click once in this area, and zoom in to the area to the right of the southernmost lake until you reach a scale between 1:15,000 and 1:25,000.
18. Navigate to and then click on Line 6,376, Column 1,851 (we will call this Pixel 1).
19. From the menu bar, click on *Window*, then *New Selection Graph*.
20. Resize the chart as needed to view the graph and the information along each axis.
21. From the menu bar, click on *Window*, and open a second *New Selection Graph*.
22. Navigate to and then click on the second pixel located at Line 6,405, Column 1,831 (we will call this pixel 2).
23. Resize the chart as needed to view the graph and the information along each axis.

Pixel 1 (Line 6,376, Column 1,851) reflects significantly more Band 4 energy when compared to pixel 2 (Line 6,405, Column 1,831).

a. True
b. False

Pixel 1 and pixel 2 represent different types of tree species; one represents conifers and the other represents deciduous.

Based on the spectral signatures that you plotted and the knowledge you have gained in class, which type of tree should be located at Pixel 1 (Line 6,376, Column 1,851)?

a. Deciduous
b. Conifer

24. Exit all applications.

INDEX

CPSIA information can be obtained
at www.ICGtesting.com
Printed in the USA
JSHW022059020822
28828JS00005B/43

9 781524 9896